FATAL CHOICE

FATAL CHOICE

A PILGRIM'S GUIDE TO HELL

JOHN TIMMERMAN

CASCADE *Books* • Eugene, Oregon

FATAL CHOICE
A Pilgrim's Guide to Hell

Cascade Books
An Imprint of Wipf and Stock Publishers
199 W. 8th Ave., Suite 3
Eugene, OR 97401

www.wipfandstock.com

ISBN 13: 978-1-62564-737-5

Cataloging-in-Publication data:

Timmerman, John.

Fatal choice : a pilgrim's guide to hell / John Timmerman.

xvi + 214 p.; 23 cm—Includes bibliographical references.

ISBN 13: 978-1-62564-737-5

1. Hell—Christianity—History of doctrines. 2. Arts and religion. 3. Hieronymus Bosch, -1516—Criticism and interpretation. I. Title.

BT 836.3 T1 2015

Manufactured in the USA.

Contents

Foreword

A TOUR OF HELL guided by medieval master of the grotesque Hieronymus Bosch: you'd expect nonstop horror and torture. The good or bad news, depending on your sadism, is that John Timmerman delivers something else. The setup is pure Dante, and there are glimpses of the awful. (I will never hear the phrase "the bowels of hell" quite the same way again.) But the actual tale is more Platonic dialogue than *Inferno*: within a good story, we get an explication of and argument for traditional Christian teaching about hell. As Bosch notes, it's not what we see, but what we learn.

We get, to begin, an argument for a worry. The world's major religions believe overwhelmingly in some sort of hell. Why? Perhaps it reflects something built into human nature, a bit of cognitive hardwiring. Or perhaps it is a dim perception of a reality that forces itself upon us, a thing Christians might call general revelation. (If God designed the brain, the two stories could both be true.) It's not obvious how to rule the second out. So the mere persistence of the stories is some reason for even atheists to worry a bit. But our attitude is not entirely worry. In a way, we hope for a hell, though we also hope to avoid it. Timmerman reminds us of some of history's true villains. We naturally hope their deaths, however messy, were not all their crimes received—if they never repented. And we often hope they didn't repent, though that does us no credit. (From now on, assume that we're talking only about the unrepentant.)

Suppose that after death, everyone is there, we all have bodies, and we're all together in the same place. If the bad are still bad, they will trouble the good again. It will just be a repeat of this life. God won't have *saved* anyone.

God could of course zap the bad to turn them good: presto! and Stalin is tossing flowers. But if that was ever the right thing to do, why would

God wait till the afterlife? The fact that he does not do it now suggests that it won't be right to do it then, either. To simply force such a radical change on Stalin without his say-so would be much like brainwashing him. We know that's wrong. And God cannot do wrong.

God could of course just not bring the villains back. But then all Hitler ever gets for his crimes is a bullet in the head. Stalin and Mao don't get even that. They died in their beds, quietly, still in charge and happy. Does that seem right? If they never come back, they miss a great party, true, but they never even know they missed it. Surely they should at least learn that they were wrong, and Someone knew it. Surely they should at least come to regret what they did.

If you think Stalin should pay *somehow*, a slippery slope starts. Should someone who killed one less person than Stalin get away with it? Two less? How about just grievous bodily harm? There is no obvious stopping point. Justice applies to every size. If Stalin gets his due, then so should you. If God brings back any villains, he should have them all.

If the villains come back, the least God should do for the rest is quarantine them. Prison is to keep the law-abiding safe, among other things. If the villains are quarantined and they have bodies, there is a place they are quarantined. We call it hell.

What is hell like, if there is one? Paul writes, "Eye hath not seen, nor ear heard, neither have entered into the heart of man the things which God hath prepared for them that love Him" (1 Cor 2:9). The same probably holds for what is prepared for the rest. We can only speculate, guided by biblical images. If hell is a matter of God's justice, one thing we know is that God's justice can be poetic:

> Whoever digs a hole and scoops it out falls into the pit they have made (Ps 7:15).

> The nations have fallen into the pit they have dug; their feet are caught in the net they have hidden (Ps 9:15).

This makes it unlikely that hell is a one-size-fits-all proposition. Sins are individual; so is what they earn. Perhaps hell is different for every person in it. The center of Timmerman's conception is this:

Hell . . . is an eternal *moment* . . . one moment that lasts for all eternity.

Hell . . . is the real self undisguised . . . it is the outward revelation of what the damned have chosen to be.

To be in hell is to hate and to be hated without end . . . throughout the eternal moment the one who hates is cursed by hatred itself. Hatred is its own punishment . . . The damned's own hatred is turned upon themselves.

If hell is the real self, it is for each person as unique as he or she is. Perhaps the thought behind "eternal moment" is this: time passes in hell, but experience does not alter with it. The damned are stuck in one state of awareness. In it, they are aware of what they and those with them truly are. This is their punishment. In hell, you are stuck with what you and your like have made yourselves. You can no longer hide it from yourself or others. Hell is being hellish and knowing it and knowing only others like yourself. The punishment is poetically just: it is simply reaping what you have sown. Sin is its own punishment, and to be in hell is to have progressed in sin sufficiently to put yourself beyond redemption and separated yourself finally from God (i.e. to have made it the case that God cannot save you without doing wrong), *and* to be fully aware of what you and your like are. If that doesn't sound bad—if it seems a relief compared with devils wielding pitchforks—perhaps that's because we have little idea what these things really are. Biblical images of burning sulfur are there not to advise us to wear asbestos but to suggest the badness of whatever it is that hell contains.

In this conception (and I think correctly), God doesn't damn us. At a certain point, he simply accepts our choice to be damned, i.e., to reject him finally. (Again, his goodness may require him not to simply change us and save us despite ourselves, and his justice may preclude his letting this choice lead simply to nonexistence.) That *is* something we choose—hence *Fatal Choice*. You may well think: who would choose to be damned? And how can people reject God if, say, they've never even heard of him? Well, we don't think we are choosing hell. But the core of hell is rejection of God. We do choose that. Some reject God explicitly, taking the attitude that they'd spit in his eye if they saw him. But there are many other ways to do it, and they do not all require having an idea of God.

We can reject God by rejecting other things. I can reject Justin Bieber by rejecting what reminds me of him, or what he stands for, or people enough like him, or his personality traits. (If I was vehement enough about this, I'd also spit in his eye if I saw him.) I can do this even if I've never heard of him: I can dislike whatever would remind me of him if I'd heard of him, or what he does in fact stand for, or the personality he really has, or people who are enough like him. Reject the copies and you implicitly reject the original: if anyone *like* J. B. annoys me, think how much more the boy himself would. I may not believe there ever was a Mother Theresa—perhaps I think there's been an elaborate deception. But I can reject her by mocking nuns or being mean to the poor. I can also reject J. B. or Mother Theresa by being attracted to those unlike them just because of the things that make them unlike them. One can reject God without ever hearing his name. Any who reach the age of reason have sufficient information to do so.

Perhaps some never reject God. Certainly some do, then change their minds. But some who reject him may reach a point where they lock God out. To lock him out is to lock yourself into hell, the state of final separation from God: only those who turn the key on themselves are in hell. In giving us freedom, God gave us the lock and the key. It is simply up to us what we do with them. God accepts this choice, I think, as the price of our freedom—again, having made us free, it would be wrong to brainwash us. And he prizes our freedom because only if we are left free to reject him can we come to love him in the best way.

By the same token, on Timmerman's view—and I suspect correctly— God doesn't directly punish the damned, either. He lets them punish themselves. On Timmerman's parsing of this, God simply removes barriers that kept the damned from punishing themselves in this life, making an indirect contribution to their self-punishment. If self-knowledge is punishment, we avoid punishment by distracting ourselves. In hell there are no more distractions: God removes them. If hellish company is punishment, we avoid it by having other company, or company that tries to seem other than hellish, or institutions that keep the hellish from acting out. In hell all that is gone: God has sorted the sheep from the goats. If final separation from God is punishment, we avoid this in life as long as we have not finally separated ourselves from God. In hell, we have—and there is weeping and gnashing of teeth.

Any way you look at it, hellish company may carry punishment with it. There will always be someone bigger and nastier than you are. It's the playground again, with no one to rein the bullies in. Hell is a prison with the inmates in charge.

This is sure to be someone nastier if (as Timmerman and tradition say) hell is the abode of demons. Many Christians are a bit embarrassed by talk of angels, and more so by hell's angels. I don't see why. As Christians, we start out with one big spirit in our picture of the world. Why not more? In a way, it makes more sense for God to create angels than for him to create us. God needn't think very hard to come up with the idea of angels. Angels are just God writ small: all he need do is "diminish" his idea of himself, coming up with the idea of spirits less powerful, less knowing, and less good. But hair, fingernails, armpits, matter generally—there is nothing in God like these. They took a truly creative leap of imagination. If God could make the big creative leap, he could make the smaller one. And why wouldn't he make things more like himself? Children different from you are a good thing, but children who resemble you are nice too. Given angels with free will, though, it seems likely that some would go bad, just as some of us go bad, and voilà: demons. Further, if there are bad angels, one might well be the baddest dude of all. Voilà: Satan.

If you are quarantined with bigger, nastier sorts, bad things will happen to you if only because they want to have fun. In a good prison, you may say, the inmates are not in charge. There are guards instead. A good God would presumably provide a good prison. So you may ask: why wouldn't God provide guards? In a way, he does. He has made us able to become only so bad, and therefore only so painful to ourselves. He has made others able to become only so bad, and therefore only so painful to us. As we punish ourselves, our natures restrain that punishment within just bounds. Beyond that, the poetic justice of hell is that it gives the damned what they prefer. They prefer a God-free life, though they may have formed these preferences by preferring a life free of other things. Finally, then, God lets them have what they prefer, and they see what it really is. Being in hell is being as separated from God as can be. So there is no light, no joy, no beauty, because all of these are the Creator's fingerprints, and those in hell have opted for a life in which he is least present. There is also nothing to rein the bullies in, because protection is a way God is present. Thus if you are maximally separated from God, but still exist, God is finished with protecting you. As human parenthood teaches, after a certain point, it is right to let one's children make their own choices and live with the consequences. Fasten your seat belt, you're in for a bumpy ride. But perhaps even the bullies aren't the worst hell has to offer. Timmerman's hell includes the Outer Darkness, where you don't even get the society of the damned, but are simply stuck with yourself: eternal solitary confinement.

Two questions remain. One is whether awareness of hell and its suffering would prevent those in heaven from being joyful. They are after all perfected in love, as their Creator is, and so presumably they love those in hell as their Creator does. The other question is why the punishment of hell is eternal, rather than (say) coming to an end after an appropriate length of suffering. If you've been a rotter for eighty years, then fine, suffer for eighty years, and as much as you made others suffer—but then why wouldn't God let the flame wink out? Justice demands proportionality, and hell, says Timmerman, is a matter of justice.

Timmerman's conception suggests an answer to the first question. Since hell just is the state of being aware of certain things, if those in heaven were aware of hell's contents, they would be at least partly in hell. If that's right, the saved in heaven are not aware of hell. There is no particular reason they would be. Save for "seeing" God, they may not be able to perceive any more than we do now, and we do not now see hell. If they do know of hell, further, it may be only in general terms vague enough not to engage sympathy—e.g., that God has assured that justice is done. Perhaps in heaven, we are aware only of God. If God is all the Bible says, God is all-consuming and *stunning.* When you've got him in view, nothing else can claim your attention. Heaven is final union with God, just as hell is final separation from God; just as those in hell have no awareness of God, perhaps those in heaven have no awareness of anything *but* God. That may sound inhuman—we all like to envision picnics with the dear previously departed—but perhaps we do this only in the vestibule, and once admitted to the throne room things differ. To say that God could fail to engage our whole attention may well be to underestimate God. But if I'm wrong about this, then perhaps those in heaven are aware only of others in heaven, in the penumbra of their attention, as fellow enjoyers of God.

God, however, is the final case to consider. He is all-knowing, and so he, at least, is aware of hell, even if none of the saved are. You may wonder, then, whether this awareness would spoil the party for *him.* If it would, that suggests again that perhaps he would not want hell to be eternal. Why spoil things for himself? The answer has to be justice. God gets no pleasure from damnation. He lets us damn ourselves only because having given us freedom, he must. If he lets damnation continue, and gets no pleasure from it, he must do so only because he must. But only the requirements of perfect goodness limit God's action. God is omnipotent, and so nothing else can constrain him. The only part of perfect goodness that might push God to never end hell is justice. So if hell is everlasting, that is because justice requires it, and a perfectly good being must be just.

But this just raises the second question. Justice requires proportionality. So how could justice require infinite punishment for finite evil?

This might be the knottiest question about hell, and I am not at all sure I have a good answer for it. But here is one thought: perhaps sin requires never-ending punishment because it is a lot worse than we think it is. Perhaps something about sin has an infinite dimension.

Hell pays back trouble to those who cause it. Our sins trouble not just other people, but God. In his case, the trouble is everlasting. He sees it all, permanently. He never stops *seeing* what we do. Time has no mercy on him. And what he sees pains him more than it pained anyone else. If you hurt the child, you hurt the mother who watches you do it—in many cases, more than you hurt the child. The more she loves her child, the more what you do hurts her. Suppose her love for her child were infinitely intense. Then if the more the love, the more the hurt, the hurt would have to be infinite as well. Thus, in God's case, the hurt is infinite in intensity and endless in duration. Proportionate "payback" for this would be another infinite hurt endless in duration. But no finite creature can in any finite time absorb a literally infinite hurt. So the only way to achieve this is for the creature to absorb a finitely intense hurt over an infinite period of time.

If God too has a right not to be hurt, a perfectly just God must do justice for himself as well as for others. This isn't revenge. If God is perfectly good, his motive is not personal payback but an abstract requirement that the moral scales be balanced. It is particularly not revenge because it hurts God to allow this more than it hurts the damned to suffer it—if he loves them infinitely, a never-ending hell multiplies his troubles. Of course, those who accept forgiveness are forgiven the pain they've caused God along with all else. (God the Son, on the cross, forgave the pain his crucifiers caused.) But those who refuse forgiveness take the consequences. And God also absorbs the consequences of his justice. He did so on the cross, after all. This might seem to imply that the more hell endures the more the damned owe, because the longer it goes on the more they hurt God. But we do not wrong another simply by letting him see us in pain.

Timmerman gives us an interesting, vivid take on the traditional doctrine of hell. I can't quite say "Enjoy!" but you will.

Brian Leftow
Oxford, February 2014

Note from the Editor

WHEN MY FRIEND HANDED me this manuscript, he told me to do with it as I wished. He wanted only to remain completely anonymous. I understand that, given his prominent position in art history at a leading university. Upon first reading the manuscript, however, I was both troubled and puzzled. Troubled by the dramatically raw nature of the material, puzzled because I failed to understand many of the references that he apparently took for granted.

Consequently, I put myself once again in the position of the graduate student. That is how we first met, after all, with him as teacher and me as student. I researched those references and bits of information that eluded me at first. Many of these I entered directly into the manuscript; others I entered as occasional footnotes (there are few of them—don't feel obligated to read them). This is, first and foremost, not an argument, not an essay, but a story. Or as the narrator, my art historian friend, mentioned to me once when I consulted him about some details, it just might be a myth.

—Lincoln Jefferson

CHAPTER ONE

The Ransom Library

THE ELEVENTH STORY OF the Ransom Library is the highest level of the tallest building within a hundred miles. Very few people use that level, dedicated as it is to archives in one section and art history in the other.

On the tenth floor reside the philosophy, religion, and classical holdings, but no carrels. Perhaps in some earlier time all the former, aging carrels, these small wooden desks with a privacy screen of two shelves at the top, must have graced the former library throughout. Now they were only on the eleventh floor. The wood was nicked and grooved, requiring a legal pad for backing. But one could stack and sprawl a dozen books across the wide desk and shelves.

The Ransom Library was originally intended to be eight stories tall, which in itself would have made it a formidable structure. This would have been in the 1990s when enrollment at the university exploded and donor money rolled in like waves to the "capital campaign." All this had been started a decade prior by a 50 million dollar bequest from the estate of C. Hugh Ransom, owner of Ransom Energy, primarily a strip mining industry for coal. With the building of several nearby motels, the architectural adventurers added two floors for conference centers and one for a computer technology center. These, of course, took up floors two through four, above the lobby and office floor. The library itself, in traditional terms of stacks and carrels and periodicals, didn't start until level five. Students generally referred to the whole monolith as Ransom's Folly.

The eleventh story of the Ransom Library had another advantage beyond quiet and carrels; through its windows one could see for miles over some of the most spectacular scenery imaginable. Indeed, even though I was moving at a good pace to finish my dissertation, I often found myself gazing at the ever-shifting scenery.

One day the sun might shine brightly, with only a lone, wandering cloud casting its shadow on the river valley below. I could trace the shadow to where it disappeared into the Appalachian foothills, which I knew from my roaming in the countryside to be miles away. The river valley, sinuously winding around the southern edge of the university, most mornings wore a coat of fog that sometimes didn't burn off until noon. Then the river sparkled in its rocky throat as if someone had taken bags of diamonds and cast them from the rooftop of the Ransom Library.

Having been at work on the dissertation for a year now, I had watched the landscape below me float through the seasons. Autumn colors ran like streams along the hills and the valley. Winter days were mild. We were just far enough south to be spared the worst of winter, just far enough north to catch a couple of inches of snow occasionally, enough to cover the rusted roofs of trailers and tin-roofed shacks that showed through the empty trees in the further hills. Spring came with its slashing storms blown up from the Gulf of Mexico. Then the river, despite the ceaseless attention of the Army Corps of Engineers, would once again overflow its banks in a broad, brown swath.

Now it is a summer day. Early. Fog lies in the river's throat. I have walked up the long hill at the top of which the Ransom Library stands. It will be a warm day. At 8 a.m. I am sweating as I enter the library. As part of my routine I bypass the elevators and take the stairway up. Here is the other advantage of the eleventh floor: in my briefcase are a thermos of coffee and a bottle of water. Nobody checks on the eleventh floor for prohibited goods; all the grad students carry them.

Once a young assistant from the netherworld came up to fetch something from the archives. He must have seen our cups and water bottles. The next day a very small sign was posted by the elevator: "No Drinks in the Library." It created a round of jokes.

I knew everybody here by sight; three I called close friends. We often took lunch breaks together on one of the benches on the college green. Each bench bore the name of some alumnus or alumna who had, no doubt, made a donation worthy of the inscription. We wondered, sometimes, about the wisdom of naming these benches after donors, making up our own variations such as "The Bulle's Seat of Knowledge" or "The Martha Hinkerson Estate." Anything to set the tensions of the dissertation writing in perspective.

I was fortunate. I had had four of my five chapters approved and was planning to defend before a very generous committee (enamored more by my creative ability than any intellectual acumen) in September.

We did talk about each other's work, about the job market, about dissertation committees. The job market, despite the then-booming economy, was as depressing as ever. In fact, I would begin my search that fall while teaching three-quarters time for the art department.

Perhaps it is important to understand that I am not an artist. I couldn't draw a straight line between two points if they were an inch apart. I'm an historian. That is to say, I'm concerned with how art develops from age to age, how it grows out of an age, how it responds to an age. But most importantly, at least for myself, I'm concerned with how religious beliefs and the culture of the time influence an artistic work.

This is where I'm blessed in my committee. Not one member of it, insofar as I've determined, is a religious person. It's not that they're opposed to it; in this postmodern age they are required to be tolerant, after all. One especially tolerates anything but absolutes, which, by assumption, are intolerant.

Nonetheless, while forced by their own principles to tolerate my perspective, I have also found them to be genuinely curious, even fascinated, by some of the arguments. Even in these members exists some vestigial cultural religion a generation or two removed in their lineage. As I consulted with them I found their questions of me like a scratching at some disconcerting itch. Somewhere between the shoulder blades where one can't quite get at it.

I enjoyed that intellectual give-and-take, even though in my own mind the dissertation was no more and no less than a union ticket to the teaching career I longed for. Perhaps for that very reason I thoroughly enjoyed my work on it.

A poet named Marianne Moore once wrote about her own profession, "There are things that are important beyond all this fiddle." For many, I have discovered, the important things are countable things, showable things. Religion, on the other hand, is important because it can't be meaningfully counted, nor can it be shown like an automobile on parade. That's why I enjoyed my dissertation. It allowed me, there in the aerie of the eleventh floor, to delve into the unknown and test mysteries.

The whole business ultimately amounted to just four words: This Just Might Be.

But I wander. I had decided long ago, while a college student, really, that I would write my dissertation on Hieronymus Bosch. It so happened that I had spent a sophomore semester in Europe in a study abroad program. As an art history major I visited all the great museums, from Italy to Spain, from Holland to the Hermitage in Russia. Scattered throughout—Lille, Madrid, Geneva, Paris, The Hague—appeared works by Bosch. It grew to the point that while wandering through a new museum, my eye was drawn to one of his paintings with magnetic force. For some reason I saved the Netherlands for last. I went first to the Rijksmuseum, of course, where I spent three days tracing the brightest constellations in the history of art.

It was warm on the top floor today. The air conditioning on the first few floors chilled one to hypothermia. It lost its force by the eleventh story. Usually the musty stacks lent a peculiar, rich coolness, but the sun had now slanted over my carrel, tinting the pages with a bright glow. I couldn't help looking out the window. It was the drowsy hour.

I was staring down into the river when his face, the face only, appeared before me.

You know how it is on those hot summer days, when the hour approaches noon. Everything shimmers with light and the very earth finds it difficult to breathe in the sultry air. The river, winding far below like a sinuous brown serpent, now glittered with light on its back—an incandescence like the sun's flame. I imagined its sound, like a scarcely audible rumble from the earth's core. One has to listen closely, for all the surface sound is the tinkling of water along pebbles in the river's throat. The growl lives deep within.

Of course, up here I heard nothing.

I was dozing off, I believe, mesmerized by heat and light, when he appeared. Or rather, his face. I recognized him immediately. A wizened little monkey's face, really, with the bold eyes peering from a myriad of wrinkles. Those eyes! What horrors they had peered upon, and yet they searched out, forcefully and unafraid. His cheekbones were strong, as was his perfectly aligned nose. His upper lip was thin, neatly pursed over the full lower lip and the large, square jaw. Power, that's what I saw in his features: power and an utter lack of fear. As if the features weren't enough, one could easily identify him by the long, sweeping hair flowing beneath that odd painter's hat he always wore.

Anyone could identify that face. I know I could. But then, I had looked upon it countless times. It was the painter Hieronymus Bosch, dead now for over four centuries.

Self-portraiture might well be an interesting art history study in itself—something I quickly filed into a crease in my memory bank for some future reference. An article, perhaps, on the devious path to tenure. Some of the old masters are as styled as if in a beauty salon, as though the painter were acutely aware of the face he portrayed for future centuries. On the other hand, some moderns were as opaque as colored glass, as if a bubble of emotion flowed below every inch of the surface, or as if to say "The thing inside is the real person." Of Bosch's self-portraits, one observes only an intriguing honesty, a fusion of personality and feature. The eyes capture a wry and fanciful spirit, the facial features an acute sense of realism about himself.

As the mirage shimmered briefly before me and mercifully disappeared, somewhere between the river and the arc of light, I mentally scanned the introductory chapter to my dissertation—a short history of Bosch and his work. I think it was to verify impressions I had formed.

To be truthful, there is not a great deal to say about Bosch's life. Even the dates of that life (1450–1516?) are uncertain. And although he signed many of his paintings, he didn't date them. We do know that he lived on this side of the great Black Plague, which seemed to cheapen life to the point of frivolity. We do know that he was a member of the religiously orthodox Brotherhood of the Blessed Lady.[1] In fact, he painted altar pieces for the Order. Why, then, are his paintings beset and besotted with the hideous faces of evil? The psychologist Carl Jung called Bosch "the

1. The brotherhood was not an ascetic monastic enclave, hermetically sealed from the world to thwart its temptations. Monastic asceticism of the time treated the body with contempt, something base that must be subdued by the spirit. There is more than a hint of Aristotle here, who believed that all evil desires are spawned by the flesh, particularly its lower regions. To the Brotherhood, such an idea was sacrilegious, lying contrary to the New Testament teaching of a body-soul unity. This did not, of course, provide an excuse for living "according to the flesh," but instead insisted that the body, with the soul, could be sanctified. The narrator's argument was that for precisely this reason Bosch had depicted the soul in captivity to the flesh. The suffering of human (and bestial) creatures in the paintings portrays a "flesh" indulged in without restraint.

master of the monstrous" and the true "discoverer of the subconscious." Others call him a painter of nightmares. I wondered sometimes why I had even selected this subject.

Like all essays a dissertation required a thesis—a point you intend to prove and then discourse on those proofs. It sounds simple; the trick simply lies in a clear thesis. In this case, I was attempting nothing less than to demonstrate that Bosch's work demonstrated a systematic theology. It sounded simple at first; then I had to explain to my committee what on earth that term meant.

But that term also can be drawn out of the airy height of abstract language and made simple. This much I had already learned from Bosch, the master of earthly details. Basically, a systematic theology holds that all parts of a sacred text must be congruent and noncontradictory in the knowledge it presents about God. It relies heavily on pattern, prophecy, and fulfillment. For example, the Bible has an inherent pattern of God's perfect creation, humanity's fall from perfection, Christ's redemption of that fall through the crucifixion, his reign through the resurrection, and his restoration of a new heaven, earth, and humanity through the second coming. The pattern acquires strength through historical and prophetic events fulfilled in the advent of the Christ. Shelves of books have been written on the subject, although few of them are in the Ransom Library and most of those are shelved under Philosophy.

That didn't matter. The fact was that Hieronymus Bosch painted depictions of each of these key theological arguments, a pattern hitherto undiscovered. This pattern is what I was attempting to prove. The problem was the hideous awareness of evil, snarling through distorted faces and forms, at each event. A satire of fallen humanity with its pretensions of perfection? A portrayal that in this life none of us, not one, escapes the cold claws of suffering? Or a mockery of religious belief itself, a delusion that crumples like fine china under the elephant footfalls of unbelief? That tension was the challenge I was trying to decode.

But I apologize. I thought I was done with dissertation talk.

I felt a shake of my shoulder, then a sudden, sharp rap of knuckles on the back of my head. I opened my eyes. The river shone, but the sun had slanted sideways. An embarrassing trickle of drool had slid down the corner of my mouth, spotting the yellow tablet, and my left cheek bore a crease from the tablet's crisp edge.

CHAPTER TWO

Unicorns and Myths

"WHOA," I SAID, WIPING the back of my hand across my wet cheek.

"*Whoa* is right. You were mumbling away over here in your sleep."

"Lincoln?" He was standing behind me. I turned in my chair, rubbing my eyes.

"We better get some coffee in you."

"Got some right here," I said. I reached out for the thermos.

"That's okay. But take it down to the bench. Take your lunch, too. It's almost one o'clock."

"Man! I must have slept—what? An hour, maybe?"

"Don't ask me. I wasn't the one jabbering away, drooling all over his tablet. You going to turn in a dissertation of pure slobber?"

I got up. We walked through the pewter light of the stacks toward the elevator. Like the air conditioning, electricity never seemed to reach up here in full force. The elevator would be slow. Most of the carrels were deserted for late lunch. A book shelver who looked impossibly young was pushing his cart up and down the aisles. Lincoln caught a glimpse of a tousled fall of auburn hair from a woman bent over a carrel desk. "Hey, Janie-girl. You had lunch yet? Come on down and be queen for the day. You can eat with two handsome men."

She stood and broke a wide grin. "Great! Where are they?"

The three of us waited for the service elevator. Slower, but fewer stops. Supposedly, only the janitors and book shelvers had keys, but some thoughtful person had left a copy on the top shelf of books by the elevator door. It lay safely under a book entitled *Seventeenth Century Doilies:*

Hermeneutics of a Symbology. That's right. It was the short section of the stacks where dissertations in the fine arts were shelved. *Doilies* was the only one that was ever moved.

I'm an average height, 5'11". I don't wear a beard, goatee, mustache, or anything else like that. They take too much time to keep up. My hair is long for the simple reason that I can't sit still waiting for a barber when I have other things to do. Every time I open a door, there are people waiting in chairs, aimlessly paging through the ancient ruins of *Motor Trend, Good Housekeeping, Readers' Digest*, and *Prevention*. I wear a set of nearly rimless glasses—I hate the way heavier ones slide down your nose and crimp the back of your ears. My nose is big enough. All in all, I think I'm pretty average, which means that I don't have to waste any time thinking about it.

But riding down the elevator with my two friends, I wondered who was the odd person out. Janeen—Janie only to us—McClatchy stood in front of me, while I leaned against the wall, still thinking of the face I'd seen emerge from the stacks earlier. If I stared straight ahead I wouldn't know Janie was there. She probably didn't top either 5'3" or 110 pounds.

Although she was a third-year graduate student, people made a lot of mistakes about Janie. The worst scenario was if one of her freshman students did. Like the year Janie taught an "Introduction to Literature for Non-English Majors." Half the football team enrolled since it was offered between morning and afternoon practice.

When Janie entered the classroom, a round of chortles and whistles erupted from the back corner of the room. Did I mention that Janie is drop-dead gorgeous? She placed her notes on the podium, carefully sorting them out until the noise diminished, and then walked slowly toward the back. She stood there surrounded by a couple of tons of prime beef and put her hands on her hips. Her emerald green eyes probed each face like a lancet. One guy laughed uncomfortably.

Janie stood in front of him. At her full height she was scarcely taller standing than the athlete seated, overflowing the chair.

"Did you have something to say?" Her clipped New England accent could have laser cut metal.

"Naw, Teach."

"What is your name?"

"Ezekiel Simmons."

"That's a nice name. Do you know where Ezekiel comes from?"

"My father, I think."

The others laughed uproariously. Someone shouted, "Which one, Zeke?"

Janie waited for quiet, not unlocking her eyes from Simmons. She saw uncertainty there now. His eyes wouldn't meet hers fully.

"Ezekiel. That's a name full of dignity, Mr. Simmons. It comes from Hebrew and means 'God is strong.' In the Bible, Ezekiel is the one who dared dream great dreams and powerful visions of how things would be in the future times."

He looked at her now, his eyes hungry. "I didn't know that, Teach."

"However," she said, walking back to the podium, "My name, Mr. Simmons and everyone else, is not 'Teach.' It's Ms. McClatchy. In this class I have a few requirements. First, you will not miss a class. Second, you will each select, memorize, and recite for the class one poem of no fewer than fourteen lines. I can help you with your selection. Mr. Simmons, you may select the first person to recite. That will be, let's see, on Monday."

"Luther," shouted Ezekiel. "Luther Porter. He smart."

"Luther. Another interesting name. Luther Porter it is. See me after class, Luther. Either that or I'll email you your assignment"

"Third requirement. You will have the assignment read and ready for the date assigned on the syllabus. I don't talk to myself."

"Finally, in my class you are permitted one polite yawn. That's when you grit your teeth and squeeze it out of your ears. Of course, you may bring along the beverage of your choice to prevent that. Either that, or you'll be invited to drop the course."

After the class, Ezekiel Simmons waited as the others, including Luther Porter, filed out. Only after everyone left did he walk up to the desk.

"Say, Teach . . . Ms. McClaney . . ."

"McClatchy, Ezekiel. You know, a little like sassy?"

She grinned at him. Ezekiel towered over her as she sat on a corner of the desk, swinging one slim leg over the other.

"Say, how did you know about my name?"

"I read, Ezekiel. A lot. I want you to read too."

"I do some. Most courses all I got to do is enroll."

"Not here."

"I figured that. You read the whole Bible? The whole thing, I mean?"

"Several times. And you?"

"Nah. My mamma does. Used to read it to us kids."

"What's your denominational background?"

He reflected. "I'm not sure what you mean. Guess I ain't got one."

"How about a church?"

Ezekiel brightened. "Oh, sure. Mamma's got a church. Pennycostal, I think. Least, they sure do shout. Got dunked myself once. Don't remember it much, though. How about you? You got a church? I mean, since you know so much about the Bible and all?"

"Ezekiel. I just said I've read it several times. But I've also read the Qu'ran, the Analects, and half a dozen others."

"Why? Why bother?"

"I guess it's the same bother we're doing with everything here. Even in 'Intro to Lit.' Looking for answers."

"Find any yet?"

"Some here, some there. But only in part. Now, it's nice talking to you, but I've gotta run."

As she went out the door, Ezekiel thundered, "Hey, Ms. McClatchy. Nice talking with you."

"Bye, Mr. Simmons."

Although we were in different disciplines, Janie, Lincoln, and I shared more than one seminar together. Our fields overlapped more than I would have guessed. Some of these three-hour seminars were a celebration of great teaching and discussion. Some plodded along like a tortoise maneuvering down the aisles of Walmart. Whenever we hit the latter type of class, we'd whisper to each other, "Squeeze it out your ears."

It became a common slogan throughout the graduate department.

Descending through the levels of the Ransom Library was a curious experience—from the mustiness of the eleventh floor, to the super-cooled lobby where the student clerks wore sweatshirts in the middle of June, to the warm outdoors. This was the time of day when the humidity started to rise. Every day, whether it rained or not, it crept out of wherever it hid and saturated the air.

Janie ran over to the commons for something to eat, hair flying like the wings of an exotic bird across the green. We headed for our bench—The Hurlbut Estate.

Lincoln pulled out his sandwich, three hard-fried eggs on slabs of wheat bread, out of his briefcase. Carefully he opened three packets of McDonald's hot mustard and layered them on. He had a warm bottle of chocolate milk to drink.

When I saw him layer the mustard, I said for about the hundredth time, "How on earth can you eat that stuff?"

"Mustard? Genus *Brassica*. Did you know you can eat the leaves of the mustard plant?"

"I suppose you have. Eaten them, I mean." I found a candy bar in my briefcase. The way to eat a Snickers is to bite into the malty bottom part and slowly chew it down. Then let the caramel and nuts settle in your mouth. Give a little thought to it and it can take you twenty minutes to eat a Snickers.

"No, I haven't. Mainly because you'd pretty much have to go to Asia to find them. Cheaper to stop at McDonald's on the way home."

"Must be Janie ran into someone she knows," I said.

"Not many people she doesn't know. Janie's a walking advertisement of her own self. Wish I had a head of hair like that. Looks like Medusa as prom queen." Lincoln chortled softly. Rather, he rumbled, like a big bear scratching its back against a post.

I thought her hair was gorgeous, a rich dark hue like chestnuts, polished and glowing in the sun.

Lincoln Jefferson, a PhD candidate in linguistics, and I sprawled on the bench, finishing lunch and watching squirrels chase each other around a hickory tree. Sunlight danced through the leaves and over the filaments of moss on the brick walk. I wondered how long these bricks had been here, some broken and buckled. The path undulated across the university green, stretching little side paths like tentative fingers in different directions. Lincoln had his sandwich finished and his eyes closed.

Lincoln was just back from a major conference, paid for by the university, where he delivered a paper on ergative verbs. I knew better than to ask him what that was. Along with several other unspoken rules of the eleventh floor were these: 1) Your dissertation is boring to everyone but you; and 2) never, ever talk about your dissertation unless someone is stupid enough to ask. Except for close friends, who commiserated, bounced ideas off each other, or prodded each other to "kill the calf." The last was a reference to just getting the thing done, quit thinking—"mental whining," we called it—and deliver it to the sacrificial altar before the committee.

If Janeen McClatchy possessed the flashiest mind in the graduate departments, a reputation very likely true, Lincoln Jefferson was hands down the most brilliant. That he came from near a tiny dot of a town, called Maggie Valley, in western North Carolina, was less surprising than the fact that he was born and raised in a cabin about six miles west of Maggie Valley. It was easier to say he was from the town, although few people knew about that either. Lincoln told me once that you knew you lived in a small town when you had to drive over ten miles to buy groceries. The cabin, he said, was on a mountain called Black Gap.

At age sixteen, Lincoln had taken every class offered at Maggie Valley High School, and they had no choice but to graduate him. He waited a year, then took a full scholarship at the university, where he stayed on to do a PhD in Linguistics. During the year he took off between high school and college, Lincoln did an intensive study of the Cherokee language. His father was a full-blood Cherokee who worked as a tour guide for the Cherokee historic sites in western North Carolina. His daddy also raised a couple of acres of tobacco and a small herd of goats on the rich upland pasture of the mountain gap. By his senior year of college, Lincoln had published three essays on the Cherokee language. After his first year of graduate school, he spent the summer developing his master's thesis, *The Language of Spirituality in the Cherokee Nation*, into a book, and published it with a prestigious national press.

Nonetheless, when I looked at him sloped along the bench like a fallen hickory limb, he looked like the least ambitious candidate on the eleventh floor. A newcomer might be tempted to ask him to get back to his janitorial duties and free up a carrel. At second glance, on taking in the size of the man, he would have moved on. Lincoln seemed to face the world half asleep, as if his heavily-lidded eyes caught half of what was going on rather than 110 percent. With his shining black hair, cheeks like planed wood, and large sloping shoulders, he might have crawled down out of some mountains. Which he had. And he loved to play the role if someone looked at him askance, peppering a North Carolina drawl at times with a "might could have done that," or a "sure ain't no kindling offen my tree." The one dead giveaway was his set of glistening blue eyes, inherited from his German mother. "She's a Kentucky girl," he explained. "They're the sassy sort. Think they're uppity."

"What took you so long," he grunted.

I had thought he was dozing. His eyes were open a razor's width as Janie walked up.

She opened a small brown bag and withdrew a bottle of strawberry-kiwi Gatorade and a pint jar of marinated herring. "Omega 3" she observed. "Commons had 100 percent grease today so I went to the Corner Mart."

"The market on the corner?" Lincoln asked innocently. "You could have had some of my sandwich."

"Yuck. Move over, Lugnut."

"So," I asked, "how you doing?"

"I can't write another word today. Zilch. You know when your handwriting looks like a drunken spider?"

"Mine looks like piles of dead ants at that point," I said.

"Whatever. I've got to finish writing this paper for Swardley on Milton. Then I have to grade twenty-seven papers for 'Intro to Lit.'"

"Any good?"

"Geez, I don't know. All the women want to write about topics like 'The Price of Freedom in *The Awakening*' or 'Female Dreams in Anne Sexton.' They sound like a broken record."

"Janie girl. You amaze me. Aren't you supposed to encourage the tender gender?"

She stabbed a piece of herring with the toothpick, tipped her head back, and dropped it in her mouth. "That's just the problem," she said while she chewed. "That's exactly what they expect and they can't see beyond the topic or the gender. They make little prisons for their minds."

"So," Lincoln rumbled. His eyes were open now, a bright contrast between his striking blue and Janie's fiery emerald. "What is the 'cost of freedom' in *The Awakening*?"

Janie could eat like a horse. She had the empty herring jar to her lips and was drinking the creamy marinade down. She used the toothpick to nab the last few onions. "In that case," she said, "death. Edna, the hero, doesn't get her way so she walks into the sea and drowns herself. Cool, huh? These twenty-year-old girls really get off on that. The solitary, persecuted female, you know."

"Sort of like me," Lincoln said. "Solitary. Persecuted. Gorgeous. Walking toward the grave."

Janie slugged him in the arm. “Ouch,” he said.

“And what about the Milton paper,” I asked. “Turning over any chestnuts like the twin keys or Eve’s will?”

“Spare me,” she said. “Hey, how do you know about Milton?”

“Hey. I went to college. Graduated even.”

“I forgot. I’m writing about the reversal of values in Book 9 of *Paradise Lost.*”

“That would be Satan’s temptation.”

“Right. Problem is, the book plays all kinds of games with the Genesis account and Swardley is dumb as a rock when it comes to religion. All he talks about are ‘hermeneutical’ and linguistic issues.”

“Like how the language changes from courtly to common in Book 9,” Lincoln offered.

“Good grief. You’ve read it, too?”

“I graduated from high school. My daddy’s got a paper somewhere to prove it.”

“Oh, stuff it in your ear.”

“Sorry, I can’t. I was squeezing out a yawn.”

“Okay, okay. I’ll shut up. But, I mean, how *can* you understand Milton unless you understand the whole Reformation thing and certainly the Bible?”

“Speaking of which,” Lincoln said, “you done with that Bible of mine yet?”

“I’m sorry. Give me another week,”

“Like it?”

“No. I hate these paraphrase things. They cheapen everything, including the story.”

“And you’ve read . . . which others?”

“King James, Revised Standard Version, the New International Version, and last summer the New Scofield.”

“Why on earth,” I interjected, “did you read the Scofield? Isn’t that the one—”

“Yes, I know. Everyone hears Scofield and thinks Apocalypse and Armageddon and all that crazy stuff. But that’s why I like it. Scofield finds the central story and places another interpretive story alongside it.”

“But it’s just a story.” Lincoln inflected this halfway between statement and question.

“Of course. A myth. Just like Gilgamesh. Just like Zeus. Just like your own native myths.”

"But maybe one of them is true," Lincoln said, again with the midrange inflection.

"Or none of them. They just represent the reachings of the imagination."

"I think we've had this conversation before," I tossed in.

"So what? I don't think we ever settled anything," Janie said.

"No, we haven't. I think we're sort of predisposed—by tradition, parents, a church—to believe certain things."

Lincoln was shaking his head.

"What? What's with you?" Janeen asked. Her eyes squinted as she turned toward him. When the leaves shifted, the dappled sun fell full on her face. Pale freckles dusted her nose and upper cheeks, like cinnamon washed across the milky cream of her skin. They started again on her neck and curved wonderfully into the V of the oversized denim shirt she wore. It flapped like a blue sheet on a clothesline over the tan cargo shorts. I sometimes imagined the freckles were alive, playing tag over a beautiful playground, then hiding in secret places.

I realized that my eyes had shifted up and down her body. Self-consciously, I felt her bright eyes fall upon me. She was smiling, and she lifted her hand and did this thing like a wave and said, "Hi."

Lincoln looked half asleep. He hadn't missed anything.

"Listen," Janie was saying to him. "You probably don't believe in unicorns, do you?"

"I can see where you're going," Lincoln said, "but I'll play along anyway. No. Unicorns don't exist."

"And why don't they exist?"

"Because of the biological and anatomical impossibility of crossing a horse with one long, spiraled horn, itself quite a trick, with a lion and a stag. Three species and one abnormality there."

"Right. Especially the lion in there. That does complicate matters. Yet the unicorn of mythology does have a lion's tail. Now, the harder question. Might unicorns exist?"

"No," Lincoln said. "For the same reasons."

"But," said Janeen, and in one quick motion she crossed her legs and sat on the bench in some kind of lotus position—it always amazed me how small people can so easily get into those contortionist positions—"they do in fact exist."

Lincoln simply raised one eyebrow. It was expression enough.

"They exist," she continued, "in human art and the human imagination since antiquity. And, most interestingly, of all the works of the human imagination, the unicorn is one figure that is relentlessly good, pure, and courageous. In fact, it's associated with virginity, and in fifteenth- and sixteenth-century tapestries, is often shown with the Virgin Mary."

"Lots of religious symbols popped up then," I volunteered. "Artwork is full of them. For example, in the twelfth century the first black Magus appeared in an adoration painting, probably because new trade routes opened with Africa. Relics were on the rise. The Reformation was waiting in the wings."

"Sure. But long before that, the unicorn is described as a real being. Greek writers were convinced the unicorn was alive and well in India. Aristotle described two different one-horned animals.[1] Of course, by the time we got to the Christian era, church fathers turned the unicorn into a symbol of Christ.

"And so now you see my point?"

"Why don't you make it clear?" Lincoln said.

"The unicorn isn't real, but it does have meaning. In fact, the human imagination creates the symbol as a kind of vessel to hold values. We need those. They give us an idea of the right way to live."

"Well, there is a problem with your argument."

"Lincoln, you'd find a problem with the Gettysburg Address."

"No, not really. Everything you say, while said in your customary spritely and winsome way—"

"Thank you."

"—is from one perspective: the limited search of the human imagination to locate and identify a repository of values. Right? Furthermore, you argue that this search endures in similar forms through the course of centuries. The streets bear new names; the town is the same."

"I don't know if I'd put it quite that way."

"No. It's more the way Eliade put it in his book on myths.[2] He distinguishes between sacred myths and what we might call fables. I prefer the distinction as one between who we are and what we do. Now, consider this. Suppose that the myths, as you call them, are not just projections of the shared imagination, but are in fact 'received.'"

"Like signals from alien spacecraft, you mean?"

1. Aristotle, *Historia Animalium* ii.I and *De Partibus Animalium* iii.II., in *The Basic Works of Aristotle.*

2. Eliade, *Myth and Reality.*

"Ah, touché, McClatchy. One can't be too careful with language. No, I meant that something in humanity itself, maybe it's the imagination, maybe the soul, apprehends pictures of how life should be. And these pictures are *given* by the Creator of humanity himself."

"But humanity wasn't 'created.'"

"Well, that's really a separate discussion. Another way to put it is this. Where do these ideas, images, and stories come from? Perhaps they all have their source in one reality toward which all the myths and stories point. Lewis had things to say about that."[3]

"Pretty far-fetched, Lincoln. Easier to say that we're born storytellers and have been doing it rather well for several thousand years."

"Easier, but is it better?"

"Aargh!" I shouted. "Just give me a good bedtime story."

We laughed like a bunch of lunatics. Who could mistake us for graduate students?

"And so the Christ, like the unicorn, is simply an imaginative projection to nail down our values upon?" I asked.

"I'm not saying that at all," she protested. "Besides, it wasn't our values that nailed him down."

"Have you ever seen the tapestry *The Unicorn in Captivity*?" I asked.

"No."

"The unicorn in hunted down, apparently killed, and brought back to the castle. But in the last panel of the series the unicorn is shown bloody but alive and rejoicing, chained to a tree in a garden of flowers."

"The resurrection," Lincoln said.

"My point exactly, then," Janie said.

"How so?"

"Another projection of the imagination. The wish for a life beyond this. At best, a garden of flowers to romp in for all eternity."

"And at worst?" This time it *was* a question. Lincoln leaned forward on the bench, dwarfing Janeen next to him.

"Yes. At worst. That's the question we don't like to consider, do we?"

"Except Dante, maybe," Lincoln said.

Or, I thought, except Hieronymus Bosch. How did he dare? Dante's carefully structured hell was nothing like Bosch's. It was as if Bosch was actually *there*—in the very place of horror and distortion.

3. The allusion, insofar as I can determine, is to C. S. Lewis, who constructs similar arguments in several essays in *God in the Dock* as well as in *Mere Christianity*.

I found myself looking down at the sun-splashed bricks of the walk. As the leaves above shifted and the sunlight flickered I felt I could almost peer far beneath the bricks, shift them aside like a glass, and see those revolting, grotesque creatures cavorting in the flames.

But then I saw the shadows on the bricks clench together, like a chiaroscuro portrait, to form that too-familiar face. It was as if he floated an inch or two above the surface of the brick, and the self-portrait was precisely the one he had used in *The Temptation of St. Anthony*. I gasped. The leaves flinched. He disappeared.

I became aware of Janie's hands kneading my shoulders. "Are you okay?" she said.

Lincoln was standing up. Precisely on the spot where I had seen the face.

"No. I thought . . ." What? Preposterous. They'll think you're crazy.

Maybe I am, I thought.

"Listen," Janie said, "we've worked hard enough for today. Let's break and have dinner at my place. I can get pasta going."

"I'll pick up the breads," said Lincoln. "Why don't you call that friend of yours?"

Janie laughed, "Think she'll want to see you when she's got a test tomorrow?"

"Try? Please?"

"I love it when you beg. See you about six?"

I nodded, but my stomach felt twisted like ropes.

CHAPTER THREE

Lincoln's Address

By the time I retrieved my books and notes from the eleventh floor, it was after four. Too late to walk home, pick up the car, and drive to Janeen's apartment. Her apartment was just six or seven blocks down Church Street, down where the whole edge of the small downtown seemed to dip and slip toward the river.

My room, on the other hand, was a three-mile hike.

I had an apartment once, but left it midway through my first year. During that time, when the brightest days felt like midnight, I couldn't stand to go into the apartment anyway. Professor Hollis and his wife had a big old house with a spacious second-story room. It so happened that the current roomer dropped out of school during my own hell and I moved in for a pittance in rent. Fifty-five dollars a month. Janeen, Lincoln, and a couple of others loaded their cars and moved me in on a Saturday morning. I was surprised that Janie showed up. I had thought she was a closer friend to Shelley than to me.

Quite honestly, the Hollises were a saving grace to me. They had come to the university thirty years prior. After several term appointments, then tenure, they fully expected to settle down and start a family. To that end they had completely restored this grand old turn-of-the-century house. When the children never came, Professor Hollis began breeding King Charles Spaniels and Mrs. Hollis ("Now call me Pat," she always insisted) kept one of the most creative gardens I have ever seen. Three seasons a year it prodigally overflowed its stakes and fences. Now, in summer, perennials galloped in waves of varied hues and sizes ("No straight rows," Mrs. Hollis said. "Life is never like that").

Indeed. To me the airy second-floor room was restorative; the garden my private recovery ward. The room overlooked the gardens and a hill full of angular trees. It had built-in bookcases floor to ceiling along one wall; I gave away my old bricks and warped boards that had served as shelves. A coffee maker, a small refrigerator, and my banged-up desk that I bought for thirty-five dollars from the Salvation Army during my first year of college still left plenty of room.

Despite everything, I don't think I was ever lonely there, and when the blackness did start chewing on my psychological heels like a red-eyed hound, I simply walked the grounds. A small brick patio, built like a lopsided circle, sort of oblong really, lay at the end of one path, and on those mornings when I woke too early I would head out there to the surprisingly comfortable wrought iron bench. With my coffee mug and my legal pad at hand I would work.

I would say that much of the actual writing of the dissertation, at least during passable weather, occurred right there. I used the Ransom Library for research and notes.

Beside the fifty-five a month, which I doubt covered electricity and water, my only obligations were to watch the house and the Spaniels when the Hollises made one of their many trips. Professor Hollis was in the history department—the American Civil War was his speciality—and he headed out often to poke through battle sites with his maps and metal detectors. In the basement he had several 4' x 8' plywood tables laid out with battle scenes.

It seemed, in time, that I became one of the family, whether reading the paper in the Victorian living room or weeding the garden on a sunny afternoon. And the Hollises were more than happy to permit my friends over if they were going out.

Many Saturday evenings passed with Lincoln and I, Janeen and her friend Rosetta Lara, whom we called Rose of course, hard into a pinochle game—men versus women, always. When we fell behind, Lincoln would pull out his black, calabash-shaped pipe and light up his daddy's tobacco. Within ten minutes Lincoln was grinning and our heads were swimming.

I wondered if it was passing the time, or an escape from time.

But it was Janie's face I saw in my mind now, as I walked down the street to Gerabaldi's Bookstore, where I thought I'd pass a few minutes. Their used book section was the best anywhere—everything from cheap paperback westerns and romances to signed first editions.

Maybe I'd pick something up for Janeen.

Besides the Hollises, she, Lincoln, and maybe Rose, who I didn't really know very well, had been my lifesavers.

She had held me, then, that Friday after I called her in a panic, late into the midnight hours, while I alternately paced or sobbed in her arms. And it was Janie who finally shoved a couple of Tylenol PM down my throat and forced me to bed. I awakened groggy and mentally incoherent to the smell of bacon and eggs frying and for a minute my heart jumped.

Shelley was back! Even then I would have taken her back in a heartbeat.

When I stumbled into the kitchen, wearing the same T-shirt and jeans I had fallen asleep in, it was Janie at the stove.

She tried to smile at me. It was the first time I had ever seen her eyes fail. She looked at me and tears coursed down her cheeks. We met halfway across the kitchen, grabbing on to each other for dear life.

She had slept that night, or tried to, wrapped in a shawl on the old couch.

I had forgotten that while I had lost my wife—I almost wrote life—Janie had lost her closest friend.

"I have to go," she said.

"I know," I whispered. "Thank you."

She looked up at me and smiled, rubbing the back of her hand across her eyes. "The eggs are probably burned," she said with a choked laugh. "I turned the burner off."

"I like them that way."

"I'll never forgive her," Janie said. "We were friends and she never breathed a hint of it."

"Me neither."

"She violated my trust. I can't forgive that."

I just nodded. I was too numb to think about it, yet it was all I could think about. "Her choice," I mumbled.

"I'll call you later today," she said.

No, I hadn't expected it either. A bolt from the blue. An earthquake. What do we have at such a times but clichés?

I had come home from class, carrying Italian takeout from Angotti's. Cannelloni, one of our favorites. And I bought a cheap bottle of Sangria. It was Friday night, after all. We needed a break. I had just prepped for exam week, and, as was my fashion, would do little more than scan my notes and get a good night's sleep before exams. I was ready. But not for this.

Shelley had found a job as a receptionist in a busy dental office, and although she enjoyed it, I know it wasn't her ideal. It was definitely not what she had gone through college for, majoring in graphic arts while I did art history.

All the clues were there, looking back. I hadn't seen any of them at the time—the Saturdays when she had to go in to work, the mornings she left early or afternoons she stayed late. Why should I notice? I, at least, was wildly in love with her and unbelievably happy. We married at the start of our junior year in college, supported ourselves on two part-time jobs and what we made during the summer. She was a National Merit Scholar; I had a small scholarship and a fistful of loans. Regular gifts from her well-to-do parents helped.

I wonder if she began to feel she married beneath her station. "Art historian" sounded so profoundly dull.

The "whys" echoed like waves all weekend. Janie took me out to lunch on Saturday.

Lincoln came over Saturday night. He sat on the old couch, one we had bought second hand in college. He didn't waste any time commiserating. "Give me the note," he said.

"Why on earth—"

"Trust me. Give me the note."

"But . . ."

"Give. Me. The. Note. Now."

I pulled it off the shelf in the kitchen and watched as his big hands shredded it. He got up and flushed the pieces down the toilet.

It didn't matter to me. I could never forget a single word. It was short, and had no heading or closing. Just an objective statement, as if I were a dirty rag she had used and thrown away.

> I find that I no longer love you. I'm not sure I ever did. Maybe we were too young, and it was childlike infatuation.
>
> But I have found love now, and I know that it is real. John's attorney will be taking care of the divorce papers and will contact you soon.
>
> Throw out or keep whatever you want here. I'll never be back. Don't try to contact me. Don't call either of us.

Monday morning, before Lincoln picked me up to make sure I took my exam, I checked the list of names at the practice. Only one John. John Knuckles. I almost laughed aloud. Shelley Knuckles.

Then, as I lifted the phone, my heart was hammering.

"I'd like to speak with John Knuckles, please."

"Dr. Knuckles?" said a whiny voice. "Doctor isn't in."

"When can I contact him?"

"Do you wish to make an appointment?"

My voice was getting angry. "No. I have to speak with him on another matter. A very important matter."

"Who did you say this is?"

"When will he be in?"

"Oh . . . not till next week. He's on vacation."

I slammed the phone down and stood there panting until I heard Lincoln blaring the horn of his big, purple, fourteen-year-old Ford Crown Victoria.

Two days after exam week I had moved into the Hollises' room, dropping off almost everything we owned at the Salvation Army.

I signed the divorce papers, said goodbye to two-and-a-half years or courtship and the same of marriage, and tried not to look back. I did nearly every day, wondering what *they* were doing, if *they* had children (we were going to wait until graduation). In time the stone in my heart had worn down some. It helped to work on the dissertation. It helped to have friends.

I glanced at my watch. It was 5:30 already. I had been standing in an aisle looking at a row of book spines, totally unaware of what they were.

If I hurried I could stop at the bakery for something. Cheesecake. When in doubt, buy cheesecake.

"Terrific," sighed Lincoln. "Probably the best cannelloni I've had in ages."

"Since the last time you were here and scarfed it down," I said.

"This would be true," he replied. He slipped his big black pipe out of his pocket and fingered the stem. "Don't worry, Janie girl. Just my worry beads until you break out that cheesecake."

"You know how allergic I am to the smoke. Just the sight of that thing makes my eyes run."

"Mine too. Tears of pleasure."

"Why," I asked, "does it smell so much worse than Hollis's? He gets this stuff. Amphora Full Aromatic, I believe, sent from Canada. It makes the whole house smell sweet. And it's the only reason he lets you smoke there."

"Easy answer. All that commercial stuff is flavored up, shot through with chemicals. My daddy's tobacco has the taste of good North Carolina soil. Home grown and cured.

"Course those four acres have other good stuff mixed in too. Compost. Manure. Which reminds me of our talk today."

"Just compost and manure?" Janie asked. "Probably so."

"Maybe so," said Lincoln. "I was thinking more along the lines of cultural-injected or artificial concepts of what's real, and the thing that is real in itself."

"Whoa," I said. "Before Lincoln orates, let me cut the cheesecake. Coffee's made, isn't it?"

"Right. Why don't we sit in my drawing room?" Janie said in reference to her tiny living room. Her whole apartment—kitchen, bath, bedroom, and living room—would probably just fit into my one spacious room. I had nine windows in my room alone; Janie had a double in the kitchen, something like a porthole in the bath, and a double in the bedroom. Lincoln shuffled toward the largest, overstuffed chair. His feet seemed to threaten the opposite wall. Janie carried in the coffee while I sliced generous pieces of cheesecake.

"Okay, Lincoln," I said when we had settled in, "what's weighing on that fragile brain of yours?'

"Ah. Eternal weight. It is so light that we are seldom aware of it. So heavy it buckles us to our mental knees."

"Are we getting discourse or preaching?" Janie asked with a grin.

"Feel free to say amen at any time."

"Amen," she said. "Go for it, Lincoln."

"I'm still troubled by what I perceive as relativism in your comments this afternoon."

"Well? Isn't that a teacher's role? To raise questions for students to search out their own answers?"

"I'm not so sure, my admirable McClatchy. Although I admire the fact that you have the highest evaluations in the grad school so you must be doing something right. But look at it this way. Are your students in your class to 'learn' or to 'receive'? You see, if all they do is sit in a room and talk, then they all believe, individually, pretty much what they want.

"Now, on the other hand, instead of 'facilitating discussion'—a truly abhorrent term, full of contradictions—let's say that the very term *professor* means what it says. That is, one who professes."

"Professes what, though? Any old angle she chooses?" I asked.

"You're getting warmer, but still wrong. The answer is knowledge and belief. The facts and the way we hold those facts—as warranted, or privileged, or whatever. The point is that these are received by the students as that upon which they form their judgment of rightness or wrongness."

"So you favor the old lecture method?" Janie asked.

"No. Don't misunderstand. I don't care if a prof stands on his head and asks questions, as long as she remembers that she is professing. Knowledge and belief. Which brings me back to this afternoon. Your argument . . ."

"I wasn't arguing, Lincoln. I was cajoling, facilitating, charming," Janie interrupted.

Lincoln laughed. The pipe was out again. Janie shifted her eyes meaningfully.

"Yes," he said. "What you were saying was that all values, our very sense of right and wrong, are projections of our imagination and collected in stories. The 'myths,' you called them."

"And?" She had a way of arching one eyebrow that I found either endearing or amusing. Janeen could do more with one facial gesture than I could with a half-hour lecture. Which was why I leaned back against the only other chair from my position on the floor. Janie was in the chair, I was sipping coffee, following the conversation, waiting for a chance to jump in, and nervously mindful of the proximity of her slim legs. Hardly a freckle on them.

"And I suggested the reversal," Lincoln said. "That all these 'myths' were incarnations of one true story that we have received from one divine source. Or put it like this—God has revealed enough of himself to make the myths meaningful. *Myths* and *mystery*. Myths provide stories about the mysteries of our spiritual nature."

"God?"

"Yes. I did use that one impermissible term, didn't I? I can't think of a better one, though, since it is the central term of all myth since the beginning of the written word. It's there in the ancient philosophers, too," Lincoln added. "Heraclites had his Logos. Aristotle had his Unmoved Mover. Plato had his Ideal."

"And Christians took over the concept, like Plotinus," I tossed in for the sake of company.

"Not necessarily," Lincoln said. "Christians *humanized* the concept because their central story is that God himself was born as human. Moreover, that this human, Jesus Christ, claimed to be God, for which, we remember, he was killed. A tendency of humanity, don't you think? When our gods get too close to us, we get uncomfortable. We despise them. They make demands on us. But the real point of my thinking—"

"Amen!"

"Stuff it, McClatchy."

"The cheesecake?"

"Sure. You eat like a horse and never gain an ounce."

"Lucky genes."

Lincoln pointed the stem of the black pipe at her. "Pipe down," he said.

She laughed aloud.

I got up to pour more coffee. The real stuff, fresh ground Columbian as dark and rich as earth. Maybe like Lincoln's tobacco. When I sat back down he took up again without missing a beat.

"If, as you say," nodding toward Janie, "truth is relative to this life—to our individual imaginations—then what of an afterlife?"

"Another myth?"

"Well, it has to be, given your premise. But suppose, looking at it my way, from the perspective of 'received' rather than 'projected,' then we have to examine this more carefully, for part of the imparted truth is that this life isn't the end of the matter, but the beginning. Nearly all of these myths, I might add, story the afterlife. For some, like the Yankton Dakota Sioux, who spent little time on evil in their stories, the afterlife was, literally, a happy hunting ground. That's why the dead were often buried with their favorite treasures—a special pipe, some pottery. Perhaps their favorite pony sacrificed at the burial site. Thus they could have their favorite things when they rode with old friends in the land of Wankantanka, the Great Spirit."

"How about your people?" I asked.

"Well, since the 1830s we have had a pretty good sense of evil," he said. He smiled, but it was without humor.

"The Trail of Tears," I said.

"Somehow the term doesn't seem strong enough today, though," he said, musing. "Tears acquire significance in comparison to the joy my people felt. They were a happy people, in harmony. Maybe it would have been better if they fought, rather than submitted. But they submitted to spare the women and children, the very ones who suffered and died on the forced march to Oklahoma. But enough of that."

I wasn't so sure. What he said about tears acquiring significance in comparison to joy stuck like barb wire in my mind.

"Here we have to do the hard thing," he was saying. "We have to entertain the notion of an afterlife. And since we see how values are relativist and skewed in this life—Jackson must have believed he was doing the right thing in sacrificing the Cherokee, after all—we have to admit that this afterlife answers not to some human judgment but some absolute justice."

Janeen groaned. "You're not saying . . ."

"Indeed I am. A heaven and hell. As real, physical entities. Let's set aside for a moment—although I know it's hard—the Greek and Roman mythologies of the *underworld*, generally assumed to be a place where the dead dwell. Nothing more, nothing less. No sense of punishment or endurance of suffering."

"Wait a minute," Janeen said. "Aeneas meets Sibyl in hell. Aeneas even makes an offering to Pluto and Persephone and encounters the suffering dead there."

"True. Which proves my point. Even the pagan imagination receives glimpses of divine truth. But remember that Aeneas escapes. Of course, as you well know, the mind of Virgil echoes through the ages. We have Dante, who adopts Virgil as his guide; Milton shows the celebration in hell in *Paradise Lost*; C. S. Lewis measured *The Great Divorce* between heaven and hell; John Paul Sartre closed hell up in *No Exit*. Where do all these stories—pagan or Christian—come from?

"But we have another question to ask, because all these pictures differ. And the question is this: What do we mean by *hell*? Consider the biblical answers, and I'll point out why in a moment.

"First, the common reference in the Old Testament is *Sheol*, a word that seems to carry a meaning similar to those of other early cultures—the place of the dead.[1] Like Hades. The logic was simple: the 'person' is not here, but only the body; therefore, the 'person' is somewhere other than the body; therefore, the 'person' is in Sheol, the land of the dead. So far, much like the other ancients."

"Mere oblivion," I added.

"Precisely. But that's where the biblical understanding of Sheol differs. In the Old Testament, those in Sheol are cut off from a relationship with God. You see, humanity has an awareness or consciousness of God unshared with the animal world. Helmut Thielicke was insightful on this.[2] So, from the outset Sheol suggests not just oblivion, but separation from God. That's why David prays, 'For thou dost not give me up to Sheol, or let thy godly one see the Pit.'[3] That separation would be the very worst thing he could imagine."

"Hang on a second, Lincoln." Janie jumped up and went into her bedroom. She reemerged a few seconds later.

"Yes. I thought I remembered it this way. Here in the NIV it says, 'will not abandon me to the grave.'"

"Remember that I said the Hebrew origin was uncertain. "Grave" is another close translation, a synonym really. You'll find the same form throughout David's Psalms.

"But I lose track. On the first point we see that Sheol is not mere oblivion but separation from one's relationship with God."

1. A brief but authoritative study of the linguistic implications of Sheol and related words appears in Block's essay, "The Old Testament on Hell," in Morgan and Peterson, *Hell Under Fire*. See also chapters 18–20 of Anthony Hoekema's *The Bible and the Future*, wherein he traces the linguistic implications of the Hebrew and also Jesus' references in Aramaic.

2. See Thielicke, *Death and Life*. On humanity's awareness of God and death, Thielicke writes: "Only men know this. Only he with his solitary awareness of death protrudes above the creaturely realm and thus has a different form of perishability, as though he were raised to a higher power. He alone must pose the question of the meaning of God's action that comes to expression in his death" (*Death and Life*, 138).

3. Ps 16:10.

"And if there were no relationship?" I asked.

"Well, David makes that clear, doesn't he? 'Abandoned' to the grave. Yet he believed *he* could be rescued from Sheol.[4] Interesting, no? This is what makes Sheol different from, let's say, Hades, which literally means 'the unseen realm' or 'the land of no return,' or 'The House of Darkness' in the Gilgamesh epic. But I transgress by digression."

Janie sat down in the chair behind me. Suddenly I felt a shiver. I thought it was an ant on my neck, and I was going to slap at it. Her fingertips, lightly tracing lines. I nearly groaned. What was happening? As suddenly, she withdrew her hand. A friendly touch? A subconscious reaching out? Then once more she touched my long hair with her palm and patted it smooth. Well, why not? I had more waves in that than an ocean. Maybe I should just cut it down, smooth the waters so to speak, set the harbor calm.

It was a few moments before I could pick up the thread of Lincoln's discourse. As quickly as I did, Janie interrupted.

"You know what? These undergrads we teach? On a Friday night they're out partying their socks off. And we're . . . what? Talking about this *mythical* place of Sheol? Not that I don't find it fascinating, Lincoln. I really do."

"What do you want me to do?" he asked. "Want me to run out and buy some beer and drown the *reality*?"

"I wouldn't ask that. You might forget your train of thought and wouldn't sleep all night looking for it."

"That would never happen. I'd just be wondering where Rose was."

"I told you she had to work. Remember? She has this little itty-bitty scholarship and is getting by on loans and work. Anyway, remember that I told you I had proofread an issue for the literary journal?"

"Twenty-five dollars and a bottle of wine!" I shouted.

"Twenty-five is long gone, but the bottle is in the kitchen. I put it in the refrigerator to chill."

I reached under me and pulled out a bottle of Merlot as big as my calf. "Holy smokes!" I said.

"It's got some French on it," Janie said. "Maybe that means it's good." She was laughing. "Do the honors. I'll find some clean glasses in this mess."

The dinner dishes were still stacked in the sink.

4. See Pss 30:3, 49:15, and 107:20.

I opened the wine after several awkward attempts. "Ah," I said. "It has good nose."

She had found three clean jelly glasses.

"Madame," I said, "after you. You may carry the crystal."

I poured and settled back against the chair. The glass chilled and beaded.

"Hey, not bad," Lincoln said.

"A fine wine, just on time," I said.

"Hmm. Just on time," Lincoln mused. "Like my mom used to say—probably still does—'God, he don't always come just when we call on him, but God when he comes he is always just right on time.' Which reminds me. We were talking of time and eternity."

Janeen groaned. "You were talking. We were thinking about Merlot."

"Yes, well. We got as far as Sheol—the place of the dead, but also the place of complete separation from God and therefore evil."

"Evil," I said. "How did you get to evil?"

"It's all in Augustine, really.[5] But think about it. If God is all good, then evil is conceivable. That is, if there are positive properties or concepts, there have to be negative ones, at least as ideas. If there is anything like justice and truth, then there has to be something like injustice and falsehood. Furthermore, there has to be consequences for them respectively—heaven or hell. The idea isn't unique to the New Testament, of course; it's there in the Old, too.[6] The difference is that the New Testament introduces the Christ prophesied in the Old—the deliverer or rescuer."

"But I thought . . . " Janeen said, leaning her elbows forward on her knees. When I looked up, wisps of her auburn hair nearly brushed my face and I caught the faint herbal scent of her shampoo. "I thought that the New Testament 'hell' was Gehenna. You know, the garbage dump?"

Lincoln sipped the Merlot and refilled his glass. He smiled now. The linguist was on his home turf. "The origins of Gehenna actually go back to the time of Jeremiah, about 600 years before Christ, when the whole Middle East was in upheaval."

"As always," Janie said.

"That's about the time of the Babylonian attacks, isn't it?" I asked.

"Right. And at that time the 'Valley of Ben Hinnom,' later Gehenna, was renamed the 'Valley of Slaughter' because of the sacrifices to Baal.

5. See Augustine, *City of God* Book XII.

6. Cf. Isa 1:27–31.

People threw their sons into raging fires as offerings. Therefore the association.

"The actual term *Gehenna*, however, first appears in the Pseudepigrapha, books written about a hundred years before Christ. There it generally refers to the eternal extermination of sinners—annihilation by fire. But in some texts it refers to eternal punishment of sinners by burning.[7] Here the reference gets tricky because it's based on metaphorical qualities of the 'accursed valley' of Gehenna, the garbage dump outside of Jerusalem. When Jesus refers to Gehenna for the first time,[8] everyone associated it with that place. But also by Jesus' time Gehenna had become ingrained in the Jewish mind as a place of eternal punishment and torment."

"Quite a leap of the imagination," Janie quipped.

"Actually, more grounded in history than imagination," Lincoln said. "Gehenna is located by Bible scholars in a huge, deep pit southwest of Jerusalem. Because of the surrounding topography, it never contains water. At its lowest end there are many rock tombs, built for paupers' graves."

Maybe this was the pit into which Judas flung himself.

"Its history goes back much farther, though. In the days of Ahaz and Manasseh it was the site of child sacrifices to Molech. It was probably the place where God slew 185,000 Assyrian soldiers to save Jerusalem. The Israelites had to dispose of the health threat in the fastest way possible and stacked up the bodies, swarming with maggots in the heat, and burned them in one great conflagration. There are many more examples, like the Roman slaughter of the Jews in AD 69–70, but they all lead to the same end—torment and punishment."

"I don't know about you," I said, "but my brain can't take in one more thought."

"That's because you're quiet tonight," Janie said. "All the thoughts get blocked up in there if you don't let some out."

"Mental constipation?" I asked.

She smiled at me.

"No. I've had some really weird thoughts lately. I don't even know what to make of them—how to put them in words."

"If you reach that point, you know who to call."

"Thanks," I said. "Mercy. It's almost one."

7. See 1 Enoch 27:1–3.

8. See Matthew 5:22: "Anyone who says, 'You fool!' will be in danger of the fire of hell."

"So what?" said Lincoln. "Tomorrow's Saturday."

"Well, the wine's all gone," Janie said. "Lincoln, you want to suck on the bottle? Drain every drop?"

"Nah. I'm loopy enough."

"Agreed," we said in unison.

"Hey, Lincoln," Janie said. "Why don't you go outside so you can fire up that coal stove you call a car?"

Lincoln went outside, stuffing his pipe as he left.

"I really don't need any help picking up," Janie said.

"I'd be glad to help you."

She walked with me toward the door. "It relaxes me. Really. I like the soap and hot water."

"Okay. I'll see you soon. Like Monday, I guess."

She put her hand out and touched my elbow.

"I haven't asked you for a while." She smiled up at me. She put her hands on my shoulders and I wrapped my arms around her thin waist. Did she have any idea what this did to me? I tried to remember, pounding it into my brain, that we were friends. "But how are you doing these days?" she finished.

"I'm doing. Better every day."

Her eyes glittered. "Like the old song: 'I'm bruised and battered, but I'm healed.'" She sang it. I joined in the second line even if I couldn't carry two notes in a wheelbarrow without a major accident: "I'm down and defeated, but I'm healed."

We both laughed. She snuggled against me. Her hands had slipped behind my neck. Then she tilted her head back, a cascade of auburn slipping to my hands at the small of her back. She looked me right in the eye and said, "I should have told you this long ago, and I'll probably regret telling you now. But I think you're the most wonderful man I've ever met."

Her small hands bent my head. I closed my eyes and felt her parted lips pressed to mine. A second time, briefly, then she said good night and I was outside while the door closed softly.

"Hey," I heard a grunt and spotted a plume of smoke by the curb. "Need a ride?"

"I think I'd like to walk, Lincoln."

"Have it your way, my man."

The big Ford sputtered and bucked down the street until all the cylinders caught. Then it sounded like a runaway train.

CHAPTER FOUR

Reflections on the Pond

On Saturday mornings I generally slept in as long as I wanted to, which guaranteed that I usually awakened at my regular time of six.

That strange inner alarm tripped and told me I had to be doing something. By the time I had coffee made I had no idea what that something was. Just as I had always had the policy of not studying the night before an exam, believing that a good night's sleep was the best preparation, I also had a policy of not working on Saturday mornings.

When Shelley and I were together, we had an unspoken division of chores. I liked to clean or do dishes. She liked to do grocery shopping and wash. It was an easy pattern we had fallen into during our brief marriage.

I wondered what she did now. Whether they—the Knuckles—hired a maid. I wondered if she had a child, or children. I had deliberately never looked up their address, pretty easy to do on the computer or in the phone book. But I admit that sometimes I walked downtown and thought I saw a certain shade of hair color, or a body turned just so, or heard laughter at my back and my heart would hammer and my throat constrict.

Now I found myself thinking less and less even of the possibility. Some people call it healing. I called it learning how to forget.

Surely this Saturday morning other things were on my mind.

This was a traditional university town, pure and simple. Most livelihoods here somehow spun off of the university or its students. At its northern perimeter, however, near the highway to the state capital, developers had cookie cut the land into vast, treeless developments with all their quaint names purportedly evoking a long tradition that none of them had. "Homestead Estates," "Brighton Meadows"—that sort of thing. They all looked the same to me, some varied in size, some of vinyl siding (earth tones being the preferred colors), some of brick or stone. Some even lay behind gates barely disguised by little oval gardens of marigolds and salvia. Probably the Knuckles lived there somewhere, their house cooled by air conditioning. My room was cooled by a mammoth hickory tree on the south side. Past the swamp of developments, two malls girdled the highway—a traditional one on one side, built like a village of stores, and an outlet mall on the other side.

To the south was Old Town, a jumble of student rentals, blue-collar workers, and some grandly restored old homes like the Hollis's. For some reason, beyond a grocery store and a Citgo station, there had never been expansion to the south. It just sort of hung there suspended in time, the air thick with the past and the scent of flowers. When a neighbor cut his grass, you could smell it a block away.

And just past the grocery store, countryside and small farms rode together into a jumble of hills. I had walked those country roads for over four years; I would rue the day when I did so for the last time.

I was walking now along a ridge on a one-lane, gravel road. I had left my car in the tiny parking lot of a small church. Its bricks were painted white and it stood solemnly in the shadows of some old growth oak and hickory. A white fence enclosed a cemetery. The oldest stone had the dates 1801–1862. I know. I had walked through the well-kept yard often. I had even entered the church upon occasion. In its darkened cool space, with light fractured by a rose window over the altar and rippling glass from the early last century in the side windows, the interior was utterly peaceful, perfectly quiet.

That's also where I first met Ed Nolan.

During the Great Depression, the Works Progress Administration had dug hundreds of farm ponds through these hills and farmlands. They ranged in size from a small area where runoff from two or three conjoined ridges was dammed up, to ponds of an acre or more. Each was contoured to the land, appearing like a smooth part of nature. Routinely they were stocked with largemouth bass and bluegill, although some farmers with deep ponds later added perch fingerlings.

I already knew three farmers who let me fish their ponds. In fact, they were more than happy to have me. The ponds tended to get overrun with fish, even with raccoons and birds taking their fair share. The standard rule was to keep the bass and throw the bluegills in the field. The smaller fish were so aggressive here that sometimes they'd battle the bass for bait. I actually liked the gills better than bass, and generally kept some pan-frying-sized ones. Bass tend to keep the taste of the water they're in. After I filleted them, I'd rub kosher salt in, soak them in cold water for thirty minutes, and freeze them.

When I first met Ed Nolan, I felt that I knew a whole lot more about fishing than about art. In fact, Ed Nolan had probably taught me as much about art as anyone I had ever met.

I don't mean those dates and artists and techniques of artists that now, after years of scholarship, I could run through in my mind like a PowerPoint presentation. I mean art itself—the real, stunning vitality of it. Like that language deeper than words because of its sheer velocity of symbol, suggestion, and arrangement.

And I never would have guessed it.

The very first time I met Ed I was driving back roads in my worn Toyota—162,907 miles and counting on the odometer. The turnoff to the chapel and a glimmer of white through the trees caught my eye. I turned off from one gravel road to a narrower gravel road.

This was before the breakup—that nice, neat term for the cataclysm in my soul. I stopped driving and was walking among the crooked stones in the chapel cemetery, when an old Ford pickup trailing a spume of dust came down the dirt road and pulled off by the chapel.

Several inches shorter than me, Ed had a set of barrel-sized shoulders that bunched against a faded denim shirt. His arms were thick and layered with the same curly, black-gray hair that flew in all directions from his head. He hoisted a red lawn mower and gas can out of the truck. A large German shepherd bounded out of the truck bed, sniffed around, caught my scent, and ran over to me.

I froze. The dog sniffed me carefully, then sat down. Its tail was wagging, which I figured was a good sign. I held out a hand, palm out. A great pink tongue came out and slobbered it in one good stroke.

When Ed walked toward me, I thought he was going to tell me to get off the property. I'd been told that before on these back roads, once with a shotgun.

"Reckon you made a friend," the man said. He stretched out his hand.

"Always use another," I laughed.

"Ed Nolan," he said.

"Ed Nolan? Didn't you used to—"

"Right. But I retired from the u. some time ago."

"When there was some trouble . . ."

"Yeah. They didn't want my work. Wanted more commercial stuff. Easier to retire. So my wife and I bought this old farm and moved out here. Nobody I got to please no more. Except my wife."

Sure, I'd heard of Ed Nolan. He was a legend in the art department. He was considered a throwback to the Renaissance, and he openly condemned, with Goya being one of the few exceptions, most of the art of the twentieth century. Still, from former colleagues, there was a certain reverence paid to Ed Nolan.

"I'm really happy to meet you, Mr. Nolan . . ."

"Ed. I'm a farm boy now. Have been for twenty years and never happier."

Twenty years? He hardly looked a day over fifty. I found out later that he was seventy-two.

I explained to him that I was working in art history, specifically on Hieronymus Bosch. He lifted an eyebrow at that and smiled.

"Maybe you'd like to see my place," he offered.

We walked along the ridge, the dog gamboling like a frisky lamb into the overgrown woods. Ed whistled, "Come here, Jackson," he called. The big shepherd bounded up.

"Heel," Ed commanded softly. "Got into a skunk back there once," he said. "Had to sleep outside for three nights."

"Jackson? After Stonewall?"

He laughed. "Jackson Pollock."

"You like Pollock's work?"

"I think a dog could paint better."

We came out of the trees. To the west, slopes of pastureland fell away to a lower stand of trees. Two large, palomino geldings nuzzled for clover, turning their serious eyes toward us while they chewed.

"My wife's," Nolan said. "Chaucer and Milton. Although we don't ride them as much as we should. I see you're married. Why not bring your lady out and ride."

"I think Shelley would be terrified of horses."

"Doesn't matter. Claire would be happy to give lessons."

But what had caught my attention was down where the hills converged, just before the tree line. It was one of the largest ponds I'd seen. Better yet, it angled in several directions, contoured to the land, instead of the traditional oval.

"What a pond!" I said.

"Like it?"

"One of the nicest I've seen around here."

He smiled and paused. The air was fresh, like washed clothing hung out to dry. I could hear the buzz of crickets. One of the horses nickered. When I breathed deeply I felt that my lungs were being baptized.

"That was my first project when we moved here. The pond was a mess. Pure algae and weeds from top to bottom. Hardly any fish. But its contours were beautiful. Such harmony. So I drained it and dredged it with a backhoe, rebuilt the dam with clay and rock. When it filled, I restocked it."

"With what?"

"Bass and bluegill, of course. Got to keep the raccoons happy. But I had dredged it down to fifteen feet through the center so I put perch in too. Last I heard, they were doing fine. Feel free to fish it if you want. Just—"

"If it's bluegill, keep what you like. Toss the rest on the bank."

He laughed. "You've done some farm pond fishing."

"Not in water as clear as that."

"Probably not. The whole pasture here is fallow land now; no phosphorous ruining the water."

We started walking again. I hurried to keep up.

"A neighbor cuts it for hay twice a summer. And Claire keeps some sheep for her weavings. Does everything herself. Sheers, washes, everything. I stack some hay for the horses, the neighbor takes what he wants."

The farm buildings lay in a copse of trees at the end of the road. Along the way I learned that Ed had started with twenty acres, and over the years had bought up whatever additional land he could. "Anything to keep the developers away," he said.

The house itself was a modest affair. The only apparent indulgence was a long porch strung along the front, hung with a profusion of basketed flowers of all kinds—wave petunias, lobelia, New Guinea impatients, and the like. The pole barn sat further back, rimmed by several attached buildings that I took to be livestock stalls. We cut across a sparse yard where several free-range chickens rooted for insects and headed for the barn. So what do I want with hay, I thought.

The large double doors had been framed in with conventional doors, and rows of Thermopane windows stretched across each side. The first floor was laid with old board, but it was swept and washed clean. I could see how they had reframed the walls, insulating and residing the inside rather than the outside. Cabinets stretched everywhere.

Nolan strode briskly toward a twin staircase. "This is my side," he said. "Claire's studio is on the left."

We climbed up into a spacious loft stretching the length of the barn. There was one door in the dividing wall leading to Claire's studio. It was shut. "Working," he said. "I'll introduce you some other time."

But I was dazzled beyond belief. I knew, through rumors in the department grapevine, that Ed's work now sold for extravagant prices. The studio artists spoke of it and the prestigious awards Ed had gathered with envy. Here I stood, centered where the works were made.

The space floated with light. Six large skylights opened the roof. The polished oak floor glistened like the surface of water. Against the dividing wall stood more cabinets and two large stainless steel sinks. Somewhere an air conditioner hummed softly. Sturdy wooden work tables stood here and there, their surfaces littered with paint tubes and mason jars full of brushes.

But all that paled beside the paintings. I was stunned. Speechless. One finished work along the back wall was huge, six feet by eight according to my reckoning. Most compelling from this distance was the way Nolan had worked with shadings of gold. Some of it glittered with gilding. It was a Pietá, set not on the bleak summit of Golgotha but in an exquisite garden. Truly the figures held the dark hue of mourning, but the painting seemed to explode out of them. Even from here, though, from this distance, I sensed something wrong, something eternally awry in the Madonna. I stepped closer. Her pale skin, I now noticed, was disturbed by discolorations. Along the side of her jaw a greenish-purple bruise crawled like a snake. Her arms bore bruises. I nearly gasped. She wasn't suffering only for her son, but for all the suffering, all the abused, through history. She shared her son's pain in her flesh. Not the beatific lady, then, but Our Lady of Sorrow. I stepped closer yet.

The longer I looked among the ecstasy of flowers, the more I began to pick out tiny figures, like the kind on overhead posters in dentist's offices, but with a much finer degree of subtlety. A pair of startled eyes between the leaves. A tiny dun-colored form that could be mistaken for a leaf. Its nose almost seemed alive with twitching whiskers. I picked out hummingbirds, the scarlet of a cardinal's wing that I first thought was a flower. I found myself standing closer by the minute to the large panel.

"Don't they tell you to stand back to view art?" he said with a chuckle. "There are no rules. Stand as close as you like. Walk into the work with your mind."

I found myself leaning forward. I stood up with a crick in my back.

"So what did you find?" he asked.

"Ha! That's a trick question. Do you mean did I find Waldo?"

Nolan laughed. "That would be fun."

"I also found paradox," I quickly added.

"Aha!"

"The Pietá is always a lamentation. You certainly capture that in the abused Madonna. But it's also bursting with life. It almost reminds me . . ."

"Of whom?"

"Not a similarity, really. Maybe a contrast. Remember in Hieronymus Bosch's *Garden of Eden* Christ stands there with Adam and Eve. Adam is just waking up. Christ takes Eve by the wrist to introduce her to her mate. It's the epitome of joy. But even at that moment, there are dark shadows all around."

"The odd creatures feasting in the pond?"

"Yes. And it gets worse in the background. The ravens fly out of their hutch."

"The owl in the fountain?"

"A symbol of evil, isn't it?"

"Not necessarily," Nolan said. "Bosch uses it as a symbol of wisdom also. The symbol of Sophia. But what do you make of it all?"

"I honestly don't know at this point," I said. "I'm just starting out." I turned from his expansive painting, looked about the room as if some clue would pop out of a cabinet.

"I'm not sure I do either," he said. "But think about this. Every painting, or every good artist I should say, uses the physical to search the metaphysical. For painters, symbols, colors, light, and such are cobblestones on that road.

"Then too, my Pietá frames lamentation with joy. I'm not as extravagant as Bosch. But consider this. If there is evil in *his* paintings, the common charge, then we must always ask what frames it. What holds it in check? For example, already at Bosch's creation, in his *Garden of Eden* painting, evil is at the gates, but there is an order that prevails against it."

"What about his *Descent into Hell*?"

"Yes. There order gets sucked out altogether, doesn't it. Chaos. Maybe that's hell—life without rules.

"I don't claim to know much about Bosch," he added quickly, "but I think the key lies in the eternal."

"The eternal?"

"Essentially he's a mystic. Always looking for the point where time and eternity intersect."

That first meeting had been three years ago. I didn't see Ed Nolan often, only when he came down to greet me at the pond. I wouldn't think of disturbing his work. Sometimes he would invite me up to the studio to show me new work. Sometimes we would join Claire on the front porch for coffee and some of her baked goods, the making of which she was an expert at. Often she invited me to bring Shelley along.

But Shelley was busy. Shelley was working early. Or late.

I had returned home from Janie's apartment late that Friday night, with little hope for sleep. When I tried, my eyes stared blankly out at the ceiling and I saw Janie's face and my whole body seemed to throb. I wished I could seal the taste of her lips, feel their softness again as they parted gently. But she's only my friend, I thought. Or was she? Surely my closest friend.

Three years ago my closest friend, the one I trusted, the one I had exchanged vows of commitment with, divorced me. Without a care. Were all vows meaningless? Could I trust what I felt when my defenses, so carefully arranged with gates padlocked, told me to never again trust my feelings? This didn't make sense!

After several hours of tossing, I got up, made coffee, and filled the old green Stanley thermos. My rod and tackle were in the trunk. I headed up through the hills to Ed Nolan's farm.

Jackson runs up to make his greeting before dashing off into the pasture. We are old friends now. Sometimes I remember to bring him a treat. Not this morning.

Dew splashes up to my knees. The field sparkles like a blanket of diamonds; each cobweb strung up in the Queen Anne's lace is strewn with jewels.

The water is perfectly still. The valley is capped in humidity and mist floats off the side of the pond that the rising sun has not yet touched. I imagine someone under the water breathing softly.

Dragonflies knit the air with blue wings. They are so delicate, yet so haughty. Two of them perform acrobatics in the air and I imagine the whole pond applauding. A fresh green breeze arises from the woods below. By midmorning, the air will be perfectly still.

I attach a hula popper. Sometimes I keep the bass when they're in the nice thirteen- to fourteen-inch range. I broil them for a pinochle night when the Hollises are gone. The lunkers I always toss back. Today I will not keep anything. Today I am just at the pond.

By the cattails on the east side where I fish, I find two fish skeletons. The raccoons aren't fussy. When they finish with their catch, the small animals come. We all seem to be walking the rim of another world in a tense and fragile peace.

I lay the popper alongside the cattails. Almost immediately the bass charges, arcing a foot out of the water in a fury of silver spray. I play the fish lightly and release it. It's a fine thing, this tense and fragile peace.

I had reeled in the hula popper long ago. I sat now with my chin on my knees, arms wrapped around my legs. A hunched up rag doll, I thought. What had Janie said? Wonderful? Not hardly. I had lived in a world of fear for three years, my dissertation my only safety net against collapse. People marveled at my pace. I felt if I didn't work I'd die.

The sun rose higher, touching my shoulders. The crickets sawed like a classroom full of Suzuki violinists. I was drowsing off.

I heard his voice speaking, softly. "Good morning, pilgrim."

I rubbed my eyes. He stood on the water not ten feet in front of me.

"No. Go away," I groaned.

"You have sought me for a long time now. Now that I come, do you want to send me away?"

"Leave me alone." Curiously, the apparition looked nothing at all like his other self-portraits. Then I recognized it. It was "The Rescue" from *The Temptation of Saint Anthony*. Was he toying with me? He wore the same scarlet cloak over a silver undergarment. The black, calf-length boots, the headdress that looked eerily similar to the Muslim kaffiyeh. In the painting Bosch is in the lead, directing Saint Anthony, while two other rescuers assist on either side. Supposedly they are three monks, leading Saint Anthony on the straight road beset by crooked bypaths into degradation, the occult, and despair. I also thought one had to be dim-witted not to see the Christ-like qualities in Bosch's white crown of hair, the scarlet and silver-white garments, the thick-leather boots of battle. What it meant in this moment of delirium, I had no idea.

What struck me about this apparition on the water was the sheer magnetism of the figure; the fierce concentration pictured in the wide mouth; the straight, pointed nose; the grimly set lips. But especially those large dark eyes that fixed on me like some dog on the hunt.

"Leave you alone? Surely, if you wish. I can't force you to do anything. I can only offer."

"Offer what? You're a . . . ghost, a figment."

"Actually, I'm a servant, but we can discuss that some other time."

"Are you something in my brain? I feel like I'm going crazy." I hugged my knees. I was trembling.

"I assure you I am *not* in your brain, although some of your doctors might say that. We're conversing with our minds."

"I prefer language."

"Very well." His voice was surprisingly gentle. He smiled. "How many times have you asked, 'I wish I knew what he was thinking here,' or 'Could he have meant this?' Shall we investigate the questions?"

"I don't want anything to do with you. I'll finish my dissertation and never think of you again."

"Truly, you do have much to think about, don't you?"

"Shut up. It's ridiculous. What are we going to do, anyway? Sit on the bank here and talk? Maybe drink a little wine?"

The inflection of his voice never wavered. "I hope we can do two things. At least, I think that's why I was sent. One can never be sure until one starts." He held up a hand to stay my retort.

"First, I hope we can find wisdom. What you have found so far in your work has been knowledge. Hints of wisdom to be sure. The theology part. But you don't really know what to do with it."

"Enough to get my degree."

"Precisely. Enough knowledge. Do you remember my owls?"

"Of course. I mean, they're in all kinds of your paintings."

"And how does conventional 'knowledge' construe them?"

"Well, they're predators, so most see them as evil omens, ready to feed on disaster."

"I don't know about 'most.' I no longer need to follow my following. One of the advantages of having passed from this life is a relief from gratification. But, suppose that for me it's a different symbol."

"Like what?"

"Well, this doesn't make the critics wrong, or me right. But suppose for a moment that the owl does represent the predator—the razor talons, the hooked beak. But the owl also has the great, round, liquid eyes that always appear to be searching inward. Now, put it together, my young scholar."

"I can't. They're contradictory qualities."

"Ah, but consider that the claws and beak are also symbols of humanity's search for knowledge. It has always been part of our nature; Sisyphus lives in each of us. But the eyes, the beautiful eyes of Sophia, represent wisdom—what we do with knowledge, how we act upon it or don't act upon it."

"So you want to teach me wisdom. Not a bad trick. I need it. What's your second trick?"

"To teach you wisdom, I have been sent to be your tour guide."

"Sounds promising. New Zealand? Chile? I've been to Europe. How about Canada? I'm a bit partial to Canada myself."

The smile faded slowly. "To hell," he said.

I rose to my feet. "Get out!" I screamed. "You devil! Leave me alone!"

I had fallen in the water, thrashing among the cattails and screaming, when Ed Nolan and Jackson came running down the hill.

The apparition had disappeared.

CHAPTER FIVE

Knowledge and Wisdom

I awakened Sunday morning with a start. I fumbled about uncertainly—a strange pillow under my head, a quilt over me. My bladder ready to explode. I got my bearings, wondering for a moment what I was dong in her apartment. It all came back as I padded in my bare feet—when did I take my shoes off?—to the bathroom.

When Ed Nolan grabbed me, I had passed out. My torso on the bank, my legs sprawled among the cattails. Not until later, when I was wrapped in a blanket and sipping Claire's herbal tea, did I learn that that strong old man had picked me up and carried me to the house.

"You're kind of long," he joked later. "I just sort of draped you around my neck like an old polish sausage."

I insisted that I had just passed out because I hadn't been able to sleep the night before and was startled awake by a dream.

Ed was skeptical. "It was more than a dream, wasn't it? You were afraid of something."

I shook my head, wondering if it wouldn't be better to tell him. He offered to drive me home, but I insisted I was okay now. Within a few minutes I was knocking on Janeen's door. It was automatic. I didn't think about it. Only later did I wonder what she thought with a madman pounding at her door.

With my mind dredging words out of the whirlwind, I tried to tell my story. Finally she shushed me and put me to sleep on the sofa.

I felt better this morning. Thirteen hours of sleep had something to do with that. Janie was gone and I had no idea where. But coffee was left in the pot and the red light was on. It couldn't be any more stale than the sludge I sometimes reheated three or four times. This wasn't bad at all. I found some Honey Nut Cheerios in a drawer and ate them dry with my coffee.

I decided to put myself to work doing the dishes, cleaning the counter. My old impulse for cleaning continued. I folded and stored the quilt and pillow in Janie's closet. I looked around her room—the rumpled bed, clothes strewn in a corner. The desk and chair were the only neatly arranged objects in the room. Stacks of books lined up along the desk like soldiers in formation. In a peculiar moment, I caught her scent in the room. It made my head swim.

I went to the living room and switched on the TV, flicking past a million church services before finding CNN.

Seven people found murdered in a New York apartment.

Twenty people killed by a car bomb in Iraq.

A hurricane approaching the Gulf Coast.

Randy Johnson pitched a one-hitter for the Yankees. I turned it off and was about to put a CD on when Janie walked in.

"Hi."

"Hi," I said. "I guess I ought to be going."

"Don't be embarrassed. I'm glad you came here."

She was dressed in white linen pants and a deep rust-colored top that made her emerald eyes flash.

"Thanks for taking me in."

"You can pay me back. Pietro's has a buffet on Sunday at noon."

I laughed. "Sounds great. But I'm still dressed in fishing clothes."

"Doesn't matter. Everyone will be looking at me." She grinned.

Did she know how stunning she looked? Of course, I thought. And why would she want to go out with me?

"Jump in the shower," she said. "You still smell like pond water. We can swing past your house and get some less smelly clothes. There's a towel on the bar."

"Where were you?" I asked as I turned to the bathroom.

"Lincoln asked me to go to church with him. I did."

"Oh? How was it?"

"I'll tell you over lunch. Now get showered or I'll drop you off at a fish market."

Pietro's not only had the best Italian food in town, but very likely the best in the region or the state. It was a long step above the pizza and sub joints that dotted nearly every corner of a university town and a step above Angotti's takeout. We had just finished our second trip through the buffet, sampling the pizza and hot dishes until we felt like stuffed turkeys. The place was jammed now. Nonetheless, we ordered spumoni and coffee, relaxing in the cool air.

"So. You were going to tell me about church."

"It's not my first time in a church, screwball. You make it sound like some exotic adventure."

"The skeptic's Sabbath?"

"Please. Just because I like to argue things doesn't mean I don't believe some things."

"Lincoln believes it's the truth."

"Maybe it is."

"But you don't know."

"You should come with us sometime." She could deflect a meteorite.

"Janie . . ." I stumbled. "About . . ."

"Yes?" Her eyes smiled above the rim of the coffee cup.

"About Friday night?"

"I've wanted to do that for a long time," she said. "It wasn't impetuous."

"I thought you . . . maybe . . . just felt sorry for me. We've been friends a long time."

"You're the only person who can feel sorry for yourself. I think you're past that point, getting stronger every day. I wouldn't have dared do it a year ago, even though I wanted to then already."

She set down her coffee and leaned toward me. Her hands were folded on the table. A thin gold bracelet dangled from one wrist. It was the only jewelry she wore. "It used to kill me to see what she was doing to you."

"You mean while we were married? You knew?"

"Of course I knew. Oh, I didn't see it firsthand, but a woman knows these things."

"Why didn't you tell me?"

"I didn't want you to hate me. And you would have if I were the one to tell you. You asked me what I believed. I believe hate is a sin we commit against ourselves."

"Did you really have feelings for me? I mean . . ."

"I know what you mean. No, quite frankly. Not then. I would never permit myself to be attracted to the husband of my friend."

"But you were my friend too."

"Of course. And my task as your friend was to support you. To be with you. There's something about honor in there."

"I've got to admit, Janie, that at first I hugged you because . . . I needed someone to hug. Someone to comfort me. And then it became different. I wanted to hug you because I wanted to hug *you*. You know what I mean?"

"Yes." Janie smiled as if we were sharing a secret.

"It grew to the point where I didn't want to let go. As if something . . . . Someone, I forget who, once read a line to me—'As if my soul were making love with your soul.' But, you know, we were friends so I thought I better back off."

"Being friends is great," Janie said. "There's no reason why we can't be more than that. But there's no hurry."

"Oh! Let's hurry," I said. We were both laughing when we left Pietro's.

When I dropped her off, Janie said through the open window of my car, "Thanks for coming to me last night. I'm glad you trusted me."

"If you have any answers, let me know."

"No," she said. "I don't think that's my place right now. But I'd encourage you to talk to Lincoln."

I left that night happier than I'd felt in months.

Monday I awakened feeling like a new person. I walked up to the Ransom Library in the cool morning with a bounce in my step for the first time in years. When I opened the eleventh-floor door, I crept quietly along the stacks and spotted her in her customary carrel. I put down my briefcase, walked softly behind her, and kissed her on the cheek.

"Hmm," Janie said as she nuzzled her cheek toward me. "You're early this morning. What if some other red-haired woman was sitting here? Or do you greet them all that way?"

I laughed and moved across the room to my window carrel. Mist hung over the river. Funny, I thought, because this morning I had a clarity of thought that seemed frightening. When I started writing it seemed like every word had been perfectly scripted in my mind. For the first time I thought of the "red zone," the last twenty pages of the dissertation. I believed I was near it now.

Janie had a noon consultation and Lincoln hadn't been in yet today. I spent lunchtime chewing on a sack of carrots and celery I had thrown together and thinking about the afternoon's work. This is really a beautiful campus, I was thinking. The colonial-style buildings were framed by old growth trees, mostly oak and hickory. It rained often here and the grass stayed lush and thick in all but the driest heat spells. With some surprise I realized that I hadn't thought of Saturday's nightmare once.

The next morning, Tuesday, I decided to work on the garden bench at the Hollis's. I didn't decide so much as follow an impulse. I wondered sometimes if I weren't too deliberate, charting out my life in segments like a AAA flip map. Life wouldn't have it that way. It threw sudden detours, even drop-offs, in our way. Maybe a better course would be to take the slow way along the detour, get off the interstate, savor the woods and lakes of unexpected countryside.

Like my academic career. I was a compulsive perfectionist. In college I'd go into a sulk if I got an A- or, horrors, a B+ instead of an A. I could have been the poster boy for a convention of psychiatrists on obsessive-compulsive academics. Indeed, as I mentioned, I had an outline for my dissertation by the time I was a senior in college. Everything so very neat, so very pigeonholed.

Just like the very neat and very brief marriage to Shelley, I thought as I settled onto the bench in the rose garden and poured coffee from the Stanley thermos. Except it wasn't. And I felt like I couldn't fully go on until I made some sense of my own feelings. In a sense, I didn't want to think about it this morning. I wanted to write.

Why did I see Shelley's face this morning? Although I confess that her features were less clear every day. I had nearly succeeded in my task—forgetting the past. Almost. What I hadn't arrived at was understanding. Perhaps I never would. Perhaps I didn't care anymore.

Yet I wondered how such a good thing—what I thought had been good—could have gone so bad.

It wasn't surprising to me that I hadn't been in a church since the day Shelley left. This was not the way things were supposed to be. After all, wasn't that why one went to church? God's in his heaven; all's right with the world. At least that's pretty much the way I had learned it growing up.

But *goodness* itself? If things happened that weren't supposed to be, what did that imply about the way things should be? On the one hand, the question was easy to answer. Janie was good. I chuckled. What did I mean by that? A thousand answers tumbled through my mind. She was also a self-professed skeptic. Can there be a skeptic who is nonetheless good? Of course. That was easy. But how does one measure that good? By what standards? I called her my "recovering skeptic."

And, beyond a shadow of a doubt, Lincoln was good. More, I believed, he was a thoroughly *noble* man; that is, he lived his goodness. I found it very odd how he seemed attracted to Rose, a migrant girl from Texas who believed above all in her own power to rise above her status.

But Shelley? I had thought her goodness incarnate. Yes, I had virtually worshiped her.

Curiously, I found myself jotting notes on my yellow tablet. I still have the sheet—twenty pages from the end of the dissertation.

Proposition:	Shelley was good.
	But, Shelley committed a sin.
Question:	What was the nature of that sin?
Answer:	She divorced me. But that wasn't the sin itself. What was it? Broken vows. Against whom did she break those vows? This: "from this time forward, for richer or poorer, in sickness and in health . . ." Against me. No. Rather the violation was against God, before whom the vows were taken. The pain against me was the consequence.
Conclusion:	
	This is nerve-wracking. If against God, does her sin have eternal consequence? If the pain against me is temporal and consequential, does that mean I have to release it? Forgive it? Grieving is natural—a part of human nature, a means for dealing with pain. An emotional act.

> Forgiveness is an act of the mind, a rational decision to release oneself from the pain.
> But I can't just "put it away."
> Of course not. There can't be, in human terms, "reconciliation." The divorce sealed that. She chose against me.
> And I can choose to accept that and choose to live with what I have been given in place.

I felt that I wouldn't be doing much writing on Hieronymus Bosch today. And I wanted to talk with Lincoln before our pinochle game on Friday with Rose and Janie. It would be at the Hollises's this weekend. They were in Alaska. No Civil War battlefields there, but Professor Hollis confessed to me that he couldn't die content until he had seen grizzly bears catching salmon. I haven't figured that out either.

I walked up to the university without my briefcase. I was taking a day off. At the beginning of the work week. I'd make my deadline easy. Twenty pages.

Even so, the graduate school had a program where their new PhDs could teach three-quarter time for a year if they chose. The idea was to bolster their resume in the competitive job market and give them time to send out applications. Sending out fifty or sixty apps and traveling to interviews wreaked havoc with writing the dissertation.

The exceptions, of course, were people like Lincoln, who were already being courted by prestigious schools and could take their pick.

I ran into him when he was coming out of Ransom for his lunch break. I hadn't packed anything so we stopped at a corner sub shop and I picked up a sandwich before we walked to the Hurlbutt Bench.

We ate while exchanging common chitchat. I reminded him of the pinochle game Friday. He finished his Vernor's in one long swallow, set it aside, and said, "Now. What did you want to tell me."

I stared at him.

"I know you well enough to know you've got something on that big ol' brain of yours." He pulled out his pipe, packed it carefully from the leather pouch, and lit it with a Diamond wooden match. I started at the beginning, with the first time I had seen Bosch's face.

Not once did Lincoln interrupt me. Except for the occasional strike of a match, he watched and listened. When I finished with the nightmare at the pond, he was still sitting there, staring pensively at the leaves overhead. I began to feel the flush of embarrassment. It was all . . . ludicrous.

"It's had one good effect," Lincoln observed finally.

"What's that?"

"It's brought you and Janie together."

"Did she tell . . ."

Lincoln held up a hand—as big as a fielder's glove. "Janie would never betray a confidence. Not ever. Let's just say that I've seen this unfolding for a long, long time. And it's different now, isn't it? I often wondered how blind you could be."

He shook his big head languorously, in mock pity. "Does she know about this?" he asked.

"Yes."

"But we're not talking about Janie here, are we?" He brushed his hand aside in a motion of dismissal. He knocked the dottle out of his pipe against the sole of his shoe and reflected. "Very interesting," he murmured.

I waited for him to go on.

"The Cherokee," he said, "like most other Native Americans, worshiped one Supreme Being. Some nations made fine distinctions, as I believe I have pointed out before. Something very much like the Christian Trinity. Now, the duty of man in this worship was to live in harmony with the world around him.

"That was part of the torment of the Trail of Tears, by the way. Why did the white man want their land? Because gold was discovered there in 1828. In 1830 Jackson signed the Removal Act.

"But I digress. If man lived in harmony with the land, then the land reciprocated. It provided nourishment. It provided symbols of connection with the Supreme Being. For example, the hummingbird feeds on the nectar of the tobacco plant. And the tiny bird was credited with bringing tobacco to the Cherokee. Thus tobacco was smoked in councils, in preparation for war, for medicinal qualities. All in the belief that it linked one to the Supreme Being. Like the smoke that rises. The Israelites had a similar belief, by the way—the altar of incense.

"Even so, in Cherokee religion, there had to be accounting for wrong. Or, in this case, disharmony."

"You mean 'evil,' don't you?"

"Well, the term doesn't fit Cherokee belief exactly, but yes, it's close. For example, the eagle was the great sacred bird. To kill the eagle properly—and only one person was designated as 'eagle killer'—was an act accompanied by sacred prayers and rituals."

"Then why kill the eagle at all?"

"Since the eagle was sacred, its feathers, worn only by a select few, provided an intercessory connection with the Supreme Being. And killing an eagle indiscriminately was an act of sacrilege that could ruin crops, bring sickness, and the like.

"On the other hand, the creature to be feared was the great serpent, the Uktena. A huge and revolting creature, it was vulnerable to killing only if one placed a shot precisely in the seventh ring under its head, where its heart and life lay."

"Fascinating, Lincoln. I have absolutely no idea where you're going with it."

"Patience. Don't trust answers given in one sentence. The Cherokee believe in harmony with a Supreme Being. That's a theology. Some people believe that way today. They believe in living in harmony with others and the natural environment. That's an ethic. The practical application of one's belief.

"But what does one do with Uktena? Can the monster really be slain? Does it keep returning? Does it have to be slain over and over again?

"Uktena appears in all our lives. We call it doubt and fear. We call it sickness, death, divorce. You see what I mean?"

"I guess so. I just don't see the point."

Lincoln started repacking his pipe and nodded. "There's a lot of truth in the old stories," he said. "We all have to live in harmony. With God, with nature, with others. Those who choose not to do so disrupt the entire order. Look at the effects on your own life."

"You think I have these visions, or whatever you want to call them, because I'm whacked out of harmony? Well, call me a wacko, but who in grad school isn't?"

Lincoln chuckled. It was that rumbling, bemused sound like water cascading to stony ground. "Never would I say that. In fact, this whole story I have told you is simply to make the opposite point. I think you are thoroughly, disgustingly sane."

"Thank you, Doctor Jefferson."

"This is not a nightmare. At least I don't believe so and you did ask my opinion. I think it's a vision, and a sacred one. A revelation much like the old stories of my nation. So, I don't think it does much good to reject it."

"So what am I supposed to do?"

"Perhaps follow it." As I was about to protest, he said, "Are you thirsty? Let's get a beer, maybe sit inside."

We walked several blocks, bypassing student bars and hangouts until we got to The Oak Room. It was a long, log cabin affair, probably not constructed of oak, set back from a gravel parking lot. We had been there before, particularly when they had their "eat all you can" specials. Frog legs were their specialty. The beer on tap, of uncertain origin, was seventy-five cents a glass. The décor was ramshackle 1950s, complete with red vinyl on the bar stools and plastic red and white checkered tablecloths.

We took a table by a window. Across the parking lot and past some bramble, the river lay like it was sound asleep.

We were popping salted-in-the-shell peanuts while I waited for Lincoln to take it up again. Suddenly that horrifying sound of squealing tires pierced into The Oak Room's quiet interior. When we stood to look outside a pickup truck was perched sideways on the road. A weary-looking basset hound crossed into the parking lot unperturbed by the fact.

"Uktena?" I asked.

"Eagle feather," Lincoln laughed. "Not for the driver though."

"You know, I'm sort of surprised to hear you talk about these old stories and visions. I thought you had converted to Christianity."

"First, I never converted. *Conversis*—to turn from. The stories helped lead me there. You've heard me go through all this before."

"Oh, yes. You argue that they all contain bits of a truth."

"Well, Christianity did change some things. But back to you. I told these stories merely to point out that you may be at the edges of a vision. And a vision is not to be feared for it is given to one. It opens a veil on truth. Nearly all Native nations believe this.

"Listen," he said. "Here's one way to think about it. Did the figure in the vision come to offer something or take something?"

"To offer. That's what he said."

"And did he say what he would offer?'

"Knowledge. Knowledge and wisdom."

"Now, isn't it true that evil beings—persons or apparitions or whatever—come to take?"

"Right."

"And benevolent beings come to give."

"Like a blessing or something. Sure."

"Then there's a second reason to accept the offer. And I don't know that knowledge and wisdom are such bad offers. Especially when you're writing your dissertation on the guy's works. I mean, isn't that what you're after?"

"I'm not sure. Sometimes facts and theory are safe."

"Precisely why our age relies so heavily upon technology and theory. In fact, our technology often outpaces our theory. Instead we find this new appliance and we wonder how it could be *used*, rather than thinking about consequences."

I finished my beer and sighed. "Yeah. Consequences. That's what I'm worried about, I guess."

"Rightfully so. I wish more people would."

"Tell me honestly, Lincoln. What would you do?"

"Honestly? I can't tell you. That's not my task, not the job of a friend. My advice, for what it's worth, is that I believe this is a revelation, not a nightmare, and that it will grant some wisdom."

"What exactly *is* wisdom?

"That's easy. Knowledge is of temporal things. Wisdom is how one relates them to eternal things."

"Not exactly my interest anymore."

"Let me put it this way. I think you can trust this apparition, as you call it. But I am most certain it will not come to you again unbidden."

"What! I've got to do some hocus pocus?"[1]

"No. You have to desire the knowledge and wisdom offered. It has to be reciprocal."

I decided to remain noncommittal. I didn't need this kind of nonsense in my life. By the time of our pinochle game on Friday night, I had finished the twenty pages in a blast of energy. My average had been about five pages a day. A good average. I had blown that out of the water. And it was good stuff. Now it was just the mechanics, finishing the typing, proofing, and such.

1. I don't know if the narrator was aware of the linguistic phenomenon of this term, one called "pejoration." In this case, the term derives from church history when the priests performed the Eucharist. During the time of transubstantiation, the priest would murmur the words "*hoc est corpus (meum)*"—this is my body—from behind a scrim. The penitents heard the garbled words as "hocus-pocus." Thus, it became associated with any conjuring act. The point was a twist from where God met man to where man conjured God.

By the end of the week I wasn't even thinking of the vision or dream or whatever it was. For the first time in years, I felt good, really good. Like I had some purpose and meaning.

I surely didn't feel that I needed *wisdom*.

CHAPTER SIX

Crossing the Threshold

PERHAPS YOU KNOW HOW it is—you finish a long project and then take a deep breath and walk back through it wondering what you missed. So the house painter does a final walk around, hoping that he hasn't missed a spot on some unfortunate peak. The auto mechanic checks for a stray wrench, the medical doctor for a scalpel or clamp. The sense of accomplishment is always hounded by the dog of anxiety.

It's a good trait, I suppose. Certainly we wouldn't want to drive off with one sparkplug missing. Although I don't think my old Toyota would know the difference.

So too, I spent the next week poring over a paper draft of my dissertation. I also had it on my hard drive, a backup disk, and my original longhand, which only I could decipher. As I looked back over my Fraenger, I realized I might have missed some things.[1]

Of course I had to be selective of works to support my thesis. I thought I had done a good job. For example, I had started with "The Third Day of Creation" pane and its widely reputed connection to the cycle of the six days of creation on the high altar of the Cathedral of St. John. Unfortunately, the altar itself was destroyed, but the painting gives clues to the conception. In the work God sits enthroned on high. In a

1. My friend pointed out to me that, while nothing can compare to viewing the actual paintings, by far the best collection of plates appears in Fraenger's *Hieronymus Bosch*. The advantages of Fraenger's work over others, he added, lays not only in the large number of full color plates, nor in the lucid analysis accompanying them, but also in the detail plates where the viewer can study the intricacy of Bosch's brushwork.

crystal globe, surrounded by the outer darkness, vegetation unfolds under a rainy sky.

From there the progression follows naturally, and biblically. In the *Millennium* we find the creation of Adam and Eve in Eden, the fall, and the vision of hell. *The Hay Wain*, although seemingly mired in a headlong journey to hell, also makes use of the ichthys[2], or fish symbol, representing the resurrection.

With the theological foundations established, I turned next to the Christological paintings—and they are many. For the nativity scenes, I chose *The Adoration of the Child* and the stunning *Epiphany* triptych. Then there's the odd *Child Jesus at Play.*

The ministry years are represented by *The Marriage at Cana*, a work I had always found strangely devoid of emotion, and the powerful *Prodigal Son.*

The passion week is amply represented by four works of *Christ Carrying the Cross*, along with *Christ Crowned with Thorns, Ecce Homo*, and several others.

I had pinned a fair amount of my argument on a relatively lesser work—indeed, one sometimes scorned by the scholars as "immature"—and that was *Table of Wisdom.* This curious work had a strange pull on me. The tabletop painting consists of a number of circles. The largest lies centered upon the square surface. At the center of that circle lies an inlaid sphere with Christ radiating light. Beneath the Christ appear the words *Cave, cave, dominus vidit.*[3]

The larger globe encircling Christ represents the earth, and it is segmented in seven parts depicting the seven sins. What I found interesting there was the fact that the segmentation gives equal weight to the deadly sins, while from Aristotle to Aquinas they were seen as hierarchical.

Situated at each corner of the square appear smaller circles, or "medallions." From the upper left, the first medallion represents "The Hour of Death." Moving clockwise, it is followed by "The Resurrection of the Dead and the Last Judgment," "The Kingdom of Heaven," and "Hell."

There is far more to say about the painting, of course—for example, its intricate mathematics that I only partly understood—but what gripped

2. The ICHTHYS was an anagram used by Christ's first-century disciples, most of whom were fishermen, as the sign of a believer. The Greek letters ΙΧΘΥϾ, or Iota, Chi, Theta, Upsilon and Sigma, are used to shape the body of the fish. Furthermore, the acrostic letters signified Jesus Christ, Son of God, Savior.

3. From the Vulgate, Deuteronomy 32:19: "Beware, beware! The Lord sees you."

me now was just how little attention I had given to Bosch's depictions of hell in my study. How could one not?

After mulling it over, I think I understood. For one thing, hell is overdone by most Bosch scholars. For another, the depictions of hell, with their grotesque demons and unrelenting suffering, were easier to avoid than engage. I hadn't wanted to go there. The whole idea of my thesis was to counteract that, to show that all disorder is framed by order, all evil by good. And I thought I had demonstrated this by the systematic theology approach. The dissertation could probably stay intact—each stage had been approved. But quite possibly I was shortchanging myself. Really, I reflected, any theology that asserts a Creator, Sustainer, Redeemer, and Judge is solipsistic unless it also includes a theodicy—a vindication of God's goodness and justice in the experience of pain and suffering. That argument drew its sharpest lines when it came to hell.

I was trying to think of Lincoln's outline of the basic ways people viewed hell, and couldn't remember a word of it. Unfortunately, he had headed home to North Carolina to help his father at the farm. Janie also left for her summer trip home, to Maine. She had invited me along, but I demurred with the excuse that I wanted to wrap things up. We had talked almost daily on the phone and she had nearly convinced me to come up to Augusta for a week at Christmas break.

"Just think," she said, "it's only a short drive to Portland where you can see the homes of Longfellow and Stephen King."

"Wow," I said in a flat voice.

"Okay. If you don't like that I'll get you up in the mountains skiing."

"Janie. I've never skied in my life. I don't even think I've seen snow more than a few times."

"Don't worry. I started when I was three. I still have those skis. Maybe you can use them."

Then she had added, "My parents would really like to meet you."

I didn't know if I was ready for that. Maybe because I wasn't sure what it meant. Although Janie was never far from my thoughts, I knew I had to go slowly. Even so, I fell asleep at night dreaming of her in my arms.

I guess I was the black sheep among my friends when it came to visiting home, even though my family only lived 212 miles away. Maybe it was because when I went home, even though everyone was super polite,

I had the feeling, "Oh, you're here." Ours had never been a household where joy ricocheted along the walls. And it had gotten icier since the divorce.

My mother had adored Shelley. Well, so had I. But when I broke the news to my parents my mother grew vindictive. At me.

"But, Mother," I protested, "Shelley divorced *me*."

Still, I was made to feel it was my fault. Out of a sense of duty I still made a few weekend trips a year. Once I got halfway there and turned around.

We lived in different worlds. My father had become successful in business and my mother tried to spend the money as fast as she could. Even when I was a teenager I already referred to her as the Mall Mama. I'll hand them this: they constantly offered me money, resisting my plea that I was quite comfortable on my stipend. A game of pinochle, a dinner at Pietro's or The Oak Room, gas in the Toyota that seemed to last for weeks since I walked everywhere. What more could one ask for?

Maybe some fish from the farm pond. I called Ed Nolan and got Claire. After chatting for a bit, she told me that Ed was still in the studio but intended to quit soon for dinner. Why didn't I come up and join them?

Ed was still in the studio when I got there. Claire asked me to cross over and tell him to get cleaned up for dinner. "Why don't you?" I said, pointing to the intercom.

"Ed hates that thing. He turned it off in his studio. Besides, he'll want you to see what he's working on."

Ed was scrubbing his hands and arms with that gritty pumice from a large bottle of orange cleaner. He used a fingernail brush to get at the paint layered down under his nails.

"I like it," I said. "Kind of abstract, but actually quite meaningful in its sum total."

"You ought to see the drop cloth," he laughed.

"I know. I'd like to inherit it. Must be worth a fortune. Just make sure you sign the corner."

Ed rinsed and toweled.

"What's this?" I asked. On a work shelf stood two brass sculptures, already toning. A boy and a girl, seated apart but facing each other. Each was about three feet tall. "A gift from someone?"

"No, those are mine." He came up alongside me.

"I didn't know you did sculpture."

"I try not to. I set the price so high it scares people off. This was commissioned by a lady in Boston for her English garden."

"Well, I do like them."

"That's work, my boy. Not art. Would you believe I got more for that than my Pietá? But a hundred years from now the lady's heirs will be wondering what to do with them and the pietá will be hanging in a museum."

"Claire said you were working on something new."

"Over here, although it's just building."

He showed me a canvas—smaller than the Pietá, maybe 4 x 3 feet.

"I'm structuring the background mood. Seeing if it fits the picture in my head. The feelings I have about it."

"Any idea what it will be?"

"Of course. That picture's complete. But you never know what you'll stir up along the way. Have you read Robert Frost's poem 'Mowing'?"

"If I did, I can't remember it."

"It's one of Claire's favorites. I'll ask her to recite it for you. But I remember the key lines. He's talking about the hard work of mowing hay—or writing poetry—and he wrote that the labor was not without 'feeble-pointed spikes of flowers / (Pale orchises), and scared a bright green snake.'" You have to understand art is like that. You're executing your plan, but then surprises come jumping out of the subconscious. Quick. And you have to be ready to catch them.

But we better get over to the house or Claire will give us something cold."

As we stepped out of the barn I caught the scent of fresh baked goods in the air. Smelled like cinnamon rolls.

"You never told me the subject of your new painting," I mentioned.

"'Jesus wept.' From John 11:5 when Jesus raised Lazarus. I don't think anyone has ever tried to capture that. Yet it has to be one of the most powerful verses in the Bible. And a great mystery—sorrow paired with a resurrection act. Anguish paired with new life. Somehow it captures the rhythm of all life.

But now, enough shop talk. If we smile nice, Claire might let us eat."

As we opened the door, Claire said, "I heard that. But you didn't really think I'd go ahead and plan on you two being on time, did you?"

After dinner I told Ed about my concern with the hell imagery in Bosch. I wondered if my dissertation would be "complete" without it.

"First of all," he said, "no dissertation is ever 'complete.' Polish your argument and let it go."

"Moreover," he added, "hell has been done to death in Bosch. That's why I liked your idea. Hell is all most people ever see."

"Or don't see at all for the preoccupation," I said. "Still, one has to make sense of it. The punishments, for example."

"Let me guess. The arrows shot into men's buttocks?"

"There's a good example."

"But rather an obvious one. Bosch hated contempt for the flesh and also denigration of the flesh. In this case he thought it apt punishment for homosexuals."

I nodded. We had walked to the studio and turned around. Jackson yapped at a tree squirrel.

"Another one," I said. "Remember in *Millennium* where a man defecates gold coins over the mouth of hell? Think of doing that for all eternity!"

Ed laughed at the picture. "Yes, but the symbolism is clear enough, isn't it?"

"What?"

"Well, his life on earth was obviously spent accumulating and hoarding gold. What worse—and maybe fitting—punishment than to give up that gold over hell's mouth?"

I shook my head. "There's so much anger in Bosch's hell scenes. His rage pours out."

"I can't answer the questions," Ed said. "Wouldn't it be nice if you could ask Bosch himself?"

I looked at him askance. Sometimes I felt Ed gave answers that were partial to what he thought, as if he knew more than he told. Honestly, it made me nervous at times.

"I don't think I'd care for that at all," I said.

He smiled and nodded.

I didn't know where I was or why I was there.

One moment I had been dozing by the pond. It was a Saturday. I was eager for the weekend to pass. I was picking up Janie from the airport on Monday.

I wasn't fishing. I was just listening to sounds of the pond and field. Below, cardinals fluted among the trees, shooting love songs in scarlet notes.

I felt the slightest touch at my elbow and thought it was Jackson. I didn't bother to open my eyes. He'd find a rabbit in the field to chase anyway.

When the touch came on my elbow again, I looked up. His appearance had changed only slightly. He looked more youthful and vital. And he seemed to bear a greater solidity than previously.

"Are you ready to find answers?" he asked.

My heart was hammering against my ribs like I had run a long way. Indeed, I no longer recognized the place where I stood, didn't even remember standing. There seemed to be sharp stones under my feet, and they felt warm—like a shoreline with no ocean breeze. "Who are you?" I asked in a voice so calm it surprised me.

"As I told you once before, I am your guide. But then you didn't believe me."

"But guide to what?"

"To the answers you seek. Things you know only in part."

"Well, go ahead and tell me, then."

He shook his head soberly. "It isn't quite that easy. That would be knowledge without understanding, facts without wisdom. For that, you must join me. Hasn't your tutor told you? You must know with the head and the heart? You must enter in."

I nodded. I was thinking of Ed Nolan. His words precisely. And, I realized with a start, very much like Lincoln's. Suddenly, I felt trapped.

As if sensing the shift, he began to speak.

I heard sounds on my ear that seemed to come from Bosch's lips. I did understand and didn't understand, as if the words were tongued with fire that kindled their meaning in my ears:

> noli timere quia redemi te et vocavi
> nomine tuo meus es tu

cum transieris per aquas tecum ero
et flumina non operient te
cum ambulaveris in igne non conbuberis
et flamma non ardebit in te
quia ego Dominus Deus tuus Sanctus
tus Israhel salvator tuus[4]

For a moment at least, the words calmed my spirit. And he didn't appear threatening; in fact, he looked very much like Ed Nolan—a good deal shorter than I, muscular shoulders and forearms. Unlike many of his self-portraits where his hair appears gray or white, the apparition had thick, curly, black hair. The eyes were the same, and the steely set to his lips and jaw.

"You may trust me," he concluded.

I was mindful of a steadily rising sound and a growing warmth, as if we had walked closer to an ocean shore. The stones felt like spikes under my feet and I shifted my weight uncomfortably. I was aware of an advancing darkness as the sound grew.

It sounded like waves, grinding against the rocks. I stopped, listening intently. Bosch touched my elbow and led me on a few paces.

As the sound of the waves intensified with each step, the heat grew. How could there be water here? I wondered. The hot air sucked out moisture and carried it off. But I heard the waves distinctly now, moaning back and forth in their stony chains. Still Bosch led me on in the darkness, and I wondered if we might simply topple off some cliffside, fall smashing against rocks below, and be swept into a fiery maelstrom. Then I did stop. Suddenly I remembered the story—the lake of fire.

4. From the Vulgate, Isaiah 43:1b-3a:

Fear not, for I have redeemed you;
I have summoned you by name; you are mine.
When you pass through the waters,
I will be with you;
and when you pass through the rivers,
they will not sweep over you.
When you pass through the fire,
you will not be burned;
the flames will not set you ablaze.
For I am the Lord, your God,
the Holy One of Israel, your Savior.

Was this the trick, then? Was Bosch leading me to a set of chains, to be perpetually bound to the grinding flow of lava? Deceiver! I realized it now. "Trust me," he had said. Wasn't that always the heart of the lie? Trust me. The old lie.

Rather, trust no one. I had to learn that once before, then thought I had unlearned it.

"Trust me," he had said. "And you can walk through, not into." Perhaps he was saying it now, his fingertips pressed lightly to my elbow. I couldn't tell. I was hearing and not hearing a language tongued in flame by this unholy ghost.

It was all madness. Bosch, the deceiver. I should have known better. I didn't want, and didn't *need*, to see any of this. I needed my work; I wanted to see it finished.

Then I thought, well, it's only a dream. You will, you must, awaken.

"True," came his voice at my right hand, his fingers still touching my elbow. "If you wish, I can awaken you."

"What? How did you know what I was thinking?"

"About deception? Well, that is interesting, isn't it? And not unexpected. You see, this is the home of deception. The Father of Lies? Surely you've heard that? Be on guard, my young Pilgrim. Perfect trust is the only way to go through."

"And I suppose that begins with you?"

Against the background pounding of the waves, I heard his chuckle. It was as if we stood like a picture within a picture, as if Bosch had painted some vast dark background scene torn by lightning and filled like a studio with sounds. Yet, we stood inside the studio-picture, like producers of the magic show. Or like two bugs kept under a glass bottle whose sides were cracking.

"Well, yes. But we knew that from the start. Now the adventure has hardly begun. There is still time to turn back. One more step and that opportunity will pass."

"I get it. Last chance choice."

"Something like that. Remember, we are traveling through. This is not a vacation, where you go to a place and then, if it's too rainy, say, or there are too many flies, you may pack up your tent and go home. This moment, where you choose to advance one more step, which is also the final step, always comes."

"I want to see."

"But you're afraid."

"Yes. I admit it. I thought it would be like a movie."

"First, you should be afraid. Second, this is no movie that you sit back and watch. You are in it."

"It's always that way, isn't it?" My head was ringing from the booming of the waves I couldn't see. I now became aware of a heavy red light on the horizon. Small things, like crowded trees, stood darkly against it.

"How so?" Bosch said. "You don't have to rush to a decision, but you must decide. Remember that I am only your guide. I can inform, as best I'm able, but I cannot force your action. To decide is to act. One step and you begin the journey."

"What I meant," I said, "is that I won't have another chance, will I?"

"This is true."

"And if I choose not to advance, I choose never to know."

"Well, there will always be *knowing* in your human life."

"What do you mean?"

"You will always have the idea. It is the nature of the hell-haunted mind of humanity."

I nodded. "Earth too wears her secret veil. Hawthorne's 'The Minister's Black Veil.'"

He looked at me askance. Right, I thought. He wouldn't know Hawthorne's work. "Awareness, however, is not knowledge," Bosch continued. "Let me be plain. Do not step forward and you lose the opportunity to know. But the loss is not thorough. You will, by choosing not to advance, retain another opportunity. To live your life at ease."

"Ignorance is bliss?"

"Quite often. Not always. But you avoid the reality. Therefore you can live in ideas and dreams. That's more comfortable."

"And a delusion, isn't it?"

"Nor should that stop you. Most people make their peace by forming delusions in place of realities. Think about it."

"I really can't think about what other people do. Not right now."

"Tempting though, isn't it?"

I felt a certain inexplicable anger toward him. I had come this far. I had no right to be angry. Or, I had every right. He stood there several inches shorter than I, that monkey-like grin creasing his square jaw. Then I realized that he knew precisely how I felt.

"Do you know how I'm going to choose too, old man?"

"Old master, don't you mean? But, no, I don't know whether you'll choose to continue. In fact, you have every right to turn around right now. In further fact, I encourage you to do so. It would be so much *safer*."

I wanted to punch the grin off that little puppet face. As I thought it, he leaned back, laughing. *He's taunting me*!

"You have only to say the word, but only you can say it."

He *was* taunting me. Yes, that cockeyed grin. It is a sneer. The lips of the devil. He has lured me here. After all, no painter in history envisioned hell more powerfully. He was an emissary sent not to guide me but to get me. I stared at him, speechless.

"This is only a dream," I muttered. I spoke to myself. A crazy, stressed-out dream. I have three hundred pages to finish proofing and I allowed myself to get sidetracked. "Only a dream."

"I thought you'd say that," Bosch replied. "Sooner or later. It is the human response."

"Oh? That's what *I* am, whatever *you* are."

"We mustn't get sidetracked on what I am. That is not the point. Here I am your guide, and, look, you have a choice. In dreams you have no choice, do you? In fact, the peril of dreams is that your will is suspended. They crawl out of your subconscious memory and play tricks, for pleasure or peril, in your brain."

"What is this, then?"

"This, my dear fellow, is a vision. *You* sought me out. *You* applied your imaginative curiosity. *You* wanted answers. Very well. I am here now. But what I demand of you is an act of your will. To choose to continue past the threshold."

My senses were deceiving me. I dared trust nothing. The sanguine light in the background hung tremulously, not like a distant sun but something palpable and dense. It all made Bosch look like a dark villain at one moment, his wild hair a blood-tinged halo, and at the next moment an odd saint, his thick-lipped grin a sign of infinite patience under his luminous hair.

Then, a sickening, cold fear touched my heart as I felt a vague tremor in the ground. This was no ocular deception, a teasing of the senses. The ground *moved*! Rather, it shuddered, like a rough-skinned beast slouching toward wakefulness.

"Our time runs short," Bosch said softly.

"Help me," I pleaded. "I don't know what to say . . . I want to see, but . . ."

"It won't be what you see. It will be what you learn."

"Yes. That is what I'm afraid of. What if . . ."

"It's different from your wildest imagination?"

"Yes."

"It won't be entirely. Remember, certain signs have been given."

"Where?"

"Two places. The sacred texts and the life you live in."

"What if I choose to go back?"

"Hell won't change. Only you will."

"And if I choose to go ahead?"

"The same. Either way, you'll live with regret and relief. I'll anticipate your question because the answer is obvious. You will regret having gone or not having gone. Either choice acquires knowledge: the knowledge of what could have been but isn't, which is the first regret. And the knowledge of what the reality is, which is the second regret.

"Either way, also, you will find relief. Choose not to choose, and the moment for choice will be forever obliterated. What blissful relief! You shall never stand at this precise point again. You will not have to live and think with the knowledge you might have gained. Were the world to know of this moment, which it never shall, it would nod in hearty agreement. Choosing not to choose is the safe way. Ethics would tell us that it is responsible to avoid threat to personal safety or to others. It would herald that old ethical value of *prūdēns*. The good life is the prudent life.

"And think what the psychologists would say! No! Don't choose. Sanity consists in the *medium*. Stay on the narrow line hypothetically called normal. On either side of the tightrope lies the plunge into the abnormal, even the insane. Can you see them clapping their soft white hands, Pilgrim?

"Or even this—think of those great pragmatists, the politicians and businessmen. Yes, they speak of 'the vision,' don't they? But to them visions are quantifiable, or else delusional. The delusional belong in one of the safety nets they have created to maintain a stable society. The Peace Corps, say. Or put them on the assembly line, but keep them out of my boardroom. We want results, and what possible profit is there in this strange quest that you *think* you might take?

"And, finally, religion. Ah, yes, what would religion say?" Suddenly he flung his scrawny arms out at me. "Flee! Run for your life, Pilgrim. Run back to the safety net of doctrine. There are your answers, each calculated, parsed, laid out in print by some of the best minds in history. Read

Augustine, Anselm, and Aquinas. Memorize the catechisms. Therein lies safety, the surety of your faith."

He stood with his thin arms waving like a wind-tossed scarecrow, eyebrows lifted so high they seemed cartoonish.

"Faith," I mused.

"Yes. That agony. Because faith is always individual. Never corporate. Therefore never safe, always dangerous. It is, as one of the greatest thinkers said, totally absurd!"

"Absurd? You mean crazy?"

"Not at all. The sanest thing one can ever do. Why? Because faith, being wholly individual necessarily affirms the individual."

"Sounds like six of one, half a dozen of the other to me."

"I'm afraid I don't know that expression, but it seems to me a bit fatuous, like naming the same thing in two different languages. The thing doesn't change, only the sounds employed to evoke its nature.

"Well now. Back to the point. Wasn't all that helpful? Am I not an excellent guide? Didn't I paint a clear and well-designed picture?" He chortled.

I nodded. But I was not so much thinking of what he said as I was becoming keenly aware of the rocking of the earth. Not an earthquake, surely, but now an insistent tremor, as if I stood on quicksand, my feet displacing enough surface to keep me barely afloat. And it felt warmer, like hot stones occasionally churning to the surface and abrading the rubber soles of my shoes. And now I seemed to hear a dull oppressive rumble, emanating from the core of the molten red on the horizon. Was it the moaning of waves I had heard earlier? If so, it now sounded like water bursting through dikes far in the distance. It *was* warmer. Where was I after all? Maybe it was the rolling, sulfurous lava out of the great deep.

Madman! He still stood there *smiling*.

"Time is running short," he said. "Soon I will have no choice but to release you. Then you also will have made your choice."

"Is it always this way?" I asked. I think I meant to ask whether or not this was standard procedure. I think I was stalling. The warm ground rolled under my feet like a bed of marbles.

"Always? I don't know. At *this* moment there is only you."

I couldn't think of anything more to say. It was like a party when the host flicks the lights off and on. Time was running out.

"Only you," Bosch repeated. "The cruel safety of choosing."

"Ha! 'Cruel safety,'" I said. "What a stupid expression. An oxymoron, we call it in the real world."

"Careful, Pilgrim. My words are not always my own. Your faith, your trust, your choice in them depends upon that question: What is true? If you doubt at all, now is the time to speak to it. This journey will admit to no doubt. None whatsoever. You will never again in this lifetime witness a truth so raw. Understand this. You will be afforded a glimpse of eternity. You will step out of your lifetime."

"Is it getting hot, or is that my imagination?"

"It is the truth. Uncomfortable, isn't it?"

"What have I got to lose? If I go on?" I asked.

"You're curious, aren't you?" He chuckled, whether in mockery or pleasure, I couldn't tell. "Curiosity is a good thing," Bosch said.

"I'm waiting for a *but*."

"But like everything in your lifetime, it may be perverted. *Pervertere*. To turn away from the good. Curiosity is wonderful, creative, fulfilling, and oh so terribly dangerous."

"I am curious. And I'm getting hotter than . . ."

"Hell, you say? No, what you feel outside is what you feel inside. It's only a taste. The horror of hell, after all, is that everything inside is turned outside. That among other horrors, of course. This is just a taste. All you'll ever experience on this side of choice."

"But the ground. I can't even see it, but it feels like . . . it's moving!"

"Yes. Indeed it feels that way. And so too are you inside."

"Well, I really don't have anything to lose, do I?"

"Either way you have a great deal to lose."

"Damn! You don't help at all."

Momentary silence hung in the foul air. The form of Bosch seemed to waver before me, growing insubstantial. A grin like the Cheshire cat wisped in front of me.

This is what he meant. My time was short—his time was short. I felt him slipping away.

If he disappeared would I be left here? I heard words, strange words:

> Quivi, secondo che per ascoltere,
> non avea pianto, ma' che de sospiri,

> che l'aura eterna facevan tremare.[5]

That's what my ears received, distinct as daggers. But what my mind perceived was this:

> So long a train of people,
> that I should not have believed
> that death had undone so many.

And as I received them, the scarlet horizon glowed luminously and I saw the stumpy figures and I discerned arms hugging sunken chests and hands clutching bent heads and legs like stone moving in quicksand. And I understood the words I had received and perceived. These are the living dead, shuffling without pain or pleasure, ceaselessly stepping around the burning cusp of the inferno.

And I shouted out, "Yes. Yes!"

My words were lost to my own ears by a rush of wind. It tore around me like a cyclone; I stood terrified in its eye. The ground I had felt moving rumbled like peals of thunder, ever louder, shaking the earth in a dark fury. Lightning ripped through the boiling heavens. Like a curtain of blinding red light it cracked the very air.

I stood paralyzed. By my foolishness. Stupidity. Madness. What was this place? What manner of dizzying chaos? The roaring in my ears was indescribable. Like an avalanche of splitting, cracking boulders, the noise swept over me.

I thrust my hands over my ears, squeezed my eyes so tightly that they protested in pain.

Something touched my elbow. I recoiled. Firm fingers wrapped around my arm. I pitched toward him.

The silence was so profound I heard only my heaving breath. I don't know if I spoke the words out loud. Breathed them, rather.

"What happened?" I asked.

I heard his chuckle first. I turned toward him. He stood there solid as a rock in his linen peasant shirt.

"You have crossed the threshold," he said.

5. Dante, *Divine Comedy*, IV, 25–27.

CHAPTER SEVEN

The Soccer Game

We traveled only momentarily it seemed through some intermediate zone. A plane of twilight cut open a flat field nearby. From this distance I could make out what looked like bright bubbles darting to and fro across its surface. They reminded me of a goldfish bowl I had when I was young. The fish would hang defiantly in the water as if suspended by a spider's thread, then dart about in their own game of chaos.

As we neared, at a slow hover, I discovered the analogy was close to the truth. There were miniaturized versions of fish boats beneath us. They seemed to flit over something like a playing field, somehow constructed out of this nothingness.

"Could we get closer?" I asked Bosch.

He didn't speak, but, as if I had communicated with the large fish boat itself, I sensed us slowing and descending. And descent it was, as if at this one place physical laws were restored. For it was a field, a playing field with soccer-like goals at each end. I saw now that in each small fish boat was seated a baby, steering the fish boat with the utter abandon of a new toy.

"They're all kids!" I exclaimed.

"Very observant," Bosch chided in his cynical way. "The oldest is only two years old."

The tiny fish boats swam in dizzying patterns. There seemed to be two sides. Yes, of course. I could pick them out now. One set of fish boats was blue-hued, the other bore a ruby tinge. Now as the teams—for so I thought of them—separated, I discerned a rather large and very dark sphere. Something within appeared to be jostling to get out. The sphere clearly changed shape, not radically but like an unborn baby's foot or fist stretching the skin of its mother.

Suddenly, a blue fish boat darted out of line from its team. It drove swiftly on the sphere, stopping just inches away, whirling and giving it a mighty thwack with its tail. The ball soared, plummeting downward short of the goal. Then the two teams were at each other, driving back and forth across the field. Sometimes the dark sphere rose into view; most often it was buried in the scrimmage of fish boats.

We drifted away.

"Where would you like to start, Pilgrim?"

"Oh . . . where were we and what happened?"

"One question at a time." He chuckled. "I was hoping there would be a ball game on today. Always fun."

"But the playing field looked solid. Much like any field. How can it be solid if we are in the abyss?"

"Once before in your world things were created out of nothing. It is not so different here. To say we are in the abyss is not to say there is no structure. But alas, I'm no physicist like the grand Newton."

"Our universe," I stuttered, "and I suppose all universes are mostly nothing. But that nothing can be transected by physical objects. I think of a meteor in outer space, for example."

Bosch shook his head. "I only know that there are physical places, structures, in the abyss. Those who dwell here can never leave, but for some reason those in the higher realm may come here for their soccer games. And there are dozens of fields like this. You see, there are no balls like this in the higher realm. Most often, it is part of their punishment to be used so. But, now, I shall ask you a few questions.

"Why don't you just tell me? Give me a lecture like a real tour guide?"

"But I thought you wanted to learn."

"Yes, of course."

"You learn best from yourself. Then it speaks to your head and heart both. Your upper and lower consciousness."

"Ask away."

"What did you notice first about our little scene?"

"Visually? The fish boats. They were very small."

"Yes, and why were they small?"

"That's the second thing I noticed. They were all ridden by infants."

"An ambiguous term. What do you mean by *infants*?"

"Babies. Little children. I don't know. Funny, none were wearing diapers."

"Well, that's another story. You see, none of them appear as an infant in heaven."

"What do you mean?"

"They are perfect. Fully grown. They become infants only for their soccer games. Now, remember carefully. I said the games are not just about sport, but punishment. Can you think of any incident—historically—when innocent children merit doling out the punishment of someone to fulfill justice?"

"I think you're losing me here."

"Okay, then. Back to the scene. You saw first the fish boats. These would indicate an appearance from the higher realm. Second, you observed the children. Undiapered, as you say. What was the third thing you noticed?"

"Some kind of sphere or ball. Not as hard as a soccer ball. It even looked a little bit lumpy."

"Someone was sealed inside it. Sealed so he could never escape. Someone meriting punishment, else he would not be here. But meriting punishment especially from children. To punish without due cause is not just. Right? The punishment must be merited. Thus the person in the sealed ball deserves to be punished for some heinous crime, but especially for a crime executed against children. They in turn have the special prerogative of executing punishment, have they not? But, being children, their sensibilities about punishment are not fully formed. Thus the game. The children receive the satisfaction of meting punishment through competition. The man in the sealed ball gets pummeled and kicked around, for eternity, by the very children he treated so cruelly."

"Wow! It must have been cruel."

"Murder. The ultimate deprivation."

"So who was in the ball?"

"Think, Pilgrim. I'll give you a clue. This massacre occurred 2,000 years ago. A second clue. It is called the Massacre of the Innocents."

"Two thousand years ago? Would that be Herod? When he killed the children two and under to try to eliminate the Messiah?"

"Precisely. Herod the Tetrarch. Herod the Great. Herod the Proud. His own self-appointed three-in-one. And there were so many others through the ages. Think of Pharaoh, the Children's Crusades, Saddam Hussein."

"Was that Herod story true?"

"Most certainly."

"I thought it was just one of those myths of Christmas."

"A wise man once said that every myth has part of the truth in it."

"But many also lead away from the truth."

"So we consult the historical record, yes? Remember those wise men who visited from the east. Also a myth according to many. They had a very long journey to make, those wise men also called Medes. By camel through the northern trading route. A winter passage."

"A cold coming we had of it," I said, reciting from one of my favorite poems.

> Just the worst time of the year
> For a journey, and such a long journey:
> The ways deep and the weather sharp.
> The very dead of winter.[1]

"Yes," said Bosch. "And these Medes were also royalty. Kings without kingdoms. The gifts they brought financed Mary and Joseph's flight into Egypt, where the baby escaped the massacre. Herod discovered that the magi had outwitted him. In a rage he believed a baby, some baby, was still a threat to his power. So he ordered the massacre of all boys two and under."

"So the children get to come back now and get revenge on Herod."

"It's not like that at all. What does an infant know about revenge? They are exercising a just punishment, but doing it through their form of play. Which makes it all the more humiliating for the man in the ball, wouldn't you say?"

"So he's aware of that."

"Oh, indeed. Else he would just feel sorry for himself. But he can't even feel sorry for his deeds. Just humiliated and punished. And probably beat up a bit. Those little fish boats pack quite a wallop."

We were silent for some moments. I seemed to see memories of my own childhood projected before me. I couldn't get very far back. I remembered my grandfather's green wool suit because it was scratchy and had a sharp smell. He died when I was almost three.

Later memories swarmed. A skinny kid with goggle-like glasses leaning against a tree by the tar playground, hoping to get in a pick-up

1. T. S. Eliot, "Journey of the Magi."

game of baseball. Heat and shade. Later that same kid, Al Kaline glove dark with wear and oil, swatting flies in the outfield. That same kid sitting on the front stoop, an hour a day, all summer long, reading the dictionary. He left home in darkness that winter, shoveling the driveways and walks of two large houses in the neighborhood before school.

Every adult holds such memories that creep in unexpectedly in his later years. We never outgrow our past.

"There are hundreds of them, you know," Bosch broke into my brief reverie.

"Of what?"

"Such balls. Played in varying games, many that you would recognize. Adults play these games, including one where they ride boats shaped as horses and swing mallets."

"Many?"

"Hundreds. Thousands. The abyss has added many in the last few years. Hussein is now among them. This later man, bin Laden, is being prepared."

"Prepared?"

"A punishment is not just unless a wrong is redressed and unless the one being punished for that wrong understands fully why he is being punished. Often that can take some time. Pride, you see, is not an easy set of blinders to remove."

"How is this done?"

"This has not been revealed to me. I can only say it is logical."

"Logic and soccer," I murmured.

"Indeed."

The field dimmed behind us. Indeed, it seemed to be getting darker all around.

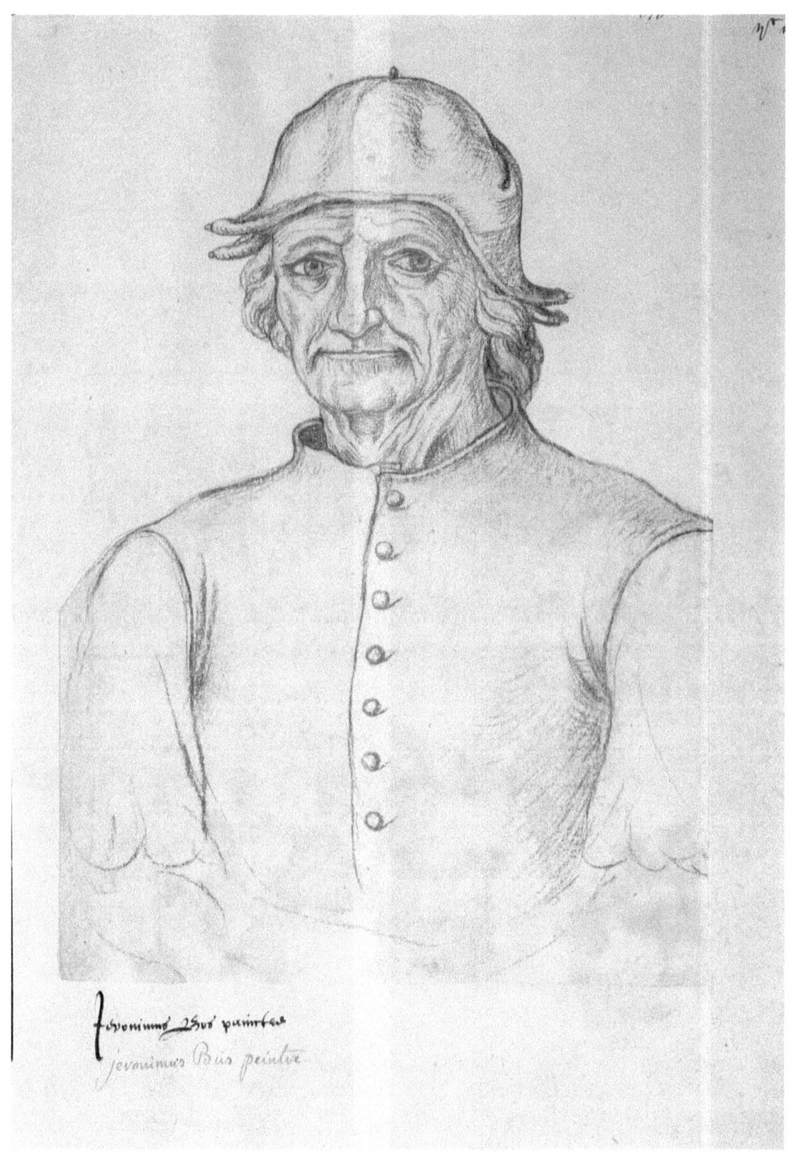

Self Portrait

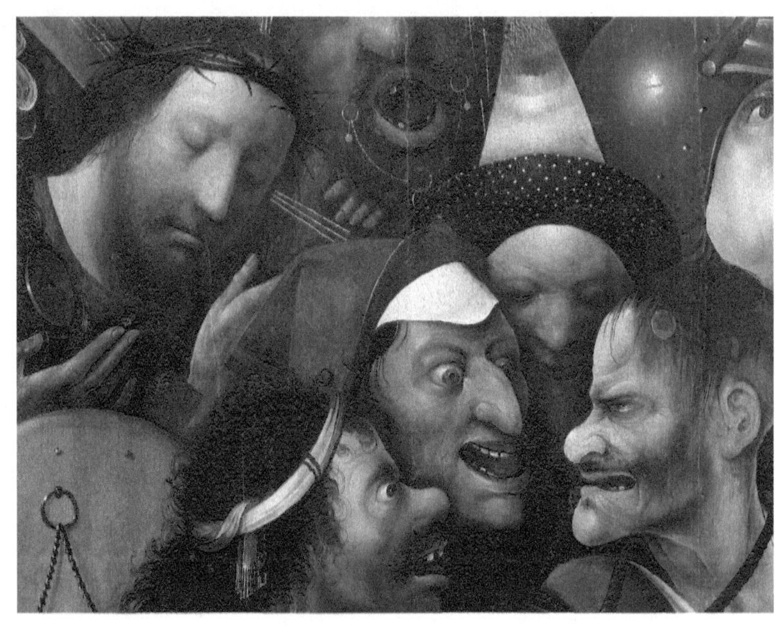

Christ Carrying the Cross

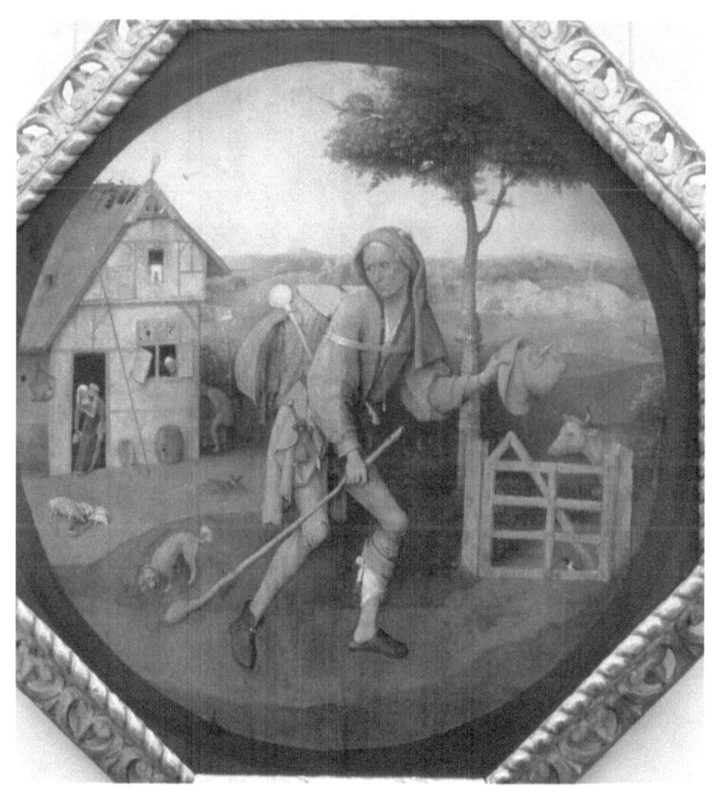

The Prodigal Son

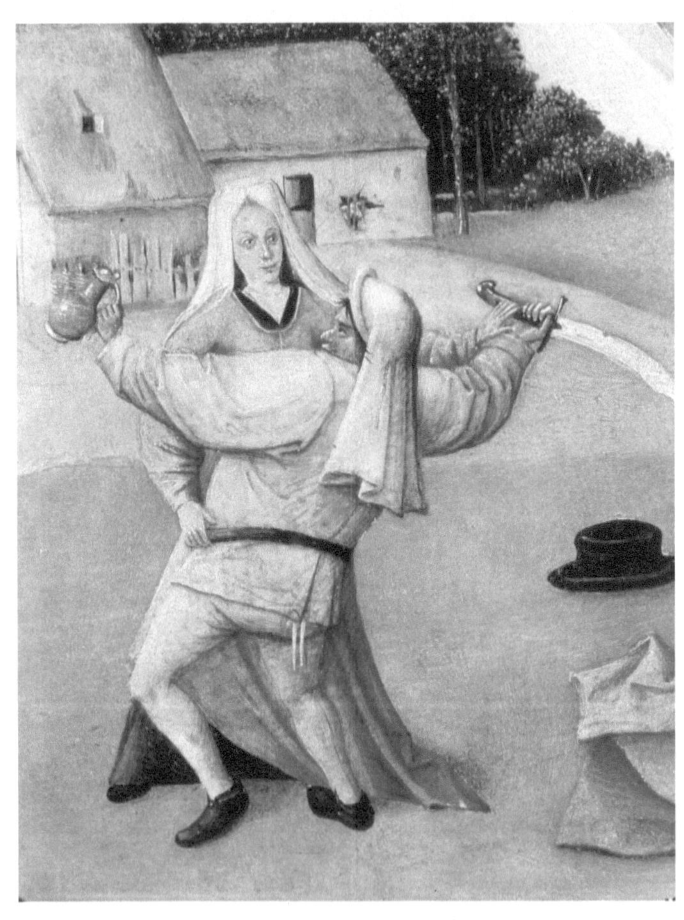

Detail from The Seven Deadly Sins

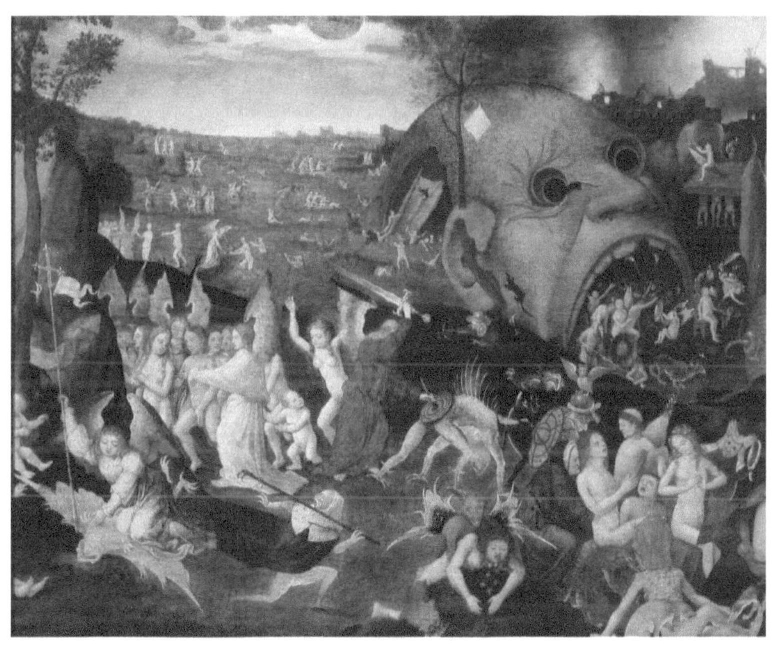

Hell

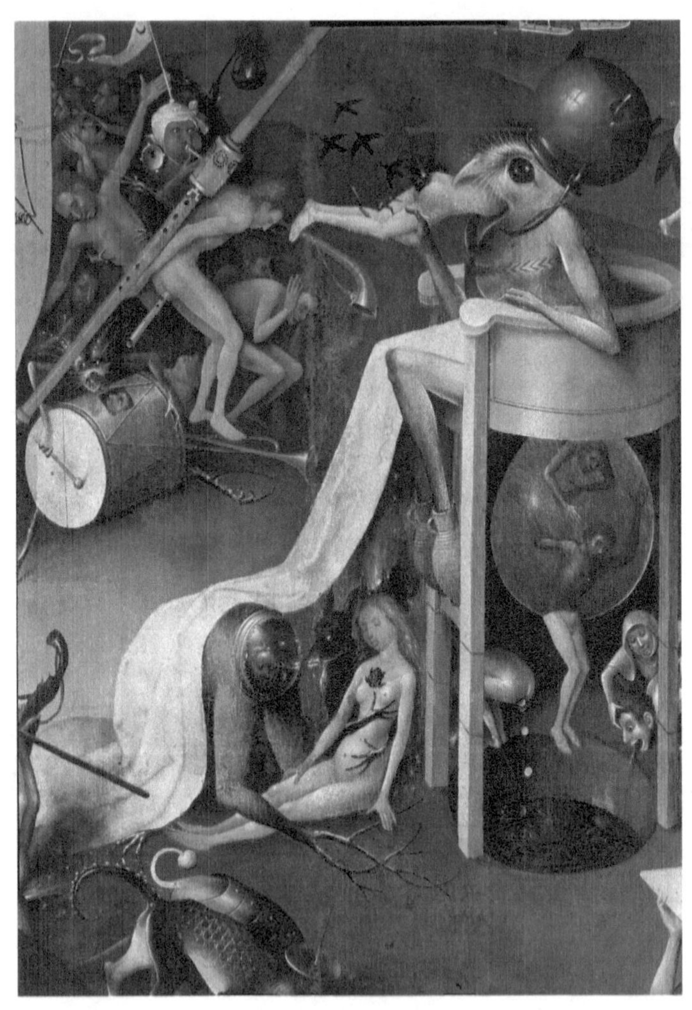

Musical Hell

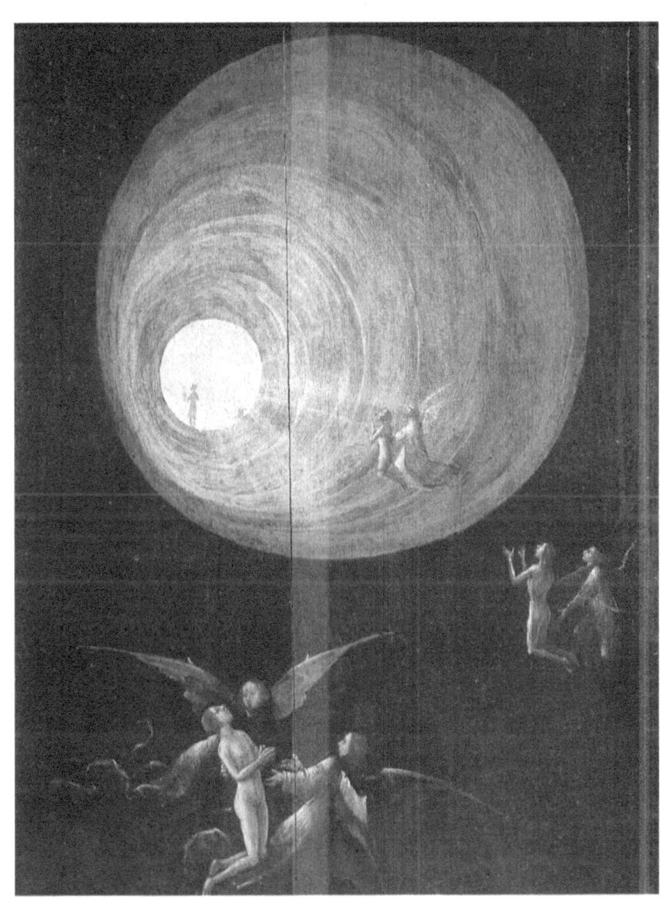

Tunnel of Light

CHAPTER EIGHT

The Outer Darkness

I HAVE ALWAYS BEEN afraid of heights.

There's probably some technical term for it, the neat pigeonholing of the emotional trigger of neurons in the brain. I know it when I feel it.

I felt it the first time when I was very young. I had ventured upon the really audacious task of climbing the monkey bars. Everyone did it; I would too. I must have been—what?—three or four at the time. I made my great ascent then sat there, looking *down*, and the earth swam to the pitch of my stomach and I focused, with a primal stare, on the bar directly in front of me as I inched back down. I reached the ground. It steadied under my feet. But my tiny heart lurched in a cyclone and I knew I'd never go up that thing again.

I dwelt in safety, for the most part, over the years of my growing up. After all, we are creatures of *gravity*; we are not made to go *up*. It is unnatural—*contra naturam*, against the nature of things.

Then that great American event called the senior class trip snuck up on me. By then Shelley and I were seeing each other. It was expected that couples would pair off at some point during the trip. They stayed in touch with the general mob, the hoi polloi, but theirs was a special place. It required strategic separation. Hand-holding walks along a flowered path. Some popcorn tossed to ducks on the pond. A souvenir or two purchased, maybe a photograph of them seated in the corny swan boat.

I could have hid out that way all day.

Inevitably, if you're going to an amusement park on the senior class trip, the mob will find you out.

I can't remember what this monster roller coaster, this aberration sprung from some demented mind, was called, but we had to ride it. It took a month or more to clank up to its apex, the creaks and groans reminding me of the tenuous link to life. Why would anyone want to do this, I thought as we transcended the apex. For a moment it seemed we had stopped, ready to plunge backward. I kept my eyes locked on the safety bar before me. No, I wasn't going to shut them. Shelley called gaily to the couple behind us, her voice strangely amplified up here. Another creak. The mad ship hurled down. Rooftops, rides, people's heads plunged upward as if to impale us. Then the coaster veered into a body-wrenching series of turns and jolts and I squeezed my eyes. I felt that the top of my head was going to fly off and my few poor brains would scatter to the winds.

My legs trembled when we finally got off. I forced an excited grin. There, I thought, I'll never have to do that again as long as I live.

Shelley poked me in the ribs. "Had your eyes closed, didn't you?"

By clever strategies, I have avoided heights, and certainly roller coasters. I have only been on an airplane three times in my life, and I took a Tylenol PM each time.

One of those flights had been to a conference in San Francisco, where a hotel tricked my phobia. Standing in a crowd of people at the elevator bank in the hotel lobby, I was literally pushed into the elevator. Trapped. And again, one of those mad engineers had the audacity to hang the thing on the *outside* of the building. For the next three days I took the twenty-two stories of stairs.

I found it odd, then, that I loved the homey eleventh-floor environs of the Ransom Library. Maybe I had been reconstructing myself from the inside out. Starting with scratch, the unrecognizable rubble like a ruined temple where I had sacrificed my love for Shelley. I had to burn it on an altar to a God unknown and suffer the purifying flame. Except that it purified absolutely nothing, it seemed. The fire left charcoal and rocks.

Yet, this was my refuge. I think that I was aware, perhaps only with some visceral yearning, that some rebuilding was underway. I had my work for one thing, and that was definitely going somewhere.

Far more important, I had Janie and Lincoln. And a cast of more casual acquaintances. The Hollises I had grown to love like grandparents. And my admittedly rather strange relationship with the artist Ed Nolan.

It was trust. A sense that they wouldn't let me down. Trust is what had been rebuilding in the coals and rubble.

I confess, though, that I will not climb monkey bars to this day. And I will not climb higher than two steps on a stepladder. Standing on a chair to change a light bulb still makes me incurably dizzy. The faster I try to do it, the more I fumble.

The reason I mention this is because I found myself next to Bosch in a thin, membranous, almost aquatic ovoid. The only way I could tell the membrane was there was its slight rippling effect, like a film of clear plastic in the slightest breeze. I was aware of a strange, steady undulation throughout the vessel.

"What is this thing?" I asked.

"You may remember it," Bosch said. "It is one of the sky boats from my paintings. In fact, if you look down, you'll see that it's a fish boat."

"Fish boat! But that wasn't real. That was just . . ."

"Imaginary? Yet, in your writing you argue that other imaginary creatures stand for something. Why not this one?"

"For starters, to imagine something doesn't make it real. If this thing is real, there's something seriously wrong with me." Suddenly I remembered a discussion with Lincoln and Janie.

"Don't extrapolate," Bosch warned.

"What do you mean?"

"The either/or lies in the truth of the thing itself. Not in the state of our own being."

"Explain."

"Yes. Suppose you awaken one morning deliriously happy. The morning sparkles after a nighttime rain. The sun scours the sky. And you conclude that this is a perfect morning. Yet, in the basement of a neighbor's house, a man lies on the concrete floor, curled in a ball, pondering the most efficient way to end his life. Is it still a happy morning?"

"I suppose it still is for me. At least, if I'm unaware of the pain of my neighbor."

"Ah, yes. Now, suppose you are the neighbor?"

"The world is pretty grim."

"Nonetheless, it raises a subsidiary question, does it not? Is enjoyment the chief end in life?"

"There's nothing wrong with enjoyment."

"Of course not. But consider the many people throughout history who have claimed it as the *chief* end. Those who have modeled governments on the principle. Those who claim it as a personal creed."

"If it feels good, do it?"

"Yes, to put it in the most crass, thoughtless terms. And to such a person, what becomes of the neighbor lying in his ball of psychological pain? You need not answer, for the answer is obvious. He is an intrusion on their happiness. Any pain is intrusive. If one's chief aim, then, is enjoyment, the pain of the beggar, the suicide, the starving, the crippled and needy, are all intrusive."

"But we can't really escape pain anyway, can we?" I asked. I asked it as a question, but it rose from my own life. I knew the answer. I had been blindsided by pain, an emotional auto wreck that left twisted metal strewn everywhere.

"That, however, doesn't prevent people from assuming otherwise. Some even make a pretty good show of it. Their fundamental error, as perhaps you guessed, is to live their lives according to the present moment. If one says, 'If it feels good, do it,' what essentially does that person mean?"

"Do it now?"

"Ah. Good. So the person chooses at the present moment, hence out of necessity rather than freedom."

"I'm not sure I understand that."

"Necessity serves oneself. When some people speak of freedom, what they really mean is the freedom to do anything they want, gratify any desire, to serve their end of enjoyment. But that end of personal gratification, or what they call enjoyment, exists in only two modes—the anticipation and the act upon that anticipation."

"Satisfying the self."

"Indeed. You learn quickly. But now let's return for a moment to your neighbor in the basement, who, we must confess, gives us no pleasure at all. Unless, perhaps, we were the monsters who caused his torment. Now the question is how one chooses with genuine freedom instead of out of necessity."

"It seems obvious now," I ventured. "One chooses outside oneself; that is, one chooses the inconvenience of helping the man."

"Oh, very good."

For a moment I felt like he was patronizing me. Then I realized he meant it.

"But incomplete," Bosch continued. "For your action isn't for the man alone. Tell me, what is the aim of helping him?"

"Why, to ease his pain." It seemed obvious. Alleviating pain had to be the principal ethic regardless of one's religious stance.

"And if that pain affected others?" Bosch mused. "Then perhaps restoration. And if he suffers because *he* inflicted pain, then restoration also. Whereas pleasure seems momentary, pain seems to gather a life of its own. And, therefore," he added, "acquires disproportionate weight in memory."

We seemed to be floating gently in the fish boat, perhaps not even with destination. In the darkness I could discern no actual movement. So too, it seemed that our discussion was going nowhere. It simply consisted of words passed back and forth as we went from nowhere to nowhere. I hardly paid attention, my answers thoughtless and undiscerning. I thought Bosch was just passing the time harmlessly chitchatting with me until something happened.

Bosch looked at me sharply. I wondered how privileged this ghost/spirit/servant was to my own experience.

"We see, then, that the free choice to enter into the need of someone else, to bear that person's pain, is future directed. In fact, freedom lies at the threshold of eternity. Do you remember my painting *Christ Carrying the Cross*?"

"Of course. I've seen it in Madrid."

"Yes. Not in the best of shape anymore. Remember, that was when we were painting with oil on wood. Did anything in particular strike you?"

"Well, so many things." I grew more alert as we talked specifics of his work. This is what I wanted. Something to take back with me and put to use. "Actually the two women in the background caught my eye first. Mary and Martha, I thought."

"Yes. What else?"

"Well, then I made a visual circle like I always do with a painting, studying the men surrounding Jesus. From the pug-faced peasants to the aristocratic Pharisee."

It was as if the painting stood before me. I was not just remembering, but it was as if I were there, in the Royal Palace in Madrid. Or as if it were somehow displayed on the aqueous membrane before me.

"I turn to the center," I continued softly. "Trace the figure of the Christ from the feet upward. That right foot, it pushes off. His body bends perpendicular to the cross. Then his face. This is what struck me most powerfully. The eyes. Christ's eyes are staring out from under the crown of thorns, right at me!"

"Yes. And what do the eyes say?"

I couldn't stop myself, even though the words choked, "This . . . this I have done. Even for the least of you, my brothers."[1]

"You read my work better than you think," Bosch said after a long silence. "That was the look I hoped for, where Christ turns to the viewer, the reader, and shares something of a Last Supper. 'This is my body, broken for you.'

"Now we go a step further. To the cross, if you will. Where Christ took on the pain of others. And to what end? The eternal end. Thereby in his assumption of pain he gives freedom. Freedom from necessity, gratification, and the rule of the moment. Freedom to choose for others, to participate in their suffering, to unlock the joy of life eternal."

His voice was quiet, musing, as if he spoke of something he himself had long desired and only recently discovered to be true.

I had nothing to say, too busy pondering the fundamental issue of my life—Was Christ in fact the Redeemer he claimed to be? Or the deluded utterer of slogans, a first-century television talk show host with some psychobabble palaver?

"And that," Bosch added after a while, "is our first lesson in the nature of hell."

"What?" I said with a start. "I thought we were talking about necessity or freedom."

"Yes. But now you may extrapolate. Or rather, let me state the matter plainly. In hell there exists only the necessity of what the person has chosen. The moment, if you will, is the climax of the desire's craving. Hell is the everlasting, never-changing prison of the moment."

"You mean nothing changes?"

"Freedom implies, does it not, the opportunity to change? Go back to your neighbor in the basement. You intervene in the hope that you can change his condition. Remember the eyes of Christ on the way to

1. The peculiar use of the phrase here struck me, since it does not appear in any biblical account of Christ's crucifixion. Indeed, the compelling quality of Christ during the ordeal was that he kept *silent*. I can only speculate that this particular vision, either Bosch's or the narrator's, is a conflation of several other well-known references of Jesus. For example, in the parable of the Sheep and the Goats, Jesus says, "The King will reply, 'I tell you the truth, whatever you did for one of the least of these brothers of mine, you did for me'" (Matt 25:40).

Calvary. They invite you in to the earthshaking change. But those in hell cannot change. They are stripped down to the essential self, the very desire that moved every thought and action."

"But I thought hell was eternal."

"It is an eternal *moment*. That is a topic we'll have to return to when we have more knowledge. But for the moment—this. Heaven has ceaseless growth. Wonder grows as new wonder is met. The imagination fully surrounds the reality and the reality fully incarnates the imagination. But understand Lesson One: hell is reversal. Not just reversing heaven, but reversal itself. That reversal reveals reality, but it is stark, brutal, and inescapable. Everything, *everything* you see is one moment that lasts for all eternity. It is bondage without hope of escape, suffering without hope of surcease, awareness locked in emotion that never tastes the cool water of the imagination. It is the real self undisguised. In short, for all eternity, it is the essence that could not be otherwise."

"I'm beginning to understand. It's like my friend Lincoln would call an antonym in language. The exact opposite."

"Yes, a good way to put it, but an opposite that can countenance absolutely none of the reality of freedom. It is completely, forever other."

"May I ask another question? I'm not sure it's related."

"Please. That's why I'm here. Although you must understand that there are things hidden from me of which I'm not permitted to speculate."

"Well, I was wondering about desire."

"Ha! Don't confuse normal, healthy desire with the craven impulse of those you will meet here."

"How do I know the difference? I mean, I really loved Shelley, but I desired her too."

"Even so. Desire was a manifestation of love, a longing for union. And now, do you feel any desire again after what happened?"

"Yes. I had to get through a lot of anger, even hatred really, to find it."

"We'll talk about anger later."

"The second time you've said that. *Later*."

"We have time. We're outside of time. Tell me, do you feel love or desire?"

"Both, I guess. I think, I truly believe, I'm falling in love anew and the desire is growing stronger."

"Desire for what, though?"

"Just to be with her, first of all. Sometimes I just want to say her name aloud to myself. Right now Janie's visiting her family in Maine.

Say, will I get back in time to pick her up from the airport?" A hideous thought dawned on me. "I *am* getting back, aren't I?"

"In no time at all. Literally. You were saying about desire?"

"Very well. I don't think you're going to go around blabbing. I still think you're something in some weird dream I'm having. Traveling in a fish boat!"

"Strange. I had the same dream." Bosch winked sideways at me. Just like Ed Nolan did.

"So," I continued, speaking more to myself really, "as I've been falling in love, I'm also . . . desiring her body."

"Have you been sexually intimate?"

"Don't I wish. Well no, that's not correct. Yes, I do wish. I want to. But I want to respect Janie. I wouldn't ever want to risk her feeling that she had demeaned herself for me. And, yes, I am frightened of another relationship."

"My advice? See the person first, not the relationship. And if you'll reflect a moment, I think you'll now understand the two different kinds of desire.

"Consider your desire for Janie. It is motivated by, as you say, the fact that you are falling in love with her. Hence, it is not just for you alone, but for her. You have a longing for something beyond yourself, a *union* with Janie. If I remember correctly, one of the church doctors once said, 'True love requires one to will another's good as one's own.'"[2]

"I don't know if I dare try marriage again."

"That's understandable. With such desire one often finds a holy fear. I found it often when I painted. The knowledge that beyond each of you—you and Janie individually—lies a transcendence that is both of you. In fact, the older church philosophers meant something like this when they wrote of the longing for God.

"But to finish the point, the craven desire is for immediate gratification. It uses the other person, or thing, or even God, to meet this consummation of desire. Such persons you will find here. Having never chosen to look beyond themselves, they are forever by themselves."

"When do we leave?" I asked. There were no controls of any kind in the lucent bubble, and, save for the slight undulations, no sense of

2. Saint Thomas Aquinas, *Summa Theologica* I, 91. See also his *Commentary on Sentences*, on love: "Love is prior to other affections of the soul, for love means the fulfillment of the affection through being informed by its object" (I, d27, q. 1, a. 1–4). Drawn from *An Aquinas Reader.*

movement in any purposeful direction. We seemed suspended from some unseen string, waiting for launch.

Bosch chuckled. I was beginning to find him quite affable. He always looked so dour in his self-portraits, jaws snapped shut like a turtle, the long, narrow beak of a nose ready to ferret out sin. "Long ago," he said now. "We left long ago. Or we left just now. Or a million miles ago. Or an inch behind us."

"Okay. You're mocking me. What good is it when I have no idea of the point?" I couldn't help smiling back.

"We can only trust personal perception to a very limited extent," he said. "Now, test it further. Lean toward the window, as you might call it. That's right. The membrane will only break if your imagination does. Further. Now, what do you see?"

"Something curved. It's moving back and forth."

"Look harder. You may have to press against the membrane, perhaps even bend it a bit, to look down. Don't worry. It's flexible."

My breath began snagging at the back of my throat. Palpitations thumped along my neck, colliding somewhere in my temples. A small portion of my forehead touched the membrane. It felt as cool as stream water, looked as bright as sunlight.

"Scales?" I murmured.

"Yes. The fish itself. I think you probably only saw the pectoral fin though. You weren't leaning very far."

"I . . . I don't like heights."

"Obviously. But you'll learn to mind our vessel less as you trust it more."

"Trust the unicorn?"

"Pardon me?"

"What exists in imagination only?"

"I'm not sure we're ready for that yet. In a way, you're just getting your feet on the ground."

"I thought we were flying."

"The fear of heights thing? Well, that's how you perceive it now. Actually, we're traveling *through*, not 'above,' 'around,' 'into,' or 'out of.' Although from within this vessel, it may very well seem to you that we are flying, as you say."

Cautiously, I pressed my forehead against the membrane. It was like peering against a giant piece of Saran wrap, but with absolutely no resistance. It seemed to move with me. Eerie. And even more eerie was the fact that, although surrounded in perfect darkness, the harder I looked the more the fish seemed suffused in a strange but radiant light.

Its sides were clearly scaled with flecks of silver. Looking closer, I saw other colors interwoven—radiant specks of cerulean blue, dapples of red, orange, and gold. The closer I looked, the more solid and real the muscular creature seemed. Peering ahead, I tried to make out the contours of its jaws to determine its species. But as the front undulated smoothly, it appeared one moment as a muskie, another as salmon, another as trout, another unmistakably as catfish with its long needle whiskers.

Perhaps this was like staring out of an airplane window. You have no consciousness of speed; towns and fields below seem like a toyland. You almost feel you could step out onto that broad wing and dance. Just as long as it's not I. I found myself looking past the fish, searching for some signs out there. Pitch black. Or, rather, nothingness.

"The outer darkness," murmured Bosch.

How about the fires I saw, back when—"

"Back when? But that was before. Now we are *proceeding* to before."

"I know. Later. What was that!" Suddenly out of the darkness a flare of red fire exploded, so red it looked like blood tossed against a black canvas. As quickly as it appeared, it winked out. In an eyeblink it was gone. But as I kept staring I noticed more of these peculiar fiery pillars, like demented fireflies burning themselves out on a July midnight. They were only momentary twists of flame.

"I think you'll see soon," said Bosch softly.

I thought to myself that he might be frightened also. Then I thought that I would not trust him if he were *not* afraid.

I was leaning against the membrane, staring out into the distance, when suddenly one of the red pillars exploded nearly in front of our vessel. The powerful fish pressed toward it in an even, unperturbed glide. I looked frantically for controls, anything to jerk it aside. Dumbfounded I looked at Bosch, who sat in disgusting calmness, arms crossed over his thick chest. His eyes didn't deviate.

Out of the pyre of fire directly in front of us emerged the most sickly, macabre creature I've ever seen. No horror film maniac could have invented this. No animator could have brought it to life.

Twisted in transparent flame, he (undeniably a "he," I felt it without knowing) was draped in flaccid skin the color of rotted suet. From a sunken chest, the flesh oozed over a protuberant stomach. An old cloth diaper draped around his loins, not pinned but locked with chains. From the waist and legs burning fecal matter flowed with the timeless, slow flow of lava. I tried to tear my eyes away from the sickening vision. I looked at Bosch again. He impaled the creature with his eyes. For the first time I looked at the figure's face. And shuddered.

There was no mistake. He had his thumb in his mouth like a lonely infant. The other hand stretched to the filthy, sodden diaper and stroked it like a blanket or a stuffed animal. But above the twitching mouth was that unmistakable mustache. The head was narrow, topped by hair frozen implacably in that right part, oiled smoothly over his brow. Beneath those beagle brows, the eyes searched out with incredible, unrequitable longing.

As quickly as the head appeared, the volcanic pyre sucked him back, disappeared, and there was once again blackness as the fish boat glided over the place he had been.

"Adolf Hitler," I said, and I felt it was the first time I had breathed in ages.

Bosch merely nodded. I gathered he was waiting for me to question. I was beginning to understand the process, but I was momentarily dumbfounded. I had to convince myself not that the apparition appeared but that he had in fact disappeared into the now gone pyre of flame. Apparition or person? What stayed in my mind were the gray, slack skin, looking like ashes, and the hopeless eyes.

"Is he the only one out here?" I asked at length. My heart still hammered in my chest. This was no dream; rather, some horrible but oblique reality. "I mean, what happened?"

"There are thousands, perhaps millions, like him flung into the outer darkness," Bosch answered, "but not one of them knows that. Each is encased by the individual pyre of flame, alone. Forever alone. Their only awareness is of their continual, unchanging debasement.

"Remember," said Bosch, "what we said about the reversal of values toward desire and satisfaction? On the one hand, necessity, in order to gratify immediate desires; on the other, freedom, in order to serve others and desire their good. Hence, it is also a reversal of being.

"Consider that that reversal extends through earthly experience. Tell me, now that we have one isolated example from the thousands—perhaps millions—since the dawn of time, what motivated Hitler more than anything during his lifetime?"

This was a trickier question than I initially thought, raising all sorts of implications, like a bowling ball knocking pins askew. I pondered it while replaying in my mind the disgusting figure I had seen. Finally, I hazarded, "Power."

"Bravo!" declared Bosch with a grin.

"I gather I'm right."

"I suppose so. That's what I would have guessed, and since we agree, we must be right."

"You mean you don't know?"

"Know? As fact, you mean? How should I know? I was never privy to his brain, thank goodness. Although I think in *The Temptation of Saint Anthony* I may have gotten a little too close, even for my tastes. Fine border, you know. Yes, well. Now where were we? Ah, congratulating ourselves on being correct. We agreed that his primary motivation—dare we call it his one aim?—in life was to become powerful. Not just to seize power, but to be power itself."

"But," I interjected, "does anyone want power *just* for the sake of power?"

"An interesting question. Example, please."

"Hmm. I have to define *power* first, I suppose. I wish Lincoln were here."

"Oh, I'm not sure that's necessary."

We continued to hover through impenetrable blackness while I reflected. I really had no clear sense if I were upside down or right side up, or what that really meant anymore. At least I knew the fish was below us. Or maybe it too was upside down. Now and then pillars of fire flared momentarily in the distance then winked out. For some of them, if I blinked I only caught a strange afterimage. I was going to ask Bosch if this lack of orientation was part of hell itself. Negation. I remembered he had given me an assignment.

"Well," I started in, "first I think I have to distinguish power from authority. One may be given authority. Or it may be a quality earned—think of King Arthur. It may be an inherent quality, evidenced by accomplishment and personality, perhaps. This is difficult. How am I doing?"

"Rambling. But we'll see where we arrive."

"Authority sounds right. I mean, it accords with ethical values, with laws perhaps. Authority looks outward. A bit like your freedom example."

"Very good, Pilgrim. You're finding your way."

"Power, on the other hand, uses position or status or some such for its own end. When I think of power, I think of a great ravenous set of jaws grinding up other people. Because of position, a person *can* do that."

"Sometimes power can be used for good, no?"

"I suppose that if I were to go to war I would want to have a powerful army rather than a weak one."

"And, assuming it is a just war, what is the goal of that army?"

"To eradicate some evil. To defeat a merciless, genocidal tyrant, for example."

"Ah, we get nearer the mark. Now what if this tyrant, as you say, wants to take over a neighboring country because of its wealth, its industry, or merely to expand his power?"

"Then he does it for his own gratification."

"To have others stand in amazement of his power, don't you think?"

"Perhaps."

"Now, what if Adolf Hitler as you just saw him, the real Adolf Hitler with all his burning greed and capacious lust and his addled, childish fears . . . what if *this* Adolf Hitler had attempted to establish the Nazi Party in 1933?"

"People would have laughed him off the podium."

"Yes. And you have seen him as he really is—the proud man made a fool.[3] Although his eyes can never see them—you noticed they turned inward like his vast ego in life—all those in hell who see him laugh. One might say he is the laughingstock of hell, but then there are so many of these once-powerful tyrants in the outer darkness. Each utterly alone, peering inward, understanding for the first time the meaning of the word *separation*. For, with no one to obey your power, and with no sycophants to adore your power, all your power is as a babe in filthy rags."

"Would it be fair to say the powerful, those who usurp office for their own aims and ends, are debased?"

"Perhaps," Bosch reflected, "it is wise to probe behind the actions of the tyrant, which all sane persons agree are despicable, to the underlying mind-set and choices for those actions. This is a mind-set, by the way, shared by many of those 'sane' people whose actions nonetheless appear to be socially acceptable. The fact is that we simply name some as notorious because of the extent of their evil."

"Hitler with some six million killed?"

"Or Stalin with some sixty million. And those figures don't include the young men they pitilessly threw to war to establish their power. But we want to know *why*, don't we?"

3. Cf. Ps 94:2; Prov 3:34.

"The everlasting 'Why?'"

"Reduced to 'Why me?' in your time."

"True. Everyone's a victim." Then I thought a moment. Truly, many people are victims. The powerless. Those without status or means. Those whose lives are ripped apart by an act of treachery that belied all promises and the very soul of trust.

"Perhaps we are better off focusing on the one example," Bosch said hastily, as if reading my thoughts.

"The modern mind," he continued, "tends to focus on the particular, doesn't it? This particular theory; that particular icon. So someone associated with that specialized thought becomes celebrated as a thinker, or a leader, or perhaps a teacher. A specialist.

"But historically, knowledge was never viewed that way. Any particular knowledge is important to a larger grid of understanding, rather than for its own sake. Instead of specialization, we have contexts, like a series of overlapping spheres all contained within one larger sphere."

"Called knowledge?"

"In my age I would have called it the 'contemplative,' but 'knowledge' will work for now. The point is that the larger orb is not fully comprehended without some understanding of the spheres inhabiting it. This is the error of so many modern 'isms.' They try to build the large orb with nothing in it but pronouncement."

"So what do the smaller orbs represent?"

"Experiences and feelings about them. Beliefs and actions based on them. Culture, society, even prior history and its later effects on the age. We can extend the list substantially to pursue those contexts of knowledge that apply to the large sphere of actions. So, in this case, behind the actions of Adolf Hitler lies the intellectual context of one Friedrich Nietzsche."

"Nietzsche! But he died about the time Hitler was born, if I remember right."

"You do. And Hitler was raised in Austria, not Germany. But one doesn't have to have a contemporaneous dialogue with a person to be influenced by the person. Ideas live on. Think of your own work. Think of your friend Ed Nolan who listens to a golden oldies station while he works."

"He says the barbaric music helps him concentrate." I chuckled, thinking of Ed's battered, paint-stained boom box.

"Nietzsche begins with the twin premises that there is no God and that Christianity is a cruel hoax foisted on humankind to keep them enslaved. This, by the way, is developed in *The Will to Power*. I wouldn't guess you've read it?"

"I confess I haven't even heard of it."

"Probably of only passing importance to our point here. Christianity is a narcotic, he argues, that reveals our emptiness. If I remember correctly, he puts it something like this: '*Radical nihilism* is the conviction of an absolute untenability of existence when it comes to the highest values one recognizes.'[4] That sort of thing.

"Of much greater influence during his time and following, however, was the book he worked on for quite some years, *Thus Spoke Zarathustra*. This work shaped a mind-set, and I have the peculiar belief that Hitler's contravention of pity, neighbor love, values, and his belief in war might very well have arisen from this mind-set. Or, at the very least, we might say that Hitler almost perfectly incarnated what Nietzsche had been thinking.

"Perhaps we should review a moment, though. First, what motivated those who now dwell here?"

"Necessity. To gratify their own desires."

"As opposed to?"

"Freedom. To choose outside of self. For others."

"And what did the tyrant choose in his lifetime?"

"Power. That is, power over others to serve his desires."

"Very good, Pilgrim. And the opposite of power is not mere weakness, is it?"

"No. It would be authority. But authority derives from some body of rules. Or laws."

"Then," said Bosch, nodding, "we stand at the threshold of Zarathustra's journey to the mountaintop of the overman—the difference between 'Thou shalt' and 'I will,' as Nietzsche put it.[5] He pictured thousands of years of values as the shiny scales of a terrible dragon. We live in fear of that dragon. On the other hand, the power of the lion rises up against that

4. Nietzsche, *The Will to Power*, 9. Bosch, it must be said, gives the work too short a shrift here. The essence of the text lies in Book Two, Nietzsche's deliberated critiques on religion and morality. Moreover, fascinating ground is covered in Book Three on the topics of individual power and power as art. One can only speculate why Bosch didn't pursue these lines of argument further.

5. Nietzsche, *Thus Spoke Zarathustra*, 26.

dragon. Yet something more is needed, he claimed. That is the child. Out of the child's innocence, and out of the 'I will,' a new era dawns."

"Okay," I said, "but what is that to the point? How does it apply to Hitler?"

"Mind you, we are not only talking about Hitler here, but about all tyrants consumed by the rage for power. And remember also that they are not just figures of state but that they appear any place—in the family home, the church, a business office, a classroom. That is critical to remember.

"Follow Nietzsche's steps. First, discredit or annihilate the dragon of traditional values. They are of no account as guides. Second, use the mighty lion to announce 'I will.' For Hitler, we could call this his vast military, but it could be any assertion of self. And, third, give birth to a new program to give that self power. For Hitler, it was the Nazi Party."[6]

"They do seem truths of any petty tyrant," I ventured.

"Tyrants are never petty. Someone always suffers from their power. To see that, we have to look at the consequences of Nietzsche's premises. What are the values that must be demolished?

"The first of these abhors pity and engages war to advance one's self. The war one fights, he argues, is for the freedom and power of one's own thoughts, liberated from social or ethical constraints. Listen to his words: 'You should love peace as a means to new wars—and the short peace more than the long. . . . To you I do not recommend peace but victory.'"[7]

I looked at Bosch, startled by the noticeable change in inflection in his voice. He seemed to be somewhere else, listening to the words perhaps or reading over someone's shoulder. Then I realized that he was reciting in perfect German, but I heard it as English. His eyes seemed glazed. I shivered at what seemed suddenly preposterous and wholly terrifying to me. Here I was, in some unworldly vessel with a ghost, surrounded by inexpressible horror. I was about to cry out, to try to awaken from the nightmare, when his seductive voice spoke again.

"'You say it is the good cause that hallows even war? I say unto you: it is the good war that hallows any cause. War and courage have

6. At other points, Zarathustra's language grows increasingly shrill in denouncing Old Testament law. On the commandments "Thou shalt not rob" and "Thou shalt not kill" he declares, "Is there not in all of life itself robbing and killing? And that such words were called holy—was not truth itself killed thereby . . . ? Oh my brothers, break, break the old tablets" (ibid., 202).

7. Ibid., 47.

accomplished more great things than love of the neighbor. Not your pity but your courage has so far saved the unfortunate.'"[8]

Bosch seemed suddenly to shudder, and released a long sigh. He turned to me with a wrinkly grin. His eyes looked very old.

"So you see the consequences of power," he said—in English now. "Neighbor love is an illusion and pity a sin."

"It sounds . . . frightening."

"Yes, indeed. For Nietzsche—and for the tyrant—love for your neighbor is bad love for yourself; your own will is your neighbor. And does that answer your question, Pilgrim? The question and more, I would say, for this is the mind of every tyrant."[9]

"I'm trying to figure out something about *authority*, the word we used before."

Bosch replied, "It might be better to start with the reversal effect. If what we have described about power is the negative act, then to what end is the positive act?"

"If we go back to Lesson One," I said, "then it would be giving sacrificially."

"Yes. And the lessons do tend to grow on each other, don't they? But think again of reversal itself. Having focused on self, the true nature of the self is revealed here. All disguises, all subterfuge is stripped away. I call it the supreme embarrassment of being."

"Well . . ." I was trying to get at his angle of inquiry. I wasn't sure where he was going, nor where *I* was supposed to go. I felt decidedly uncomfortable, like the feeling before an exam question when you wonder if you have ever heard of the topic. And worse, I wondered if that was exactly what he wanted.

"Let's see," I continued. "We've seen that reversal turns one in upon the isolated self. And whatever anguish that self suffers."

Bosch nodded noncommittally. I noticed, as I paused and looked out the membrane, that the flares seemed now to be increasing in number again.

"And we observe that the opposite action is to help others. The neighbor in the basement. And that an example of such action was Christ on the cross. Be it truth or myth, it incarnates, fully, the principle. In a sense, we are all the people in the basement."

8. Ibid.

9. Cf. Nietzsche, *Zarathustra*, 60, 290–91.

Again he nodded, now with a slight grin. Or was it a grimace?

"And what does one gain by such action?" Bosch asked.

I found this trickier yet. It would have been easy to say that I saved the neighbor and gained a lifelong friend. That I gave a beggar in disguise a dollar and he turned out to be Croesus,[10] thus showering me in gold. I knew I was off track, of course. I would do these things because I had a sense of "oughtness." One ought to help save a fellow human; one ought to help the homeless beggar. But, it crept up on me that the harder one pursued these avenues, one did receive something. That there is a certain authority in "oughtness," and that "oughtness" itself derives from an authority beyond human fabrication. Without that, I might as well leave my neighbor lying in the basement and ransack his house to *my* own gratification. By giving up more of oneself to others, one began to receive more of one's true self. That reversal led somewhere—not to momentary gratification, but to some kind of gratification in knowing what one truly stands for.

"I would call it 'reciprocity,'" I said suddenly. "Even though you may not be granted the praise or thanks of others, what you do for them is reciprocated by a growing sense of who you really are."

"You become more and more yourself," Bosch commented.

I hesitated. "But so are these." I swept my hand toward the membrane. By now flares had thickened considerably. They appeared like a network of fiery nerves thrust against a black canvas.

"Perhaps we'll understand that better," said Bosch, "when we inquire into anger, wrath, and hatred." His eyes were closed.

Suddenly his head tilted, leaned against the membrane, and he snored softly.

10. The fabulously wealthy Lydian king who died in 546 BC.

CHAPTER NINE

Encounter with Bel

WHILE BOSCH DOZED—AND IT did strike me odd that a spirit or whatever he was would doze—I reflected on his last words: "anger, wrath, hatred." They rolled about in my mind like a sack of dice, turning up odd combinations.

I don't think I could hate. I mean, I believe I'm incapable of that soul-numbing state. Hatred always struck me as a spiritual and psychological suicide.

As I thought about it, there were plenty of things I stood against on principle. These make me angry. They seem intrinsically wrong. They break what a friend of mine calls "shalom," the fundamental harmony and order of things.

So I think the pollution of streams, rivers, lakes, and oceans is wrong. When I see litter, I get angry. On more than one occasion Lincoln and I have walked the college green bagging Styrofoam, plastics, cigarette butts. It does little, but we take a stand.

I don't think anger is wrong. Maybe Bosch can help me with this.

Hatred, as I said, is more mysterious to me. I know full well that many people harbor hatreds—prejudices, for example—that twist them into a constant state of rage.

I wonder if Shelley hated me. Or was I just a piece of used debris to be cast aside?

Even in my darkest nights, I never felt hatred toward her. I felt angry, yes, and depressed and confused and lonely. For weeks I cried myself to sleep at night. One night I got up and took the pillow that still bore her scent and put it in a garbage bag. It didn't help; that side of the bed was as empty as it had ever been.

What I wondered—over and over—was this: when did that smile that I thought was for me alone vanish? Did it become an empty tic of facial muscles and perfect teeth while she gave the real things to someone else? That haunted me. And that precious body, given to me in one flesh, now given to another in one flesh. I wondered what vows they could possibly have taken.

But that seems a time long distant now. Lights break out in the darkest night. Stars appear, then dim as a sun lips the horizon. And those waves of despair finally ebb.

I'm not saying that I'll soon forget what happened, or that I'm "over it." I'm only saying that I never hated her.

I almost felt like nudging Bosch to tell him my thinking, but he was still snoring gently, his mouth open with a slight trail of drool forming in one corner. It seemed indecent to awaken him.

Then I thought—what about the person who hates himself? Or at least the condition he is in. Hates himself so terribly that he wishes to end his life as he knows it.

No one on a university campus is long a stranger to suicide. Despite the efforts of the *Campus News* to gloss it over in technicalities, three or four suicides a year occur here—that's just in my memory. Was it when the person could no longer stand to look in the mirror for fear of the other he saw there? Was it to escape pain?

This I knew not. Such self-hatred was a mystery to me.

Suddenly, as if twisted by whiplash, my mind reverted to a scene from my childhood—a mystery so profound I don't understand it to this day. Terrifyingly, as it unscrolled in my memory, it was as if I were once again *there*. Not the graduate student, but the young boy stupefied by the unknown. And his powerlessness to do anything about it.

Seen from the outside, the house looked like a skeleton draped in black rags. The doorway gaped like a broken jaw. Inside, detritus—blackened studs, a fallen flight of stairs to the second story, chunks of cinder block from a ruined foundation—littered the ash-laden floor.

There, amid the litter, she hunched over the dull orange light cast by a camping lantern, unzipped her jeans, then slowly rolled the waist down several inches. She withdrew something from the tiny purse set by the lantern and seemed to study it, passing it gently through her fingers. She leaned back. In one swift stoke she ripped a red line just below her navel, then hatched over it with another.

She held the glittering razor blade tightly, pointed against her abdomen, and struck quickly a third time. Her back arched; her head snapped back. A sound like rusted metal keening escaped her clenched teeth. Then she fell forward, hands clasped to her abdomen, making sucking sounds like someone walking in muddy water. The blade dropped from her fingers.

After a moment or two she reached into her purse, cleaned herself with several tissues that she cast aside, and tore open two large gauze bandages that she pulled very tight against the cuts. She gasped several times, breathing hard as if she had run miles through a black forest.

Then she lit a cigarette, holding the match a long time while she sucked in deeply. In the match light her face seemed very young. The match burned down until the flame disappeared between her fingers.

She finished the cigarette, ground it out on the charred floor and picked up her purse and the lantern.

"Go away," she said. But she was staring at the floor and I couldn't tell if she was talking to me or to something in the deeper shadows. Then her white blouse slipped through a slant of light and she was gone.

It had been shingle-sided once, the house one lot over from the corner of Neland and Worden. The old asphalt composite shingles that weren't supposed to burn.

When the house caught fire years earlier, the studs flamed up like a torch, caving in huge piles of shingles that hung from the ruins of the framework saved by the firemen's hoses. They should have let it go, let it all burn in one huge twisting pyre. But the vacant house had burned on a hot summer night and the dry wind could have easily spread the blaze, so the firemen extinguished it before the house burned to the ground. So it stood now, blackened and soulless. The ruined framing boards leaned against each other and groaned in the wind. The roof caved in toward the west end, the long ridge board sunken and poking out through the empty second-story window.

The city put a chain link fence around the lot and, after a while, lost interest in looking for the owner. In time, weeds grew and choked the poisoned soil. Once each summer, in late August, three men wearing orange shirts that said JAIL in large black letters came in with brush whackers to clean the mess. Neighbors made excuses to walk by and watch them. When the prisoners were done, the neighbors could see the holes cut low in the fencing, flaps easily pushed aside, where people—who knows who?—crawled through and explored the ruins. That's when they asked the city to tear down that witch house.

But whether they complained to the city or not, the house stood there, implacable, frightening, a testament of darkness. After services at the church across the street, men stood together smoking pipes or cigarettes, staring out with heavy faces at the house, bringing all the weight of their spiritual judgment to bear.

"Last crew hauled more whiskey bottles out of there than the liquor store stocks," said one. "Whole back of the pickup truck was layered with whiskey and beer bottles."

"Least the city cleans it up once a year. Gives them jailbirds something to do."

"I never see 'em. Them that fool around in there. Don't see 'em comin' in. Don't see 'em leavin'. Don't hear no noise neither."

"You live a block away, Randolph. People nearby don't go to church or we could organize them. Do something."

"What? Do what? I see plenty, I tell ya. Rats the size of beavers. I keep a coupla cats. They see them things comin', they run on home."

"That's so, Randolph," said another. "I've seen the rats. That's why I wonder why anyone would *want* to go in there."

"Maybe it's like they say, it's witches."

The truth was that the city wasn't doing a thing about the house beyond cleaning the grounds once a summer. The whole neighborhood was sinking into a black hole city officials called "deterioration." In fact, few members of the church even lived there anymore. They lived in new brick homes south and east. There the lawns were pristine green, the very air more pure. There were no rats. Some were joining new churches in new neighborhoods.

But that last comment was what my friend Len overheard, and it was why we decided we had to go to the witch house.

She crouched like a whisper of smoke in the burnt-out house. Had we not seen the quick flicker of a flashlight, no more than a firefly light, we never would have seen her. We had no intention of going *in* the house.

It would be enough to crawl through one of the gaps in the fence and say we'd been there.

The vapor lamps from the church parking lot, installed last year in an attempt to prevent vandalism, left fragments of silvery light in the yard. Gradually, like a black and white movie in slow motion, the inside of the house became more distinct. From here we could see clear through to the backside, to the broken window framing through which she had entered. We edged carefully forward, toward the cinder block foundation and the pile of rotting boards and shingles that had never been cleared.

The little flash flicked on again. It wasn't a flashlight, but one of those small camping lanterns, fed by a couple of C cell batteries. The light was dim and cast an orange halo around her shadowed face.

Why? I wondered. What is she doing here? I crept forward toward the foundation. Someone tugged on my ankle—Rick or Len, I wasn't sure. I heard a rustle behind me and saw two bent shadows sliding through the gap in the fence and I was alone.

Or, alone with *her*. The house, the nauseating smell of burnt wood left to rot, the sharp odor of rodent feces and stale urine, all faded. I saw only the white blouse, the body fragile as twigs, and so it was that I was the only other one who saw the razor first land, then plunge. Then saw her kneel forward as if praying on a burnt pew before no altar I could imagine and I saw the blood spread between her pressing fingers before she cleaned herself with Kleenex and pulled the heavy bandage tight.

Go away. To whom was she speaking? Halfway home I felt a knot rise in my throat. I ran toward the trees in the schoolyard. I fell with my face to the grass and fallen leaves and cried.

Len and Rick asked me what I had seen, of course.

"What did you run away for?" I demanded.

"We'd seen enough," Len said. "Pulled on your ankle anyway to let you know we were going."

"Yeah. Real brave," I said.

"Hey, the deal was we were going inside the fence. That's all."

"Yeah," said Rick. He was my best friend. I didn't want to argue with him. "Why? What did you see?"

"Nothing," I said.

"Then what's the big deal? Really, what did you see?"

"Nothing. Only a girl smoking a cigarette. That's all."

"She didn't take her clothes off or something?" Len asked.

"No, Len. Nothing like that. Like I said, nothing at all."

School started and the wind sawed dry leaves from the maples and blew them in little waves restless on the ground. I kept seeing her face, even if I wouldn't see it, blurred orange and shadowed as it was. When I couldn't stand the unseeing, I went back.

I picked the same night of the following week, thinking she might come on some sort of schedule. I also convinced myself that I could just hide in the shadows outside the fence. No need to go in. I knew what I was looking for.

I stayed until I suddenly found my head drooping and sleep like a blanket closing down behind my eyes. I jerked myself awake and walked home.

Not worth it, I thought. And, who cares? And, it's cold out here at night. The walk turned into a run, then I shivered in bed a long while before falling asleep.

I would have missed her save for the full moon and the church lights falling through undraped limbs of the maple trees. It was the first week of October, an unusually warm evening. There had been little rain for over a month and the early leaves—maple and birch and poplar—had fallen quickly and heavy. Inside the fence they felt like six inches of dry crust under my hands and knees.

I had told my parents, after dinner, that I was going to the drugstore to buy a comic book. This was not unusual. They also knew that I would stand there and read through a dozen or more until the owner would walk past and encourage me to make up my mind.

The clock behind the drug store counter said 6:45, but when I stepped outside it was full dark. I had bought a candy bar instead; the new DC comics were due in on Monday. I felt my steps head toward the witch house, as surely as if someone had locked an ankle chain on and pulled.

The flicker of light seemed at first no more than a shard falling from the moon's face. The dim slats of light seemed alive themselves, catching the glint and twists of leaves that shivered in the corners. Then the flick-flash turned into a muted orange glow, even dimmer than last time, if that was possible.

She wore a skirt, very short, of some shiny material, and boots to her knees, also shiny. The orange light licked up and down them and they looked dull red in the light. Like blood, I thought. I couldn't tell the color of her blouse; also dark, maybe black.

She toed a loose cinder block with her boot and sat down on it, rubbing her hands above the lantern as if she were cold. She didn't move her head. She seemed to be staring into the orange lantern as if trying hard to understand something about light. Where did it come from? Where did it go? It just hung there, tented in an orange glob.

I crept closer to the foundation, expecting the harsher glare of the razor, the sudden rippling silver. But she only sat there, immobile, waxy in the shiny skirt and boots, imprisoned in the tented glow.

She gave a great sigh and squared her shoulders. Her body was like half a person, like a paper doll in profile, so thin she was. She leaned over and took a cigarette from the pack in her purse. The tiny lighter flick-flashed and for a moment her face, large dark eyes, the small nose, the very full lips now pursed like two stones, appeared then disappeared. Smoke trickled above her, hanging like a lost ghost until it found a doorway to the outside through one of the gaps.

I was at the cinder block foundation, on my knees, without fully realizing how I got there. That's why I saw clearly what happened as she smoked the cigarette down.

When the cigarette was little more than a glowing ember, she shifted forward and tugged the small skirt up to her waist. Her panties where white, vivid like a flagged triangle in the dark. As she spread her legs wide to encompass the orange glow, they too were very white, like two bleached bones propped into shiny boots. Then she took the cigarette butt and pressed it to the flesh on the inside of her leg about one inch below the white panties and I heard her suck in her breath like "unhnn."

And I thought she was just going to tap the cigarette there and no one could do what she was doing as she pressed harder and held it there and arched her back as she had done before and her head snapped back and her sweating face stared somewhere past the black rafters.

Then she made a sound like "eehhah," high and through clenched teeth and it reminded me of the sound of the dentist's drill grinding slowly into the tooth and you wanted to make a sound like that, clenching your jaw muscles open, with tears in your eyes while the dentist said, "Just a while longer—almost done," but it wasn't and it lasted forever with the drill shattering nerves like a hammer on electric wires. Tendons froze on her neck, bulging grotesquely like icicles bearing aloft a goblet of snow.

Then she pulled the cigarette away and her body convulsed and her head slumped forward, and even through the smell of the burnt-out house the odor of burnt skin curled like a green fog through the air.

And I was standing before her with no idea how I got there and my chipped voice shattered when I said, "Don't."

She squeezed the butt between her fingers and let it fall on the ground. She shifted her hips again and pulled her skirt down but I was still seeing the coal-black eye in her skin. She panted and sweat poured from her, running droplets trembling from her chin and nose into the globe of light.

Then she said, "Don't?"

"Please, don't hurt yourself."

"What do you care? What are you, some kind of peepin' tom, likes to sneak up and watch people?" She searched for her purse, drew out her cigarette pack. "Don't worry, kid. I just need a smoke."

"I can help you," I said.

"Hah! Help me. You're just a kid. How old are you, anyway?" She lit the cigarette, eyes squinted against the smoke. I never could see her face clearly. We were both standing now, two shadows atop orange knees.

"I'm not so young."

"How old?"

"I'll be thirteen in January."

"Hoo, boy. So you're twelve."

"Why? How old are you?"

"Sixteen. But if you live to a hundred you'd never be as old as I am."

"Why do you do it?"

She was silent, casting small clouds of smoke at me. I couldn't see her eyes but they seemed to be inside me.

I reached out to touch her arm. She jerked back violently.

"Sorry," I said quickly.

Her thin arms wrapped tightly over her abdomen. One hand would arc upward with the cigarette.

"Where do you go to school?" I asked.

"I don't."

"But you have to."

"Someone can tell *them* that."

I didn't understand. "Where do you live?"

She jerked her head to the north. "Yeah, you get the idea, kid. Up there."

I felt the candy bar in my pocket. "You hungry?"

"No," she said. "I don't want to eat. Then I'll have to wake up again."

"Here. Take this. It's a Snickers. I just bought it."

She studied it in my hand a moment, then snatched it as if it might run away. She broke the wrapper with her teeth. She chewed and swallowed with choking sounds, the way a dog tears at raw meat.

"I can bring you more," I said.

"Why? So you can feel good?"

"I want to help you."

"Go away now. Just go away." She extinguished the lantern, leaving two dark shapes in the shadows.

One of them shifted toward the gap in the back wall. "I'll bring you some food," I said.

"Don't bother," she said.

Then I was alone with the dry leaves and the wind.

Once, when I was much younger, a stray Collie wandered into our yard. I wanted to keep it, of course. My parents never wanted a dog. Couldn't afford it, they said, which I knew to be true. Nonetheless, I coaxed the Collie into the backyard. I dashed into the house and got two bowls, one filled with water and the other with Cheerios. The Collie, with those spasmodic jerks a dog makes when hungry, gathered in the Cheerios, lapped out the water bowl, and lay on its side. Under the thinned coat, each rib protruded like lattice work. I rubbed her, stroked behind her ears, and thought she was sleeping. With the sun glinting on the ravages of her coat, she seemed to me then the most beautiful dog I had ever seen. I went inside to beg my mother, pledging to clean an upstairs bedroom if I could keep her. "We'll have to call the pound," mother said. "That's best."

Back downstairs, I looked out the window. The Collie was gone. I ran outside and saw her far down the street. I ran a few steps and was going to call out to her when I realized that I had no name by which to call her.

At the intersection, the Collie turned west and disappeared, just one flicker of glowing gold fur.

It had been preternaturally warm the week of the witch house visits. "Indian Summer," we called it—that time after the first frost when most of the leaves have fallen and then the temperature suddenly soars. Thursday, the next day, was actually hot. We wore short-sleeve shirts and shorts to school. In the morning a wet mist hung above the ground. The empty trees were obscure arms holding the street together. Sweat hung heavy on us in the afternoon.

After dinner I excused myself. It was already dark at 6:30. Things seemed to crawl slowly in the sultry air. Streetlamps dripped yellow light. At the grocery I bought a loaf of day-old bread—I was using my allowance. She'll want something to drink with it, I thought. What? Not milk. It might spoil by the time she gets there. I walked past the racks of juices and soda pop. All the brands we didn't get at home because we couldn't afford them. We got Faygo. I looked for my favorite—Faygo grape, and dug the coins out of my pocket. Enough for two cans. It was all I had.

I asked the grocer to wrap the bread in plastic wrap. I didn't want the rats to get at it first.

I could hear them skittering around in the dry leaves as I climbed over the foundation to her cinder block. I saw something glinting there in the muted lamplight. I picked it up—the shiny wrapper of a pack of cigarettes, nearly full.

I wondered for a minute what that meant. Had she just forgotten them? Did she want *me* to have them? Was it some kind of sign left behind? What?

I set the bag of bread and Faygo down, then placed the pack of cigarettes next to it.

I walked through streets dripping with tears on the way home, but that wasn't why my heart was pounding.

I lay in bed that night with all the windows open, trying to catch even the most languid slip of breeze. The sheets were damp.

I awakened to a long low rumble, as if someone were playing bass kettle drums. I don't know when I had finally dozed off. And now, still half asleep, I realized it was thunder, unbroken, distant, that crept forward like foothills tumbling off a mountain's flanks. The air felt like it had been vacuumed away. Nothing left. Then through the open windows I saw the sizzle of lightning. First here and there and then as the thunder drew closer it was a rain of light, a dance of berserk energy, torching around the whole western sky. It lit the black face of the mountain tumbling toward me.

Then, just as the wind slammed into the screens, mother and father ran through the halls, shaking my sisters awake, slamming windows shut, calling loudly "To the basement. To the basement. It looks like a tornado." Even as they called, the tornado siren on top of the school wailed its spiraling sound. As we hurried down the stairs, a wall of wind sucked against the house, followed by the hard pepper of hail like a giant fist hurling pebbles.

Standard policy in those days was to shut off the electricity at the fuse box and to keep a strong flashlight, a bottle of water, and some old blankets in the basement. We didn't need the flashlight. While we sat in the basement southwest corner away from its one window, lightning stroked our faces. So powerful was the thunder that the concrete walls of the basement seemed to shiver. A small rivulet opened in the corner of the window frame, sliding down like a snake and coiling into a growing pool on the floor. Father found some old work towels in the cellar and tried to jam up the window frame. The rest he laid on the floor.

I remember I was feeling sleepy—the storm was letting up and the tornado siren had long since stopped—when new sirens shrieked up Neland Street past our house.

"Fire engines," my father said. "Lightning must have hit something."

"Probably the school," I yawned.

He shook his head. "That's all brick."

"Then the church."

He grinned at me. "Time for bed, I think."

We left the windows closed. The rooms all felt cold.

Friday morning dawned to a sky clean as washed crystal. Sunlight danced on every wet thing. Lawns were still soggy, and large puddles hung in street gutters, their entrance to the sewers blocked by mounds of wet leaves. Everyone wore jackets; some younger kids wore winter coats. It was the kind of air you feel in the back of your throat when you breathed deeply.

Kids that lived a couple of blocks north were talking loudly about it. At the center was the reverend's daughter, who claimed she saw everything through the front window of the parsonage. The bolt of lightning—she said—hit the end of the rafter poking through the second-story window and rolled over the house like a fireball. "It was just like a flamethrower at Iwo Jima," her father the reverend had said, even though I knew for a fact he was never in the war, either that one or Korea. He was blind as a bat for one thing.

When we raced up there after school, though, this much was true. The witch house was nothing more than an ugly heap of ruins. The smell was awful. "Probably killed a million rats," Len said. We heard that the city had condemned the whole site because of the shingles and general mess and would come in with a special crew on Saturday to clean it out.

They were there early, the prisoners in their orange garb, armed with shovels, pickaxes, and metal rakes. A cop stood to the side with his gun in a gleaming black holster. The jaws of the yellow scoop shovel plowed over the fence and bit enormous chunks out of the mess and dropped them in a dump truck that shook under each new load. A bulldozer shoved loose debris into the shrinking remnants of the witch house. Dump trucks came and left. The scoop pried around the inside of the foundation walls, excavating below ground level. Finally the dozer plowed the foundation itself over into the hole. The dump trucks returned with loads of sand while the scoop shovel was loaded on a trailer and hauled away. The yawning prisoners smoked cigarettes, threw stray pieces of debris into the hole while the dozer layered in the sand. A private wrecking crew dismantled the chain link fence and hauled it away. There was nothing to wall out or in anymore.

Only a few hours and it was all done, as if the black knob had never been there. The sun glittered on the fresh pile of sand. In the spring prisoners, maybe the same ones, would return and plant grass there. They would come in August to cut the grass and clean up. Maybe the grass would all be worn down by the feet of playing children.

We went home for lunch, Len and Rick and I.

Len said, "I wonder if she was ever naked in there."

"Shut up," I said. "You don't know nothin."

"And you do?" asked Rick.

"No," I said. "I don't know nothin' at all."

I emerged from the memory to the sound of my own cry. Like the nightmare panic that seems to gag in your throat.

The thing had cut through the darkness like a bolt of red lightning and now fastened on the tenuous membrane. Its scaly claws, sharp and red nailed, poked into the membrane, as if one push would rip it to shreds and hurl this alien creature full upon us. Jaws agape, green-scummed canine teeth drooling red droplets, the creature's breath fogged the canopy. Most repulsive by far was the translucent flab of its belly. Whenever it pressed against the membrane it left a trail of viscous puss-like fluid. Through the translucent entrails, I could see innumerable bulges twisted and twining.

It was at the moment I realized they were maggots that I did scream.

Bosch woke up with an agonizing slowness. I dared not speak, as if I could hide behind the membrane. The creature shifted right and left, like some primeval animal searching for prey. As it turned toward Bosch, I saw wisps of a ragged patch of hair on its back, like a possum's perpetually decaying look.

Languidly, Bosch rubbed his eyes. Then he said something that could not have astonished me more. "Tell it to go away, Pilgrim."

"Go . . . go away?"

"Not me. That." He pointed, and it did seem that the creature snapped viciously at his finger. "Tell *it* to go away."

"Do you really think it will?"

"Ha! You're wondering if you need magic spells, you mean? I tell you, Pilgrim, you won't know unless you try."

Right. Well. This is just a dream anyway. "Go away," I said. It sounded shaky. I wondered if I should try again with more force.

The beast turned toward me and fixed me with one eye. I saw fires of perfect hatred and rage burning there. Its talons loosened and the beast hurtled backward into darkness. I fixed my eyes in that direction, hardly daring to breath. Far in the distance I saw a momentary red splash, as if a pebble had been cast into burning liquid.

"What . . . what was that?" My voice trembled like a child soloist.

"A demon. Bel, if I'm not mistaken."

"Demons are real?"

"You just saw one. A minor one, to be sure. If memory serves me right, Bel is a demon of beauty. But there are so very many of those."

The light was back in Bosch's eyes. That twinkling knowing with the avuncular grin.

"Beauty," I said. "That was the ugliest—"

"Remember our earlier lesson. Hell is reversal, but also revelation of one's true self. The demons' task is to lure, to seduce. They are Satan's lions, roaming the earth, masquerading as creatures of light."

"But I've never seen such . . . such pure rage, such evil."

"Precisely. Its very words are worms, eating into a person. For Bel and her kin, they are the deceitful lure of beauty. And finally as artificial as one of those lures you cast into the pond."

"What do you mean? I don't think I understand."

"Hmm. Perhaps we should try a sidetrack, as long as we don't lose the main path. What do *you* mean by 'beauty'? How do you define it?"

"Well, as an art historian, I think I would define it as harmony, a certain fittingness among the parts that gives pleasure to the viewer."

"Does my work give you pleasure?"

"Oh, yes."

"Don't be too quick now."

"Well, an intellectual pleasure. Sort of like following the plot of a good book. Like *Crime and Punishment*."

"Very good. But parts of *Crime and Punishment*, and parts of my paintings, are . . . what word shall we use?"

I hesitated. "Ugly," I said at last.

"Very good. Because we seize beauty out of a world where ugliness abounds. Beauty without recognition of the reality of the ugly is—what shall we say—saccharine? Cloying? Unrealistic, perhaps?[1] Such art is a fantasy, my friend, of another world, and therefore of only secondary value to the world in which we live. Similarly, a work that grounds *only* in the ugly obscures or dismisses the imprint of grace upon this world. But now, lest we stray too far afield on this side road, back to our main point."

"Remind me?"

1. When editing these papers, I discussed this very point with the narrator. In his estimation, many fine studies of beauty in art exist, going back, perhaps, to the ancients. But he also mentioned two works that he had found helpful in understanding beauty and ugliness. These are James Luther Adams and Wilson Yates, *The Grotesque in Art and Literature*, and John H. Timmerman, "The Ugly in Art."

"Pilgrim, I have to remember that you are human. Forgive me. Your thoughts are linear. You are not given the gift of 'overseeing,' of holding thoughts simultaneously."

I looked at him to see if he was insulting me. I was trying my best, after all. I had agreed to come on this bloody ride. "I'll admit that sometimes my head feels like it's full of fragments," I said.

"Which is the effect of linear thought. So let me help you. The issue was how this beast that we saw, one of Satan's demons, appears on earth as a figure of beauty and grace. Now, we have agreed that in hell we see the reality and the reversal. *That* is what we saw, for in hell there can be no pretense. One is revealed as who one really is. All the disguises we don on earth are stripped away. So too with Satan's servants. So the real question is how Bel and her ilk work on earth.

"Seduction. That is the key. Seduction to an unreal image, or something other than one truly is. Now, listen to me. How do you define a person? Let's pick any person. Someone you know well. Say, Mr. Jefferson."

"Lincoln? Why him?"

"Because you know him well."

"Okay." I thought for a moment, bringing his image to mind. As I did so, I noticed that with increasing frequency the fish boat seemed to bump in the air. It was like one those nauseating thermal updrafts one feels while flying on an airplane.

"Well, the first thing anyone would notice is that he's tall, maybe 6' 7" or 6' 8". And big. Honest, his hands are like grappling hooks and his chest is like a barrel."

"Very good. I'm getting some definition."

"His hair is jet black, probably because he's part Cherokee Indian."

"Aha!"

"He often wears it pulled back in a ponytail, fastened with some beaded elastic thing. Hmm . . . he weighs maybe 250 pounds, I'd say. No fat; it's all solid. He's just *big*, you know?"

"Oh, I think you've pictured him quite well. Although I have no idea what his face looks like. Rather an important omission."

"Oh. Yes. Well the thing that would set him apart in a minute would be that fact that he has dark features, Cherokee like I said, but his eyes are so blue they seem painted in."

"Very good. Now I would be able to spot him, you would say, in a group of people."

"You could spot him in an auditorium."

"Spot him. Know him. Defined."

"Well . . . "

"We missed something, didn't we? This is how Mr. Jefferson appears to the world. But that really doesn't tell us very much about *who* he is. It doesn't define Mr. Jefferson as a person at all. How might you do that?"

"The most obvious thing," I said without hesitation, "is that Lincoln is without question the most brilliant person I've ever met."

"So, intelligence. A good quality generally."

"Generally? Yes, I would say so. Why not?"

"Well, obviously there have been brilliant people who used their intelligence to quite wicked, self-serving ends."

"But that's not like Lincoln at all. He's kind. I would call him humble. He really cares about others."

"Now we're getting somewhere. Qualities of a great soul, one might say."

"And I trust him completely. That is, he's honest."

"A wonderful virtue. Now let's ask what Mr. Jefferson's motivation is for these wonderful traits. For we have agreed, haven't we, that brilliant people can do ugly things."

"Yes, but motivation? Do you mean his beliefs?"

"Yes. A good point to start."

"Well, Lincoln would say it's because he's a believer."

"A believer! Horrors. We all 'believe in' *something*. Hitler was a believer."

"I mean a Christian. He makes it quite plain."

"So a follower of Christ. Now we have identified a great deal about Mr. Jefferson, have we not? Especially as we identify his beliefs and how he acts upon them. We might call that the core reality, the essence, of Lincoln Jefferson. Now, bear with me a moment longer and I think we'll reach our destination.

"Can you, Pilgrim, imagine Mr. Jefferson as something other than he essentially is?"

"He wouldn't be Lincoln anymore if he was something than he isn't."

"Oh! Good conclusion. And now we arrive at the work of Bel and her scummy family. Their very work is to seduce someone from what they are to a longing to be something other than what they are. Essentially it's an act of murder, killing off one self in order to pursue an image of that self. The image is the tempting lie planted in the mind by one of these demons—but, of course, in their earthly appearance as figures of beauty and light."

For what felt like the hundredth time, I shook my head. "I'm sorry, Teacher. I'm not sure I understand."

"Image. A depiction. A fabrication. We had them in my day. You have them in yours. It's the lie of how we might appear better than we are. To whom? To the eyes of the world. As one grows evermore fascinated with that lie, one grows ever more discontent with what one is—physically, psychologically, spiritually. So we imagine that this or that product can deliver us from discontent. And into the hands of Bel. It is a barely noticeable process of murder as one shapes an idol of the idealized self. The real self lies in ruins.

"Indeed, some of the lies are so insidious they get planted in the brain like a hornet's stinger. A young girl watches models in expensive clothes and thinks, if only I were thin like that model, I could have expensive clothes and beauty too. She runs away from her own inner beauty on a treadmill until she arrives at an emaciated stick figure. Such is the work of Bel.

"Or, a young man concludes that large breasts are the defining quality of beauty in a woman and he twists his mind into all the back alleys of the computer until he is no longer able to love the reality because he worships the false god. The self-loathing grows each time he fingers the keys, but he is unable to turn away from the graven image. This too is the work of Bel.

"This, Pilgrim, is the earthly work of these demons. Their steps are transparent, but no less insidious. They are the same steps of Eden's fall. The object appears to be good. By participating in it, we hope to gain—what? Knowledge, fame, gratification, beauty. The lesson gained, however, is the knowledge that falsehood has thoroughly insinuated its way into one's life and beats along the arteries. We are pestilence; we despair. We wander a wasteland east of Eden. Such is the work of Bel.

I shuddered with this revelation, wondering how the grotesque creature that appeared before me could ever appear good and tempting. "I have one other question," I said with hesitation.

"Speak of it."

"It's very odd. While you were napping—"

"I was? Mercy."

"I had . . . not a dream, really. A memory from when I was a child. Someone who, at least it felt like this in the memory, hated herself beyond belief. Then when I awakened . . . that beast, that Bel, was clawing at the membrane. And the look in the creature's eyes. It was like the girl's. The one from the memory. But a million times worse. It was full of rage and hatred, and it turned on me."

"Yes. We were going to talk further about those emotions, weren't we. Before we got sidetracked by Bel's opportunism."

"Opportunism?"

"She thought I was asleep."

"Tell me this, Bosch. One more question if I may. How come the creature didn't break through the membrane? Its talons were digging right in. It seemed ready to burst."

"Pilgrim. Do you have faith that the membrane is ferrying our journey?"

"Yes."

"Then you also had faith that it would not let Bel in. Our faith bends. It is not brittle. And the demons flee before it."

CHAPTER TEN

The Choice of the Prodigal

I EXPECTED BOSCH TO set out on a discourse on his named topics. Instead he sat quietly, stroking his chin and staring into the infinite dark. I followed his gaze, seeing nothing I didn't expect from earlier experience, although I sincerely hoped no demon would tackle our fish boat. Low in the distance—I had no concept of up or down—a streak of occluded, deep incarnadine hung like a constellation.

It was very much like looking at a belt of stars on a pitch black night, when camped in some desolate area, perhaps. But here the stars were the color of thick, gelatinous blood.

This is what Bosch had been staring at. He reflected a moment longer, then heaved a sigh. "It might be helpful to our cause—"

"Forgive me," I interrupted. "But I'm still not sure what our *cause* is. I mean . . . you offered your *tour*, as you called it, and I chose to take it, but what is the purpose?"

"I'm afraid I can't tell you that. My assignment is only to satisfy curiosity. You realize, don't you, that you will never be able to carry a report? People will say you're crazy. Perhaps they will administer drugs and, in time, pronounce you 'cured.' And at that time, you will have learned to disbelieve the event itself."

"Perhaps I disbelieve it even now."

"Like a dream, you mean? Yes, that would be safe, wouldn't it? Why don't we think about it like this, for even this may be done in dreams: perhaps we should think of this voyage of ours as a quest. Not an adventure, certainly. That is the true opiate of the modern masses. For an adventure may be undertaken for any number of reasons—entertainment, diversion, excitement. A quest, on the other hand, is always *toward* something. Even if one is not entirely certain what that something is at the outset, there is a compelling need to search it out. Perhaps there is no Holy Grail in the Chapel Perilous after all, but the knowledge of that is as important as actually holding the Grail in one's hands. So, you see, let's think that we are on a quest."

"Okay," I said. I nodded, not entirely sure that I followed him.

"But," he added, "we have already come to understand this much. An adventure can also be easily changed. What are these things you young people go to called? These horrible things with cars that go on tracks up into the air?"

"Amusement parks. I agree. They're horrible."

"Yes. And the site of many an adventure. But suppose you arrive and a thunderstorm breaks out. You decide to come back another day. The adventure, you see, can be easily broken. Maybe the greatest consequence is disappointment. But that is momentary until the next adventure.

"The quest, however, is quite different. You commit yourself to the journey, no matter what the end, no matter what dangers rise against you. And why do you make this commitment?"

"To see what is at the end?"

"Only in part, because you believe the journey itself is worthwhile and necessary. Because you trust whatever directions or guides you have been given for the journey. And because you have *faith* that no matter the dangers, those guides will lead you aright."

"But the particulars," I reminded him. "Even if it is a quest, one has to set one foot before the other."

"Certainly true. And that too is the very nature of faith."

"And the particulars of concern now are anger, rage, and hatred," I said. "We've had examples. We have to make conclusions on the particulars before we can advance."

"Well spoken, Pilgrim." He looked askance at me, one eyebrow lifted, a smirking grin. "Indeed, I wonder almost who the guide is here." Then he laughed. "But you're right. Entirely right.

"So, let me ask you some questions and perhaps together we may arrive at some answers.

"Anger is something of an enigma. Understandably so since it arises from that roiled pool of human emotions."

"You said human. Don't animals feel anger?" I asked.

"I'm not privy to that, but I'd rather suspect not. Their instincts register fear, protection, safety, attack, hunger—such things as these. I doubt whether the instincts are screened by emotions or reason. But that is a side path we really need not venture upon. Safer to stick with humans."

"Fair enough. Anger. Right or wrong."

"Well, that is the enigma. Shall we agree that anger can be either a positive or a negative emotion?"

"Explain."

"Start with the negative path, as the divine doctors of my time encouraged. Negative anger is abusive. It lacks justifiable cause. It is directed at a person or conditions for reasons of self-interest. Someone might say, 'I am angry at my employer.' Why? 'Because he doesn't pay me what I believe I'm worth.' But perhaps he can't afford to pay you more. Perhaps the very worth of your work is not quite as esteemed as you make it out to be. Perhaps, in dire economic times, the person should be glad for the job he does have. Too many variables, and anger is the fell swoop that tries to brush them all aside.

"Now, anger in the positive sense is directed at a person or situation for two reasons: an unredressed need of the person or the desire to better the situation. That situation, for example, may violate some ethical value and needs correction. Didn't you tell me earlier that you stand opposed against pollution of earth's resources? Why?"

"I believe that we should be stewards of those resources. Along with the idea of Manifest Destiny, although you probably never heard—"

"In fact, I was there."

He was serious. I continued. "Along with that came the idea that we 'own' the land. We can use it however we will."

Bosch nodded.

"I think that in our headlong rush to use up our natural resources or trample on the ones available, we diminish that beauty and consequently ourselves. What we do for fun, nature pays the price."

"Example?"

"I've swum in lakes so fouled up with motor fuel that I've had to get out of the water. Lincoln and I went hiking in the back country one day and we came across a whole range of hills hacked to pieces by . . . whatever—ATVs, motorcycles. And the rains had eaten out gouges in the ruts. Or, you wanted an example? Try this. In our first year here, Shelley and I were going to go on a picnic up by Fox Lake. We could smell it a couple of miles away. The whole lake was the color of rust. It seems a slurry dam at a mine had broken and poisoned everything. The lake's still dead as a doornail."

"Yes, you do have examples. And I see you get a bit angry. A perceived injustice, right?"

"Well, when is it ever just to simply destroy something that has never harmed you?"

"Ah. Good question. I wonder if we might return to it . . ."

"Later."

"Yes. We want to be very careful here. So, the reasonable question is why do we need nature at all?"

"You can't be serious!"

"Oh, very. Why don't you help me?"

I was thinking to myself and realized of course that I would sound like a petulant child. Even if I did feel that way.

"Earlier," I ventured, "you talked about a quest. There are no certain answers, no sure directions, but the seeking itself is important. I guess that in the same way we need the idea of the wild—a wilderness, something untamed when all our lives seem too domesticated. Untamed and untouched, a pureness of creation."

"Excellent. We need an idea of another world. Even if we never visit it, never roam the Tetons, never swim in the Gulf of Mexico, we need to know it's there."

"True. I want to be able to go into the pristine wilderness when I wish. But that's not all. When we run roughshod over the earth, we diminish its beauty, its natural order. And consequently ourselves."

"What do you mean 'ourselves'?"

"We lessen our capacity for wonder, for awe. Our sense of beauty withers."

"You're doing well, Pilgrim. Anything else?

"Yes. We know full well that these resources are both limited and fragile. I read somewhere that more species have gone extinct in the last fifty years than in all of recorded history."

"Very good. Let's register these as ethical values, the abrogation of which should arouse our anger."

"I would add action too."

"You tend to leapfrog ahead of me. Grant that an old man needs to plod along the stones. Let's summarize first."

I laughed. "Go ahead," I said.

"We presuppose that nature has intrinsic merit that deserves protection. This presupposition may be held for many different reasons. A Christian would say because God created it. A Hindu would say because it evidences harmony. A Taoist might say because nature is comprised of living spirits.

"We go a step further. We observed that nature serves our sense of beauty and our sense of freedom. Finally, we said that since nature has few internal defenses against the deeds of humans, we should protect what is fragile and threatened. All these may be held as admissible ethical values—to recognize worth outside of pragmatic use, to appreciate beauty, and to help what is essentially helpless. Sufficient causes to make one angry when the principles are violated and the damage done. Now, how does one experience that anger? Lace the offending factory with explosives and blow it up?

I couldn't help chuckling. "No. I also oppose violence."

"That would be an act of rage, then. When anger steps beyond the controls of principled ethical values, the response surpasses the crime. We know it's wrong to steal, but we don't send five-year-olds to prison for shoplifting a candy bar."

"That would be insane."

"Yes. But rage also exceeds control. It is excessive, rather than directive. It abandons focus and reason. And, by the way, the word *rage* derives from the Latin *rabere*—'to be mad.'"

"Now you sound like Lincoln, the walking dictionary."

"Hmm. Yes, you've spoken of your admiration for Mr. Jefferson. May I take that as a compliment?"

"If you like."

"But why don't we follow up on that? You said you admire Mr. Jefferson's kindness. His compassion. I assume that if you admire these, they are ethical values that you also hold."

"I'm not as good at it as he is."

"Of course. You still carry bitterness, don't you? Which, I suspect, may be gone by our journey's end. Maybe that is our quest. Bitterness does tend to get in the way of positive values, doesn't it?"

"I've worked hard, for over two years, nearly three now, to get over my anger at Shelley. Or, really, what happened with us. You know, the funny thing is, my mom was angry at me when Shelley and I broke up."

"Angry at you for the situation?"

"I don't think Mom knows the difference. You haven't seen her when she's mad."

"Ah, that word again. Unreasonable, perhaps. That is, seeing a situation contrary to how good reason would see it. Seeing it emotionally, through anger."

"I would guess that's true. Although it was certainly directed at me."

"Indeed, unreasonable anger, as with ethically validated anger, requires an object. Since Shelley was only a memory, and a happy one for your mother, you became the object. Yet, it was not, I trust, anger to the point of rage."

"No. Looking at it now, I see it came from sadness. God, but she loved that girl."

"And even though the object of the anger—you—was errant, the essential cause of it, the emotions of loss and sorrow, was not. They're part of our being human. It seems to me that if God has created us emotional beings, capable of the whole spectrum from love to anger, he fully intends us to use those emotions. We have already decided that anger in itself is not wrong, haven't we?"

"How about being angry at God! I haven't been inside a church for three years. I don't even want to hear about God. And emotions, what! Was God angry at me for something? Why did he let that snake Knuckles slither into my marriage and destroy it? Tell me that!"

"I am truly sorry, friend. There is little I can tell you about the specifics. But I really don't think God minds in the least your being angry at him. The Bible, front to back, is filled with those who have felt the same. God's response to you is the same as to them."

"Oh?"

"The one answer before which anger flees: love. Think about it."

I was breathing hard, my thoughts racing. I was embarrassed by my outburst, but apparently Bosch thought little of it. He hadn't given me any direct answer that I could discern either, but then I really didn't expect that. I tried to turn my thoughts to his question. You know how you have those times when emotions get control of you and you don't trust yourself to speak. Like you're going to find a stone in your throat and your voice will squeak. Or you're afraid the pressure in your sinuses will squeeze out a tear or fill your nose with snot and you won't be able to find a handkerchief. Like traveling without knowing where you're going.

I had grown accustomed to the jarring descents and ascents of the fish boat, although I had no sense of altitude or direction. We were, as Bosch had said, simply going through. I pressed against the membrane—hard, and without fear now. The scales on the fish's back seemed subtly changed in color—from green and silver to a slightly golden hue. But when I traced the lower scales, as far as I could see them, they had taken on a ruddy color. It was true—the sanguine ring I had noticed appeared to have broadened. And thickened.

"Well," I said after some time. "This probably doesn't count, but Lincoln surely was helpful to me during my breakup with Shelley. Mostly he sat with me and listened."

"I think that counts a great deal. One might say that negative anger cancels the possibility of kindness and compassion. It also, one could say further, denies forgiveness."

"Yeah. I hadn't thought of that. What I wonder, though, is this. How about hatred? It is different from anger. Or even rage, which we said was out-of-control anger. I mean, I was very angry when Shelley broke up with me. Angry at the situation, I suppose. Bitter. Sad. All that. But I can't say I ever hated her. Now Knuckles, that's another story. I used to lie awake thinking of ways to kill him."

"Perhaps that's because all your anger focused on him. You did not in fact kill him, but he became the external object for your emotions."

"I at least wanted to beat him up."

"You probably imagined doing so."

"No more than a million and six times."

"When in reality the tables may have been turned. Or you might have been ashamed of your cruelty. If it were hatred, you didn't act upon it. Which raises the question."

"What?"

"Can hatred be hatred if it's not acted upon?"

"Sure. I think so. Look at all the prejudices people have. Some hate ethnic groups. Some hate rich people. Some hate poor people. Hitler hated Jews. He didn't think they rated as humans, so he killed as many as he could. Slaveholders didn't think their slaves were human, so they felt free to beat them. Or to lynch them if they tried to escape."

"Any conclusions, then?"

"Well. Hatred would appear to be a mental state of intense anger. It's directed at a person, like anger can be, but it sees that person in the meanest sense possible. Hatred, it seems to me, is a state of the will. It is a chosen positioning, and therefore destructive of the person who chooses. And the one who hates *always* believes he is right. That's why hatred is a corrosion of the soul."

"Right," said Bosch. "We might call it an irrational act to demean another. It always bears a sense of viciousness."

"So it bears no redemptive value other than making the one who hates feel gratified."

"Hardly redemptive."

"Then call it a consequence, for, I agree, it is hardly suitable to use the term *redemptive* here. But . . . we have witnessed, haven't we, the condition of those who live for self-gratification?"

My mind flashed back to our first encounter in hell. I shivered.

"Understand," said Bosch, "once again the *process* of eternal hell. The *condition* of hell is eternal separation from God. Consequently, it is separation from all such virtues as love, kindness, goodness, and compassion.

"But the *emotion* of hell lies in direct counterpoint to those virtues. Now, of those virtues, which would you say is primary?"

"Love. I would say the others stem out of love."

"You see the conclusion, I'm sure. The primary emotional counterpart in hell is hatred, and a hatred of the most violent, disturbing kind, for to be in hell *is* to hate and to be hated without end. Hell is separation from God, but also separation from others. There is no community in hell. The souls there drive each other apart by their unrelenting hatred for each other.

"Perhaps we should underscore one thing yet. And we should do so rather quickly, for I believe we are approaching a new revelation. We speak of emotions. We speak of virtues and their contrarieties. We should not fail to speak of the rational mind."

"What? Reasoning what is right or wrong?"

"Certainly that is a pertinent issue, and I'm sure one with which we'll have to reckon," Bosch replied. "But I was thinking of imposition of the will. The declaration that 'I will do this' or 'I will not do that.' Sometimes this follows upon reasoned scrutiny. Most often upon belief of what is right or wrong."

"I agree that most people deliberately choose to do right. It's harder to see that deliberation in doing wrong."

"The 'heat of the moment' thing? True. But don't people choose to let their passions lead them into wrong choices? Don't they put themselves in positions where the wrong act seems necessary or even right? Look at it like this: in my paintings, for example, I always had certain ideas that I wanted to give expression to."

"Incarnate? Put the abstract into the physical?"

"Something like that. Except that the true artist cannot direct the viewer to those ideas. We suggest—by figures, colors, symbols, and the like. Else the work is little more than what you would call an advertising poster."

"Nice analogy."

"Precisely. The work must be analogous; not equal to. And so the painter gives the work over to the viewer. Sometimes the viewer, as he or she enters into the making of the work, sees things similarly, sometimes differently. The artist has no control, nor should he. He hopes only for some measure of delight—by which I mean 'discovery' of personal importance.

"But to the point. As you know, my work has elicited much argument in the following centuries. I can't mind that. But I do find myself wishing that more viewers located a theme of supreme importance to me."

I hesitated. I had written several hundred pages on these works. What if he said something to discredit it all?

Perhaps he noticed my dismay, for he quickly said, "Oh, don't worry. No word from someone nearly five hundred years gone will change your work. Nor should it. That is not the point at all. Not at all."

I laughed. "Well, what is it then? This grand theme?"

"Choice," Bosch said. "The enigma of free choice. The power and the consequences of this torturous freedom."[1]

1. In his response to a reader's troubling question—"Won't heaven's joy be spoiled by an awareness of unsaved loved ones in hell?"—J. I. Packer points out that, first, the damned have chosen their place: "None will be in hell who did not effectively choose it by following in the footsteps of Adam and preferring their own way to God's. . . . Nonbelievers universally make the anti-God choice, and hell is God giving people what they chose." Thus far a familiar argument. But Packer has a second, more speculative argument—that in our transformed resurrected state, we will not be aware of

I reflected, running a mental scroll of Bosch's works through my mind. I knew them with an unnerving intimacy. "I admit," I said at length, "I can't find too many examples. The temptation of Adam and Eve, of course, in *The Garden of Earthly Delight*."

"Sometimes it's subtle, of course. Remember, an artist never shouts. It's in the whispers that meaning lies. But I was thinking, first of all, of *The Prodigal Son*. Remember that?"

"Of course. A portrait of conflict."

"Why the conflict?"

"Well, he's on the road, and, as I see it, caught between past and future."

"Explain."

As I spoke, I seemed once again to see the painting itself cast upon the shimmering membrane before me. Every detail emerged clearly.

"Behind him lies his past," I said. "His wasted heritage. The White Swan Inn has an upside-down jug above a ruined gable, a sign to me of debauchery. In the upper window, a pair of men's drawers hangs out to dry. From a lower window, with ruined shutters, a woman peers out, soliciting customers. In the doorway a soldier accosts another woman. Alongside the inn a man urinates, unmindful of who sees him. In the foreyard, pigs feed at a trough, a symbol perhaps of what occurs within. Obviously it's a house of prostitution. Obviously also the son is well acquainted with it.

"He looks back, it seems to me, with a look of—how shall I say it?—regret? Sadness? Longing? After all, he does wear on his basket a large wooden spoon, a common symbol of wantonness and wastefulness, and it is pointed *back* at the White Swan. Directly at the jug, as a matter of fact. The life he has squandered."

"There is something else on the ragpicker's basket," Bosch said. "Do you remember that?"

"Yes, I do. It's some kind of fur, a skinned-out hide. I couldn't figure out what animal."

"A cat. Symbol of misfortune. Which he bears on his back. Now you have ably described what lies behind him. But, as you say, he is on the path, pointed away from the White Swan."

"But still looking back," I interjected.

---

hell: "Remember, in heaven our minds, hearts, motives, and feeling will be sanctified, so that we are fully conformed to the character and outlook of Jesus our Lord." Packer, "Hell's Final Enigma," 84.

"Oh, to be sure. Decisions are never easy, are they? He is caught in the middle. At the moment of choice. Ahead lies his father's house. Which direction will he go?"

"There are a lot of odd things," I said. "As he looks back, he is hooded. Yet in his left hand, he holds a hat pointed forward. The tailor's awl and thread pierce the hat, and the awl points forward. His walking stick is more like a cudgel, but the small end points forward."

"A new direction?" Bosch asked.

"Yes. Toward something. But he bears the scars of his past. The torn and scruffy suit. The bandaged calf. And somewhere along the line he lost a shoe."

"How so?"

"His right foot is shod in a carefully worked leather with a silver buckle. The left is a laborer's sandal. Then there's that thing I've never understood coming out of his coat."

"What does it look like?"

I peered closely at the painting hovering before me. "Um, a pig's foot? A foreleg? It has a cloven hoof. Maybe it ties into the pigs feeding in front of the White Swan."

"But no pig. Just the foreleg and hoof."

"Yes."

"We'll get back to that. Tell me what lies ahead of him?"

"A cow. Plain old tan cow."

"Lying down. It's on the path ahead. What else do you see?"

"Green trees. Fields."

"You're missing the obvious."

"What? Oh, yes. The gate."

"Indeed, he has yet to pass through it. You would think the choice an easy one, wouldn't you? Behind him the swine-like life of dissolution. Ahead the verdant fields of his father's estate. Easy choice."

"Of course. Yes."

"No. Not at all. Back to the cloven hoof. It is not a talisman or good luck charm. See here . . ."

He pointed to where the hoof protruded, slightly below the rib cage. "It grows from within him. The lust of the pigsty remains within him, ripping him back toward the brothel."

"In the parable Jesus told he made it back home."

"Yes. And there is that hope for every prodigal. There are signals, but they are secondary, for it is he who must choose."

"Signals? What are they?"

"Well, the three magpies, for one. But they're minor. See the owl in the tree? We know from earlier discussion that that is a symbol of Sophia, or wisdom. And then one you probably aren't aware of. Not a "tan" cow properly, but a dun cow. She appears often in illuminated medieval manuscripts as a symbol of the Holy Spirit—Comforter, Protector, and Guide.[2] Of course, she lies just on the other side of the gate; the Prodigal still must choose."

"Complicated."

"Indeed. As complicated as yes or no. Or as simple."

"Are you saying then that anger, rage, and hatred are willful choices?" Even as I spoke, the painting that had been cast up against the membrane like a slide projector dimmed and disappeared.

"Just the opposite," Bosch responded. "One may choose in advance to stand against them. One can will not to be possessed by them.

"On the other side of the Prodigal's choice lies God—but, he will not know that unless he chooses to step forward. At that moment, with one fingertip on the gate, God will reach out to rescue him."

"I remember earlier when we talked about reciprocity," I said. "You gave a good example here."

"Thank you. And if he should choose to turn back, we find the principle of reversal. He would grow further from his father's estate each time he turned away until he would find it impossible to turn *toward* again."

"But aren't some choices simply coincidental? I mean, they come by habit or custom rather than deliberation."

"This could be tricky. An example, please."

I didn't have to search long. "Well, while I'm writing my dissertation, I mostly use my old, gray Cross rollerball pen. I buy black ink cartridges. Fine tip. But sometimes I use a plain ballpoint with blue ink. Sometimes I'll just sharpen a dozen #2 pencils and use them. You know, when they're all dull the work is done."

"Yes. Excellent example indeed. The use of tools. Now tell me, what is the end or goal of these tools?"

"To write the dissertation."

2. Cf. Walter Wangerin Jr., *The Book of the Dun Cow*. In this beast fable Wangerin draws upon the medieval legend of the dun cow.

"So they are tools used to enact your choice to complete the dissertation. Could we say that the tools are then neutral? That there is no intrinsic virtue or vice in black ink or blue?"

"I suppose."

"I remember that I had some brushes that I just did not feel comfortable with. They didn't balance. But I needed them to do specific tasks. Can you imagine painting human features with a stiff two-inch brush? Or a base coat with a minute brush used for eyelashes or fish scales? But the choice lies in what you do with those tools. Let's assume that your dissertation is a good choice—"

"You haven't read it," I said.

Bosch gave me a disarming grin. "Good subject though. No, what I had in mind were the ends and the consequences of choosing to write the dissertation itself. Consider. First, you believe you have something of value to say. Second, you believe, the achievement will earn something important—that is, a degree. Third, you believe this degree will lead to a profession where you can enlighten and direct the minds of others. Perhaps we should also add that you hope for an honorable career in which you can support a wife and family if such should occur, and provide you the means to contribute to helping others. These are noble consequences, yes?"

"Sure. But I don't know about the wife and family."

"Of course not. You don't know for certain about *any* of those hoped for ends. You have simply chosen, at this stage, to write a dissertation that may have those hoped-for consequences. Now, please bear with me a moment longer and I think we'll find some resolution."

"Sure. We seem to have all the time in the world. Although the ride sure is getting bumpy. Is your fish boat going through some river rapids I can't see?"

"Something like that. We'll find out soon enough, won't we? Now, your question had to do with tools. Are they choices or coincidences? Are they ethical entities or ethically neutral? And I explained that the end to which we put these tools constitutes the choice and hence the ethical judgment. Thus it was that we concluded that your dissertation was a good end, it had clear ethical value, even if, perhaps, you misplace a modifier or slip in an unneeded comma or two."

I cringed. Grammar worried me more than anything. One entire stage of proofreading was with *St. Martin's* beside me.[3]

Bosch chuckled, sensing my discomfort. "Don't worry," he said. "When I dripped a bit of paint, and I couldn't blend it, I just made a new figure out of it. So, let's get back to these tools a moment. Let's say that you used them to write a thoroughly scandalous text. The temptation is great. A publisher has offered an advance that will assure health and prosperity for your family, property, and items of pleasure. All you have to do is include in the book certain specified obscene acts, a worship of things, characters who willfully slander and even murder each other, and above all a glorification of the ethos that the best life is the self-gratified life."

"Wow!" I said. "Sounds like a best seller."

"Probably. Then might we conclude that writing that work, using the very same tools, mind you, is what we might call a 'bad' work?"

"I would say that the consequence is a bad one."

"For whom, though? Notice that the writer acquires some of the same ends or consequences of your dissertation. Security. Family. Even prosperity."

"Right. And he'll probably have a million readers, while I'll have four or five."

"Well, we don't know about that, do we? But it is safe to say that this writer's end is crass and materialistic, while yours might have intrinsic value?"

"A mighty strong temptation to go his route, though."

"Of course. And that's the never-ending tension of choice. Whom do I serve? Nonetheless, our point is that the tools in either case are the same. Simply that in some cases we wish they were not utilized because they result in moral profligacy. But, so it is in all of life. An executive might run a business for his own benefit and gratification, heedless of the misery he inflicts upon others who might stand in his way. The list goes on. But what do we conclude?"

"Well. We *use* certain tools. I suppose we choose them. We select them. But the ethical issue, the actual choice, is to what ends we employ those tools."

3. This would refer to Andrea Lunsford and Robert Connors, *The New St. Martin's Handbook*. It is a standard grammar and style casebook used in hundreds of college writing courses.

"My, my, Pilgrim. I believe we are making progress. And having done so, we may return to our beginning."

"Which was?"

"It seems to me that our point of origin here was the meaning of anger, rage, and hatred."

"Yes. Then we got into motivations and consequences with your painting *The Prodigal Son*. You were arguing that the reasonable mind can impose an act of will upon anger and rage. Which leaves . . ."

The fish boat contorted like a windblown leaf.

"Hold tight now, Pilgrim. I believe we will witness hatred firsthand!"

CHAPTER ELEVEN

The Wrath of God

WITH DISMAY, I REALIZED there was nothing to hold on tight to.

The turbulence in the fish boat was utterly unnerving. The membrane undulated like water's surface, insubstantial, tenuous, windblown. We were wrapped in sanguine clouds, deepening to the color of arterial flow. Then we began to break through.

I shrank back in my seat. I should have had some sense of the horrors of hell by now, but I confess I leaned somewhat toward Bosch. As if anything could shield us! Only this membrane that fluttered with heat waves as we approached the flame. "Trust it," Bosch had said. Easy for him to say, I thought.

It hit me with a start. Easy for you to say. You're dead! But what was I? Bosch had said we were going *through*. Very well. I had made my choice. And I didn't want the fish boat to drop me off here, for heaven's sake.

The last of the dense cloud burned off. A long, transparent tube lay before us, circling away into the infinite distance. It was impossible to judge its width; it seemed at one moment to be miles wide, at the next impossibly compressed, like a subway tube. Very slowly we glided closer.

Now I could see them. Shapes inside stumbled among large rocks the color of coal. Now and then one of the shapes would kick out at a rock, leaving a burning red-brown trail like blood upon it.

"Shapes," I called them, because at first I was unable to determine what they were. I was fully struck now not just by the horror, but by the unmitigated ugliness of what I was seeing. These red-litten shapes stumbling around in the fiery tube were, or once were, human.

"That should be close enough," Bosch said softly. I don't know to whom he said this, but the fish boat slowed its descent and glided slowly along the length of the tube.

"I thought they were demons again," I said.

Bosch spoke softly. It was as if something here saddened him deeply. "Not all demons are from hell," he reflected. "Some of the worst grow in the souls of humankind. Especially the demon of hatred."

I tried to imagine anything worse than what I was seeing, and I couldn't. I expected to see some muscular monster of the Greek underworld flailing a whip. Humbling the proud and hating, if you will. No need for such here, I realized. Hatred is its own punishment. Truly, on the earth hatred hurts those to whom it is directed. That is not the end of the story. It never is.

I saw now that throughout the eternal moment the one who hates is cursed by nothing more nor less than what that person essentially is—hatred itself. For the first time I saw clearly the differences among anger, rage, and hatred. This infernal fire rightly belonged in hell, encased in a tube. The punishment would never recede, it would never be lifted, and it would never be forgiven. The time for each had passed; they would never be permitted another chance.

Their humanity had been wrecked. I mean literally, in the flesh. For what I saw beggared the imagination. Bodies staggered about blindly, for the simple reason that their faces had been gouged open. Noses ripped away, eyes dug to decaying sockets. Lips hung askew, never to speak words of malice again. I wanted to tear out my own eyes from the ugliness, but told myself that this was why I was here. For what purpose, to what end, I couldn't say. I felt my stomach twist in nausea.

Their fingernails had grown all unheeded into long curved spikes, and toenails that seemed rotted with fungus curled over the toes, causing them to stumble. Each time one blinded figure stumbled into another claws ripped the air. Bone shone through where eyes were plucked apart. Entrails dripped green bile from torn rib cages.

When one of the figures crashed against a black rock, it seemed to grow new features, only to have them ripped apart moments later in a silent howl of agony.

"Enough?" asked Bosch.

I was hyperventilating, my head dizzy. "Enough," I said.

The fish boat veered away, gliding swiftly from the maelstrom trapped in the snakelike tube. Tormented by the image, I sat in stunned silence.

After a time Bosch asked with his implacably calm voice, "Any questions?"

"I don't understand it. I thought that with your 'principle' of reversal those who hate would be stuck into some numb, emotionless trance, unable to feel any emotion at all. Maybe with a bit of fire licking their feet that they couldn't even react to."

"Remember that I also said that in hell the true nature of the person is turned inside out. It is true that not every one here is a clear example of reversal. For example, a person who hates may operate under a smooth mask of guile, waiting for the precise moment to unleash her hatred. Or, perhaps, a person might even cultivate a friendship with the person he hates, meanwhile deliberately undercutting him until he is destroyed. Oh, hatred wears a thousand devious faces. And there lies the true reversal. Here the malevolent mind of hatred is worn on the very features.

"Now, it is true that there are those aberrations of human nature who seem to have hatred stamped on their very souls. How else do we explain the torture of Hitler we witnessed earlier?"

"How come he isn't here?" I asked.

"I can only speculate, but I think the tyrants of the outer darkness are deprived even of the small comfort of the presence of others. I trust you noticed how jammed the tube of hatred is. Yet, there's always room for more. Someday, of course, it shall be sealed forever."

"But here they are all jammed together."

"Yes. After all, what happens in hatred? Separation. The person who hates wishes to destroy the very self of the person hated. But here lies the reversal. That other person you see, clawing and tearing with such merciless enmity, is always the person's other self. Their own hatred is turned upon themselves."

I shivered at the idea, not for the first time on this strange journey. And saw again the shredded faces, the clawed entrails.

"But," said Bosch, sensing my discomfort but determined to play it out, "you appear to be missing something quite obvious."

"Whatever could you mean? It couldn't be more apparent."

"That's the way with us humans, is it not? Remember the first time you looked at Ed Nolan's Pietá? Struck by the whole, you failed to notice the Madonna's bruises, which, we must admit, demonstrably changes one's perception of the whole. Then, moving closer, you saw the figures—so full of life—in the foliage, which once again changed the perception."

I was following so intently I failed to ask how he knew this.

"So what else lay in this corridor you witnessed?" he prodded. "Think."

I did. "The rocks," I exclaimed.

"Ah. But were they simply accidental, or do you think they changed the whole?"

"I don't know. They were just . . . rocks. Jagged big chunks of some black rock. The figures kept tripping on them. Cursing and kicking them. Because they couldn't see, I imagine."

"They aren't rocks," Bosch said calmly.

"What?"

"Precisely. They aren't rocks. They are figures."

"But they were just lumps in the way."

"Think now, Pilgrim. Use judgment and reason and we will see this clearly. Assume for a moment that they are figures, quite human, enduring a very odd sort of punishment."

"Just being there."

"Exactly. They don't seem to suffer, certainly not in the way the hateful do, but they are just there. You see, while those who live by hatred are consumed by their passion, others live their lives without passion or commitment at all. These *refuse* to commit. They became stone long before they died, believing in nothing, uncaring at all times. They have never sought for and, consequently, have never found anything to act upon, to stand for. And they don't care that they don't."

"But some of these can be decent people, right?"

"Decency! What is that to the effect here? A dog may be decent. It sleeps and feeds. The truly great that we remember are great in the proportion to which they love and in proportion to the strength of their striving. If, in striving against that which besets it, a person continues to love, that person is truly great.[1] Now, please don't misunderstand me. We

1. This appears to be an indirect allusion to Søren Kierkegaard's masterpiece *Fear and Trembling*. Cf. "Not one shall be forgotten who was great in the world. But each was great in his own way, and each in proportion to the greatness of that which he loved" (31). And also, "Everyone shall be remembered, but each was great in proportion to the greatness of that with which he strove" (ibid.). See also Kierkegaard's own footnote:

> To this end passion is necessary. Every movement of infinity comes about by passion, and no reflection can bring a movement about. This is the continual

are not all great in worldly terms. It is best we are not. Nothing is quite so seductive as having the world call one great. But I tell you, Pilgrim, in the moment I snap my fingers a person's life has come and passed against the enormity of hell. No, do not strive to be great by the world's standards. Rather, commit yourself with unrelenting passion to what God has given you to do."

"It's been quite a while since I've read the Bible, but it seems to me there was a verse along those lines that I once liked."

Bosch looked at me. "Perhaps this? He said, 'Some trust in chariots and some in horses, but we trust in the name of the Lord our God!'"[2]

"It sounds sort of like it. When I was a kid I pretended, while I was riding my bike, that I was a mighty knight going out in the name of the Lord our God."

Bosch nodded.

"You seem to have strong feelings about these . . . these rocks," I said. "I haven't seen you get that worked up before."

"'Worked up'? Interesting. Yes, I suppose so. After all, there is no life lived without living for something. Else we are insensate clods, feeding, drinking, waiting to die."

"The whole thing," I said, perhaps trying to divert his strong feelings, "all those jammed-up people in the tube—it seems beyond all belief."

"Yes." Bosch's tone had switched back to his reflective calm in an instant. "No sheerly human reason can fathom it. Or, if dreamt of, it seems inscrutable. Which is precisely why such forthright warnings are given against hatred and spiritual sloth."

"Warnings? Such as?"

"This should not be hard to understand. First, they emerge from the general sense of ethical oughtness that we discussed earlier. Every society, every religion, sees the need and place for constraints. We need it to live in harmony rather than destruction, so we establish certain laws

---

leap in existence which explains the movement, whereas mediation is a chimera which according to Hegel is supposed to explain everything, and at the same time this is the only thing he has never tried to explain. Even to make the well known Socratic distinction between what one understands and what one does not understand, passion is required.

Of all passions, Kierkegaard adds in his epilogue, "Faith is the highest passion in a man" (131).

2. Ps 20:7.

according to this sense of ethical oughtness. If this specific violation occurs, that specific punishment follows."

"Violations?"

"Remember, we are speaking of ethical norms here. A positive and a negative. The positive value—my neighbor has a right to happiness and security, for example. If I should be so intemperate as to rob his house, I have violated both his happiness and security—the negative. Therefore, I merit punishment for the violation I have committed and the consequences I have caused."

"But still. What we saw . . . doesn't the punishment seem a bit . . . extreme?"

"But you agree violations occurred?"

"Yes, but not *necessarily* against someone else. I mean, not everyone who hates someone kills the other."

"No. Perhaps they only wish they could. Still, the disease of the soul is the same."

"And those stupid rocks. I mean, I can't see how they merit that. And how about all those people who can't choose to make some passionate commitment? Someone with limited faculties, for example."

"Really, Pilgrim. I had thought better. Those 'rocks' have quite deliberately chosen not to choose. They have turned their will away from the very proposition. As for those others with 'limited faculties,' as you say, do you really think God's grace so feeble that he wouldn't have some provision for the deleterious effects of sin in general?"

"No." I shook my head. "It's just that I'm getting a pretty nasty picture of God's anger here."

"That's because you *are* in hell."

"But how can this be? I mean, if God is so gracious, why doesn't he just do some purifying miracle and save everyone?"

"Oh, my. The old mushy universalism daydream. God as the great Buddha, nodding benevolently over the masses. Nonetheless, your question has merit, and we shall try to answer it. And the answer in short is justice."

"There has to be more to it than that."

"Indeed there is. We can imagine justice as simply arbitrary and expedient. That is, relative to the situation. For example, suppose you had to appear in court before a judge whose rulings were notoriously inconsistent and whimsical."

"I would say that his power had gone to his head."

"Indeed. And perverted the meaning of justice itself to the god Power. So we have to establish several things about justice. Consider. We said that differing societies and religions share a sense of ethical oughtness. But either one of those orders may be so arbitrary that it impugns the ethics itself."

"The massacres of the Crusades in the name of God."

"Or the barter in slavery along the African coast," Bosch added. "But, now let's consider further that out of these religions and societies there is one God who is just."

"What would make him just?" I asked. "It seems that God pretty much gave this world over into human hands to run. That is, I don't see his finger poking down, and him saying 'This is wrong.'"

Bosch actually laughed. "No. He has already done that once. And while it is the character of humans to repeat things ad nauseam, thinking in many words to prove a case right, God is sufficient unto himself and therefore not enfeebled by redundancy. Being eternal by definition, for God to say a thing once is to say it for all time. But we are missing the point. The tenable question here is what in God's nature qualifies him as just, or even, as some might say, justice itself.[3]

"Now, since you claim to have lost some of your familiarity with God's revelation, perhaps it would be best if I lead you to understanding. Remember our issues. Is God just? Is his wrath just? Are they accurate to the case?"

"Ah, yes. Since you put it like that."

Bosch reflected, as if studying the best approach. The turbulence had dissipated. Once again we glided through darkness. I glanced down through the membrane, half expecting the fish's scales to be charred beyond recognition. Quite the contrary. The body now appeared a sleek silvery gray. If anything, its undulations were far more powerful. One twist and it shot ahead. I leaned forward. Nothing should surprise me anymore. Nothing beyond belief. As I peered along that torpedo-shaped body, I saw the telltale seven rows of gills struck below the cunning eyes. Occasionally the fierce jaws would gape into those terrible serrated rows of back-slung teeth. Brute power, beauty, and strength—the great white shark.

3. J. I. Packer provides a short and useful discourse on the *idea* of the judge. The judge must be 1) a person with authority, 2) a person identified with what is good and right, 3) a person of wisdom, able to discern the truth, 4) a person of power, able to execute sentence. See *Knowing God*, 127–29.

"Pilgrim?"

"What?"

Bosch chuckled. "Apparently your mind was elsewhere. I had asked a question."

"That's a shark," I said stupidly.

"Oh? Yes, that's true. One does not take a bicycle through our next passage."

"I'm sorry. What was the question?"

"We were to start with the nature of a God whose wrath is just. Is this correct?"

"Yes."

"It strikes me, then, that the first necessary and sufficient condition is holiness."

"Holiness?"

"Yes. Although I admit that's a word that has lost force among many of your generation. Quite a shame, really. Or, if it is used in religious circles, it often means some idealized human state that one can achieve by certain steps. If I have regular meditations and prayers, for example, and discipline myself to refrain from wrong choices, I achieve 'holiness.' While these conditions may be admirable pursuits in and of themselves, and beneficial to one's spiritual life, authentic holiness is a state of being. And nowhere is this state of holiness perfected but in God."

"'For all have sinned and fall short of the glory of God,'"[4] I said. "Some of this is coming back to me."

"I believe so. Very good. Now, if we call this God 'holy,' what does it mean?"

"Perfect? Pure? Sacred? I don't know."

"All of those, perhaps. The Hebrew word for 'holy' literally means 'separate.' In his holiness God is so profoundly mysterious to us that we can only know him by those qualities of himself he has chosen to disclose."

"That is precisely why people have trouble with God," I interjected. "They picture this distant, self-absorbed *it* who could care less about humans."

"Oh, dear. Why ever would one think that? Would you rather have a careful explanation of how lightning works, and then enjoy its beauty and its salutary effects on nature, or to have it suddenly strike you dead?

4. Rom 3:23.

I would say God has chosen to give, first, all necessary and sufficient evidence for us to know him, and, second, precisely the right amount of knowledge to know him safely. But let's not lose our argument. Our proposition means first that holiness is God's essential being. He is separate from humanity, indeed, all his creation. Let me explain something that might also 'come back to you.'

"God is called a holy God throughout Scripture. But only twice is a very unusual word combination used, where the holiness of God is repeated three times in succession. Both times, by the way, the words are spoken by heavenly beings, those most intimate in their knowledge of God.

"The first of these occurs in the revelation to Isaiah, where the seraphim proclaims, 'Holy, holy, holy, is the LORD of hosts! The whole earth is full of his glory.'[5] The song was called by Old Testament Jews the Trisagion—the three times holy. Holiness to the third power, one might say. But we find it again in the New Testament. In the revelation of John, the scene again opens on heaven. Spiritual beings surround the throne of God and sing 'Holy, holy, holy is the Lord God Almighty, who was, and is, and is to come.'[6] It is the same song, the Trisagion, as that sung in Isaiah's vision. God, the sovereign Lord, is forever holy. His essential, defining quality of holiness never varies.

"Now then," Bosch continued, "if God is essentially holy, the essence of holiness, we should say, then it follows that he is righteous."

"How so? What do you mean?"

"If holy, he can only act in accordance with that holiness. Therefore he is righteous. He cannot abrogate his own nature."

"If he is righteous," I suggested, "then he would do anything to save us from . . . this." I waved my hand across the pit. As if in response, a bolt of red lightning pierced the darkness.

"Hold tight," Bosch cautioned, "we are nearing our destination. But you raise an interesting point, along with a few million who have raised it earlier. A response, then. First, he has done everything he can while still maintaining his essence as a holy God."

"Explain."

"One such act was the clear definition of laws for righteous living, how to live in a relationship with him. Second, he devised the most

5. Isa 6:3.

6. Rev 4:8.

outrageous plan in all eternity—before time began—to make himself the offering that would restore humans to righteousness. And his holiness.[7]

"Now the difficulty arises from a further response to your question. God, remember, cannot deny his own nature, no more than you could justly wander around the campus claiming to be an orangutan. It is not your essence. For even more than he loves us, God loves righteousness. Only that comports with his holiness."[8]

7. I believe Bosch is referring here to Colossians 1:21-22: "Once you were alienated from God and were enemies in your minds because of your evil behavior. But now he has reconciled you by Christ's physical body through death to present you holy in his sight, without blemish and free from accusation."

8. In his interesting study *How Can a God of Love Send People to Hell?*, John Benton explores the close tie between God's righteousness and his justice:

> God loves what is right. He will do everything possible to save us, consistent with justice. That is what he has done in Christ. But he will not do anything inconsistent with justice, because there is something even more terrible than sinners going to hell and that is a God who is no longer committed to justice.
>
> "Why doesn't God just let us all off?" Because we are responsible for our sins and God is committed to what is right. To say that God should not punish sin is to ask him to say that sin does not matter. It is to ask him to say that holiness does not matter. It is to ask him to be no longer committed to justice. It is to ask him to be no longer committed to right instead of wrong. Logically it is, to all intents and purposes, to ask him to become an evil God and that he will not do. It is to ask him to accommodate himself to our sin, not by dealing with it justly by hell or by the cross, but by himself becoming like Satan, not committed to what is right. He will not do that. The punishment of sinners is terrible, but far more terrible is the prospect of an omnipotent evil God. (79)

Interestingly, R. C. Sproul develops a similar argument in *The Holiness of God*: "When the Bible speaks of justice, it usually links it to divine righteousness. God's justice is *according to righteousness*. There is no such thing as justice according to unrighteousness. There is no such thing as evil justice in God. The justice of God is always and ever an expression of His holy character" (166). In my own following research into the topic of God's holiness and justice, I found one of the most helpful books to be Thomas L. Trevethan, *The Beauty of God's Holiness*. See also Robert W. Jenson's "Foreword" to *Sin, Death, and the Devil* (edited by Braaten and Jenson), where he presents the *shalom* argument that "History's whole dismal armory of sins, so impressive from a distance, is only a selection of ways *not* to be one thing, righteous. We are created to be righteous, that is, to form one community with each other *and* with the persons of the triune God, in which each of us takes her or his unique place and uses that place as an opportunity to love the rest of us. Any sin humanity can think of is simply one or another way of refusing to do this." (2)

Yet, among these various resources on evil and the justice of God, I found the most compelling to be N. T. Wright's *Evil and the Justice of God*. Wright establishes that God is necessarily a God of life: "God's justice is a saving, healing, restorative justice, because the God to whom justice belongs is the Creator God who has yet to complete His original plan for creation and whose justice is designed not simply to

"And therefore he sends people to this place?" I asked. "I mean, hell was always just sort of a vague idea to me. Sort of like a sentence in prison. But this is pure . . . *torture.* It doesn't seem right at all."

"Ah, Pilgrim. I wonder if you have learned anything at all. Yes, it is torture. It is hideous, unbearable. But remember that it is also the outward revelation of what the damned have chosen to be, in their hidden lives, on earth. That's the horror—that we shall be known, our true selves revealed. In hell, believe me, no remorse exists, no godly sorrow. They are as they appear.[9]

"But I think we have moved beyond holiness and righteousness to the very heart of our issue. You ask about God's wrath. We can understand nothing of that apart from a third quality of God—justice. If we understand that, then we are in a position to understand why God can't just sweep sin under the carpet. In hell there are no carpets to hide under in any event. The horror of hell is exposure.

"Now. How do we understand justice? It is the final weighing of right and wrong, is it not? We understand that God is holy, and only those who have been delivered according to his plan can stand in the presence of his holiness. We understand that God is righteous, and that by this same plan we are made righteous. That is to say, we recognize *our* violations of his holy will and we accept his righteous offering."

"The lamb without spot?"

"'The lamb who was slain,' as the revelation puts it. But I see that your familiarity is increasing."

"Perhaps I needed to be reminded. Things got in the way, you know."

---

restore balance to a world out of kilter but to bring to glorious completion and fruition the creation, teeming with life and possibility, that He made in the first place" (64). The ultimate signification of God as life is manifested in the resurrection. But, Wright points out: "Evil is the force of anti-creation, anti-life, the force which opposes and seeks to deface and destroy God's good world of space, time and matter, and above all God's image-bearing human creatures" (89). Thus we have a conflict that exists both contemporaneously and eternally.

9. The narrator found this observation about life on earth and the afterlife an interesting point that he now wishes he had asked Bosch to pursue further. I suggested to him some lines from Randy Alcorn's book *Heaven*: "Earth is an in-between world touched by both Heaven and Hell. Earth leads directly into Heaven or directly into Hell, affording a choice between the two. The best of life on Earth is a glimpse of Heaven; the worst of life is a glimpse of Hell. For Christians, this present life is the closest they will come to Hell. For unbelievers, it is the closest they will come to Heaven." (28)

"Yes. Unjust things, to be sure. But consider now. Infallible justice cannot be mitigated. Either one has said yes to the righteousness of God, or one has said yes to oneself."

"Whom do you choose?"[10]

"Precisely. For choice must be made, and to say yes to either is to obviate choice to the other."[11]

"But, I can't be righteous like God."

"Of course not. Why would he expect you to be? The power of the cross didn't stop at Calvary. It's ongoing, forever, into eternity. Conversely, a sin against God without repentance is an infinite sin. Remember that out of his holiness God is also a good and loving God. Everything we know about him indicates that he earnestly desires our happiness and love, and will do anything, short of denying human freedom to choose, to give happiness.

"There is," Bosch continued, "a very good reason why we raise these subsidiary questions. You see, punishment is only just if man's free will and responsibility are put in the foreground. This is what the justice of God entails—the very exposure of secrets, diversions, and guile. The horror of punishment is the announcement: This is who you truly are. Indeed, you thought to hide these things from all people. They are no longer hidden.

"This is not expedient. It is just. It lies in the holiness of God."

"Quite different from human punishment," I observed.

"Oh, indeed. Why do we humans punish?"

"To discipline, I suppose. I was grounded for half the summer once. When I shoplifted a Popsicle at the grocery store. The thing was bulging

10. Granted, the narrator's knowledge of Scripture is a bit fragmentary at this time, but I believe the reference is to Joshua 24:14–15: "But if serving the Lord seems undesirable to you, then choose for yourselves this day whom you will serve. . . . But as for me and my household, we will serve the Lord."

11. In a remarkably clear and compelling analysis of the topic "Hell and Human Freedom," Jerry L. Walls states:

> So in the end, one either perfects his moral freedom or he perverts it. In the former case, one has lost all motivation to do evil, whereas in the latter, one has lost all motivation to love God. But initially, I want to stress, moral freedom requires both the ability to respond to God's grace as well as the ability to resist it. And the latter requires the ability to deceive oneself, which entails the ability to avoid clear perception of God's relation to happiness.

See Walls, *The Logic of Damnation*, 131.

out of my pocket and melting. I never dared shoplift a thing again after that embarrassment."

"What else?"

"Hmm. Protection. Stalkers are a big danger now if you're not aware. If they break their court orders to stay away from someone, they are jailed for the person's protection."

"Sounds reasonable. Anything else?"

"Well, with the more serious crimes, the offender is put in prison for a certain number of years, depending upon how serious the crime is."

"And what is the aim of this punishment?"

"According to the courts, it would be reform. Spend some time in the clink and mend the error of your ways. Which is a joke. Most come out as bad as, or worse than, when they went in."

"Anything else?"

"I suppose I'd have to include retributive justice. This is where the biggies fall. If you murder someone, you might be put to death yourself."

"And do these forms of punishment work effectively?"

"Are you kidding! The jails are so jammed they let people out after serving less than half of their sentence."

"So it hasn't prevented crime. Nor, from what I understand, controlled it. Yet it seems an excellent system of justice, with clear levels of punishment to fit a variety of crimes."

"There have been worse."

"Indeed. Now, what is the condition of all those who appear before the courts of justice, awaiting either freedom or punishment?"

"They got caught?"

"Well, that's one way to put it. Another is that they are being held accountable."

"For what?"

"For choices they have made, and actions committed. But I would have thought we could have assumed that, since we covered the groundwork earlier. Yes, freedom requires that we live with the consequences of our freedom. But at any stage of the judicial process, things may go awry. A lying witness. Paid-off jurors.

"But now suppose the person stands before a judge who knows all these things, a judge from whom nothing is hidden, who knows fully the act and the consequences. Such a judge is God."

At that moment the fish boat literally trembled, as if hit by some kind of shock wave. Another bolt of blazing red lightning lanced the sky.

There was no ground to strike. It rived the darkness and flamed into the distance.

"This will require skill," Bosch murmured. "Skill and cunning."

"What?" I asked.

Bosch shook his head. "I think we should conclude quickly," he said. "Let me summarize.

"God's holiness demands that he stands opposed to evil. Sinfulness and holiness stand always in opposition, never, as some doctors of the mind suggest, in manageable 'harmony.' Sin, then, is the enemy of God. Because of his very nature, God cast the angel of darkness from his presence. The angel's deceit is that he still masquerades as an angel of light, pretending to be what is forever lost to him. And he knows it. Oh, does he know it. Which is why he rages against the holiness of God in perfect hatred.

"Wrath? Yes, God exercises wrath. He does so to protect and uphold the very laws of holiness. He does so to protect and uphold the very hearts of those who come to his holiness.[12]

"Let me ask you this. Suppose you have discovered that someone you love intensely has been beaten, robbed, and left abandoned to help herself. Would you be angry at her?"

"Of course not! I'd do anything possible to help her and to—"

"Yes. Avenge the wrong. To pay back the wrongdoers, but also to make sure they don't do it again. The wrath of God is a terrible thing for the precise reason that God loves even those who do wrong. He is patient beyond our conception, longing for their presence. But he is a just God, and when patience necessarily runs out, his wrath will pour out upon them."

"What do you mean by 'necessarily'?"

12. In his "Foreword" to *Hell on Trial* by Robert A. Peterson, David F. Wells outlines the case for a God of wrath:

> A God who is without wrath is a God whose Christ has no cross, and if he has no cross, it can only be because we are thought to have no need of his cross. While there have always been those in the church eager to believe such happy propositions, in the end what remains is a faith remade in the likeness of fallen human life, which, in consequence, has lost truth and reality. Not only so, but it will also have lost its hope entirely. For Christian hope rests upon the fact not that evil can be ignored, or that it will simply fade away, but that it has been judged at the cross. There is a day coming, therefore, when truth is going to be put forever upon the throne and error forever on the scaffold. (x–xi)

"At such a time as the person utterly forsakes himself in evil—gives his soul to the devil, as some say—or stands before God for judgment after life.

"But now . . ."

The fish boat bucked wildly as two savage crimson bolts shattered the darkness in front of us. I was thrust against the membrane and saw the great white shark, its angry jaws agape, twist and buck rapidly to avoid the bolts. They left an afterglow in the canopy like a sheeting of blood.

"The chains," Bosch gasped. He too had been thrown askew.

"Hold on tight, Pilgrim," he shouted.

"To what?" I screamed back.

Bosch turned his head toward me. His hair was disheveled, his eyes wide.

"To what you did before," he said in a remarkably calmer voice. "Your faith in our vessel itself."

And at that moment the vessel twisted and plunged fiercely as another shaft of crimson light cracked past the canopy. It was a cataract of blazing fire and sounded like the roar of jet engines.

CHAPTER TWELVE

A Disquisition Upon Sin

I RECALL SEEING A movie once where a skilled team of robbers attempted to steal some precious jewel. The details are lost to me, but I remember that they wore some special goggles that turned all the invisible laser alarms into lines of blue light. All they had to do was avoid the lines and success was theirs. But if one of them so much as touched an alarm light, all was lost. They had trained themselves to contort and twist and slither through the maze.

I don't remember if they failed or succeeded. Only the acrobatic, unnerving contortions.

The thickening ring of scarlet bolts had a grotesque advantage over laser alarms, for the unworldly energy bit and snapped and jagged unpredictably. As each blast reared up and roared past, the force of its energy slammed against the fish boat.

What frightened me the most, however, was that the shark was not simply trying to evade and escape. It was on the attack! It plunged with its own focused power toward the tiniest of gaps and heaved through.

I was, perhaps, even more surprised when Bosch suddenly reflected in his calm, ruminative voice, "In general, Pilgrim, people don't believe in hell because they don't want to live without their sin. In order to live with it, they find they can't believe in God, either."

Despite our jagged, pitching course, I found again that his voice itself calmed me. He was leaning back, arms crossed casually over his chest. I realized that my own hands were clenched tight. I wiped the sweat from my forehead.

"What?" I said.

"Just musing. Sin is intriguing, don't you think? Some people get a bit too whimsical and call sin 'boring.' We keep repeating the same old sins, they say. Humanity has lost its capacity to invent new sins. This is very odd."

"Why?"

"Because, while some sin is corporate, each sin is finally individual. Each and every sin issues from that moment of choice that one can never retract or undo. The only undoing must therefore come from someone other than themselves. But, have you noticed? We seemed to have gone through them again."

Indeed I noticed. The jagged bolts had disappeared. I twisted in the fish boat and craned my neck to see behind us.

"I'm sorry," Bosch said. "On this journey you are not permitted to look behind. That is past and cannot deter us."

"What was it, then?"

"The gates of hell. Or chains, rather."

"Where are we going now?"

"I can't tell you what lies in store, either. You know better."

I peered through the gloom. All I saw before me was another dull reddish patch. It was as if we had passed through the fire gates and were headed towards something smoldering at the heart of everything I had seen. This heart in the darkness throbbed with increasing urgency. Like malignancy itself, the cancerous tumor spread fibers in long waves.

"We were talking about the jaws of hell. Why don't we continue? Information can never hurt for what the future holds, can it?"

"Okay. I'm all ears."

Bosch played quizzical eyes over me.

"A figure of speech," I said. "I'm listening."

"I will admit the image and the reality are highly contrary to one's expectations. After all, the history of art, as you well know, has depicted the entrance to hell as a terrible set of jaws, an ever-widening mouth—the *absque ullo termino*—devouring the sinful. This could be figured as the jaws of the great pit, the lion, the dragon, or the leviathan."[1]

"I'm not sure what a leviathan is."

"Well," Bosch said, "the name appears several times in Scripture, but it's generally figured in art as a great serpent or a crocodile. As you

1. The authoritative study of these figures and the development of hellmouth imagery through the Middle Ages is Gary D. Schmidt, *The Iconography of the Mouth of Hell.*

can imagine, artists have pushed their imaginations to the limit to depict those grim jaws. Often the head is simply disembodied, dominated by stretched jaws and rapacious teeth.

"One of the most interesting pieces, though, is an etching from *The Psalter of Blanche of Castille.*[2] Oh, this would have been done in the late twelfth century, when such art particularly flourished. In the etching two spheres interlock. In the top sphere, Abraham, surrounded by seraphim, cradles newly-washed saints in a towel."

"The bosom of Abraham?" I asked.

"Indeed. Comfort. The assurance of salvation, for Abraham is the 'Patriarch of faith.'[3] That being so, everything in the lower sphere is inverted. Satan's animal head points downward. Fully half of the sphere is dominated by his swollen jaw. Demons bearing pincers and hooks stuff the damned into the bloated throat. Strangely, the damned show little emotion. They stare about, almost with an air of stoic defeat. One demon prepares to bite the head off a condemned man, while another man looks on dispassionately."

"Maybe," I ventured, "they realize they have received the just desserts for their crimes. That sentence has been passed. There is no further appeal."

"Very good, Pilgrim. I like your insight. What bothers me is that even as the damned are squeezed together, each seems so utterly alone."

"Like a shipwreck. All go down but the experience of going down is always final and individual. Each person faces death by himself only."

"Yes. And so it is also with eternal death," Bosch reflected. "I believe you are now tutoring me, Pilgrim."

I laughed. Small chance of that. Yet, I had begun to feel that our discussion had moved past the brain scratching that it had been at the outset. It had now settled down into my core, as if by understanding more my capacity for understanding more grew simultaneously.

"If the Psalter etching is one of the more interesting and clearest depictions," Bosch continued, "then I find one of the most masterful and intriguing to be from *The Book of Hours of Catherine of Cleves.*[4] Perhaps because it appeared only shortly before my time—in the 1440s. Perhaps because the unknown artist turned loose his imagination to capture hell.

2. See fol. 171.

3. Cf. Rom 4:13–15.

4. Ms. 945, fol. 168v.

It seemed that until *The Book of Hours*, artists held back. They wanted to bring hell to realistic life, but they hesitated lest they went too far."

"I'm not familiar with the work," I said.

"Perhaps you should be. Some critics think I stole some ideas from it. Actually, I had never seen it until some years later when I met the unknown master. He was reluctant, at first, to admit to the work, but of course there are no more secrets after death."

"What makes this work so important?"

"Basically, the imaginative construction and the depth and thoroughness of the work. This artist used the technique of the castle with twin flanking towers. Demons are flinging bodies down into the tops of the towers, which are shaped like cauldrons. Between the towers, the head of a lion shapes the castle dome. In fact, its lower jaw forms the crenellated buttress. Inside this mouth, demons hurl rocks and jeers on the damned below.

"But there's more below. As if figuring a descent into lowest hell, the artist provides another leonine mouth, its cheeks spread impossibly wide. For within it appears yet a third mouth, into which demons stuff the damned. In a nearly humorous touch, a demon carts a load of the damned to the awful jaws in a wheelbarrow. But there is no humor in hell, of course. Humor is the blessing upon those who rejoice.

"Oh, I forgot one thing. Much to the point, too. At the bottom, a fierce, creaturely mixture of lion and dragon spews forth the seven deadly sins."

Bosch sighed. "People have given me much too much credit in the history of art, you know."

"I hardly think so. No one of your period approaches your imaginative scope, your genius for playing outside the boundaries of reality."

"Is that a line from your dissertation?" He positively glared at me, then chuckled gently.

"I'm afraid it is," I said. "But I used the phrase 'sandbox of reality.'"

Bosch looked amused. "Too many people," he said, "credit me with inventing hell in art. As if I were the first to give faces to horrors. What they forget, I suppose, is that during my time, hell was an accepted reality, death an imminent threat, and the arts were supported either by wealthy patrons or by the church. That is to say, the artists lived from a spiritual center that has largely disappeared in your time.

"But how much of that concern," I asked, "also arose out of events preceding your time? I mean, the history is littered with death. Look at the Black Plague."

"To be sure, civilization appeared to be disintegrating. Remember that England and France were at war—although mostly thinking about and planning for war—during much of my lifetime. But it is true, the Black Death left effects that could not soon be forgotten. For one thing, we have to understand the sheer number of deaths. In some villages, even larger cities, well over half the people died. And they died so rapidly and horribly.

"The afflicted had ulcerating sores, as if the blackened flesh were eaten away. Some had tumors that twisted and distorted their features beyond recognition. They couldn't get away from their pain. They staggered through the streets as outcasts. Some killed themselves simply to end the misery of burning fever and ceaseless thirst.

"How do you explain it? The people of the time believed it had to be one of two things—a punishment from God or an affliction loosed by roaming demons. The afflicted didn't care, of course. They died.

"But the larger effect was abandonment. The upper class fled the cities. Physicians wouldn't get near the sick. Priests locked themselves in their inner rooms and refused to serve the sacraments. Many of the dead lay unburied. No one would lift a finger to help. Punishment by God or the work of Satan's hosts."

"That's when it happened," I said quietly.

"What happened?"

"The art world changed. At the time of the Black Plague, skeletons started showing up. Grotesque ones, even ones with sickles."

"Yes," Bosch agreed. "What else?"

"Demons. Because people thought Satan was unleashed on the land, demons appeared."

"Very good. You see, when we stand before things we don't understand—physical things—we need a supernatural explanation. Punishment of God or the work of demons."

"Of course, modern science now knows what caused the plague, and how it spread," I said.

"Hindsight helps little here, Pilgrim. You have to understand the *mind* of the times. And, you see, when the plague waned, when the skeletons picked clean by birds and dogs were buried, when the priests and magistrates began sneaking back from their hiding places, then the people also began to wonder: If this happened once, how do I protect myself by becoming right with God?

"Certainly not all people were interested in the question. For many the church was thoroughly discredited. And many turned to licentious living of the worst sorts."

"Eat, drink, and be merry; for tomorrow we die?"

"Abandon all moral law for personal pleasure. So too it remains today. But for some of those of my time, there also occurred an abandonment to morality. How did this happen? In part through an awareness of the seven deadly sins."

"Of course."

"Can you name them?" Bosch asked with a twinkle in his eye.

"Maybe. Wrath, obviously. We were just talking about it."

"Yes. But it is a troubling word. Perhaps the old word *ire* fits better. From the Latin *ira*, which is closer to your understanding of hatred."

"Okay. Pride, gluttony, envy . . ."

Bosch laughed suddenly, "Oh, yes, envy. As one of your wags once put it, the only sin one can't enjoy."[5]

"Ha! I can do you one better," I said. "Janie made me read this with her. Bought an extra book for me. She said it might get some knowledge of true art through my thick noggin.'"

> And next to him malicious Envy rode,
> Upon a ravenous wolf, and still did chaw
> Between his canker'd teeth a venomous toad,
> That all the poison ran about his jaw.
> But inwardly he chewed his own maw,
> And neighbor's wealth, that made him ever sad;
> For death it was when any good he saw,
> And wept that no cause of weeping more he had,
> But when he heard of harm, he waxed wondrous glad.[6]

"There," I said, "wasn't that a neat piece of work?"

"Neat?"

"Fitting."

5. Despite my best efforts, I could not locate the source of this quotation. I later asked Janeen. She said she believes it came from Samuel Johnson, but that she couldn't bear to open that book again and look for it.

6. Edmund Spenser, *The Faerie Queen*, I.

"Oh, yes. Nearly all of Spenser is. I especially like the toad, which turns out to be himself. But don't look disappointed, Pilgrim. I have been alive far longer than you and have talked with a good many such as Spenser. Now, please continue. You've mentioned wrath, pride, gluttony, and envy."

"Sloth. Covetousness . . ."

"Which is different than envy?"

"Yes. But I'm not sure how."

"Perhaps like this. Covetousness focuses on the object. You want something that someone else owns so badly you're willing to steal it. In some cases you convince yourself that it's rightfully yours. Envy is directed at the person herself. You resent her for what she has. You might even want to destroy that person for what she has. Let's see. We have six. We need seven."

"Ah, lust."

"Oh, yes. Lust. The one that, oddly, everyone in your time seems to think the very worst sin, yet nearly everyone does it, so nearly everyone forgets it."

"That's a bit extreme."

"No, I think lust is a universal condition perverted to one's own needs or preferences."

"Explain."

"Like so many things, it all goes back to Aristotle. You see, one of his investigations was to know the true nature of humankind. His first task, though, was to distinguish humans from animals. Sometimes, one might say, it's still hard to tell the difference. So Aristotle thought it best to see what we shared in common with animals, and that would be the sensual passions—the urge to eat, to mate, to reproduce. We would agree, I trust, that these are *appetites*."

"The distinction, then," I observed, "is that humans have will, or rational choice, as we discussed earlier."[7]

"Yes. In Aristotle's mind, that's what connected us to the First Mover. But to the point here, Aristotle arranged human nature from the lustful, animal desires that resided in the lower extremities—generally the waist down. Moving upward, one encounters the sins of the stomach—like gluttony—and of the heart—like envy and wrath. But the worst of all sins, since it perverted what was closest to God—the First Mover—resided in

7. See especially Aristotle, *De Anima* II and III, and *Nicomachean Ethics*, both found in *The Basic Works of Aristotle*.

the head and hands. The rational will and acting on the will. This was the choice, by pride of course, of one's own way over the divine harmony."

"That's amazing," I said. "It almost makes Aristotle sound like some early, pre-Christian Christian."[8]

"Well, that had to wait until Thomas Aquinas adapted Aristotle's system to the church and rebaptized the First Mover as God. But, yes. Every good philosophy is also a good theology. I don't want us to miss the point, though,"

"Which is?"

"There are actually two points. The first is this. Many people believe lust to be the most horrible of all sins. Oh, how they shudder thinking of what this or that person has done. How they poke and scratch at the sore through gossip and slander. How they delight in their self-righteousness. Or the fact they weren't caught. I tell you, Pilgrim, theirs is the worse sin. It is the sin of pride, of a will turned from God's capacious love to a Pharisaical fence of rules in which they have netted a small fish.

"And that is point two. Dare I say this? The worst sin is that of the individual mind either denying or profaning God. The act of proudly choosing self over God. It is the fist sin, the sin of Satan and the angels that rallied to his side. The sin of Eden. Pride is an act of the will that locks one in the prison of one's own bleak heart."

"With no one to turn the key?" I asked.

8. It is fascinating to observe the influence of Aristotelian thought upon contemporary Christian ethicists in their contention with postmodernism. For example, in *Ethical Reflections*, Henry Stob argues that human conduct acquires ethical significance only when related to a transcendent norm. He points out that:

> These social scientists err in failing to distinguish between the *causes of* and the *reasons for* human behavior. They assume that there is no realm other than nature and nature's forces. They fail to see that man has membership in the world of spirit, and that he has a rational will which can be engaged by the transcendent Good, attachment to which evokes behavior inexplicable in terms of natural stimuli. They think of what man does as the determinate consequence of the influences playing upon him from being; they refuse to acknowledge that man has the freedom to set himself ideals and to aspire after them; they fail to recognize that moral values are more than psychological projections of selfish interest, and that they have objective existence in a world which . . . lies above and beyond the causal nexus of nature. Against these social scientists we must declare that human conduct transcends causal explanation and has a rationale which calls for a distinctively moral analysis and judgment. (15)

"Some reach through the bars, turn the key on themselves, and draw it back in. But, yes. There is a key. It's the same key that locked the gates of hell. This is the way one of my favorite poems puts it:

'Well enough 'tis known that mankind great

First was fashioned for perfect bliss;

Our first father did forfeit it

Through an apple that he bit upon.

We were all condemned because of that food

To die in sorrow, away from bliss,

And then to go to the heat of hell,

Therein without surcease to dwell.

But for that, at once, a remedy came:

Precious Blood flowed on the rood so rough,

And blessed water; then, at that plight,

The grace of God grew great enough.[9]

"Ah yes," Bosch murmured. "A world of theology in twelve lines."

"Speaking of a world of theology in small spaces, how about your tabletop painting on the seven deadly sins?"

"A misnomer. I prefer *The Table of Wisdom*. It was an actual table, you know. Phillip II, in *his* peculiar wisdom, sawed the legs off and hung it as a regular painting."

9. I have noticed that from the earliest stages, the narrator was given an ability to understand Bosch's use of foreign languages in his native tongue. I hesitate to draw conclusions, but it does suggest that in eternal matters there is some restoration of language to pre-tower of Babel days—a universal language, if you will. Interestingly, in the narrator's account of hell thus far, there has been no suggestion of speech in hell. Sounds, to be sure, of every sort, but no consciously shaped speech.

When the narrator later admitted to me that he did seem to understand the passage, but that it seemed to have "fuzz" all over it, as he put it, I jotted down the words as he gave them to me and soon understood the source.

Flipping through a few pages in one of my books, I found the lines in Book XI, Section 54, of *The Pearl*. My text, which I still think one of the best, is Sister Mary Vincent Hillmann's edition with translation. Bosch, of course, spoke this in the original Middle English.

"Stupid," I observed. "Like hanging a painting without a frame. And with staples."

Bosch grunted. "A bit strong, perhaps. But it certainly did rob the work of the sense of working *into*. In this case, peering into a metaphysical world as one walked around the table."

"I remember that from our earlier discussion. The work was quite early, wasn't it?"

"Oh, yes. And a work later criticized as 'didactic,' if you can imagine. Then one would have to call all my work 'didactic,' which as you know is not a term I'm fond of. Learning a lesson is not the same as speaking a moral. What these later critics miss, I think, are two things. One, a table is for *use*. Not to hang on a wall. Two, the painted tabletop uses mathematics to approach metaphysics."

"You lose me there. I have trouble balancing a checkbook."

"Mathematics is one of the most creative sciences," Bosch mused. "It uses symbols to capture concepts, after all. Not unlike the artist. Few people have seen that in *The Table*. For example, 128 rays emanate from the eye of God, in the center of which, like an iris, stands the resurrected Christ. Remember Pythagoras? For him certain numerical combinations held symbolic significance, especially when the sum of their parts is equal to the product of their factors.[10] Now the number twenty-eight has both the sum and the product of seven,[11] thus the number of holiness and wholeness.[12] It is the perfect number, hence the symbol of perfection itself. Now, I'm sensing that mathematics is perhaps not your first love, and I suppose I don't have to go on at length, since better informed critics of a later date have explored this wisely."[13]

"It is generally best to approach *The Table of Wisdom* wisely," I said. "But what about the hundred remaining rays?"

"Well, here we have to turn to the Bible for help. The number one hundred, particularly in the gematria,[14] is the number of perfect completeness and fullness. For example, in Genesis we are told that Isaac

10. An example would be the number six (1 + 2 + 3 = 2 x 3).

11. (1 + 2 + 3 + 4 + 5 + 6 + 7 = 4 x 7).

12. And one appearing often in biblical literature. See particularly Revelation. But it appears in other ancient texts as well.

13. The narrator informed me that, beyond question, the reference is to Wilhelm Fraenger in *Hieronymus Bosch*, since he had never located the discussion elsewhere.

14. The reference is to the Jewish system whereby numbers are associated with physical objects or religious concepts.

'received in that same year a hundred fold.'[15] Was it precisely a hundred times more? That doesn't matter. It was far more than he could ever expect. So too, the eye of the table, with Christ centered in the eye of God, is the perfect fulfillment—the perfect, necessary, and wholly sufficient grace. I had many such principles in mind, and if one walked slowly around the table one would eventually see that."

"But the rays, if I remember right, flow outward toward the seven sins."

"Yes, they do. But the circles also force one to go around. Grace is offered, but the sins may block the flow of grace. The sins, I'm sure you also noticed, are portrayed asymmetrically. This is not to add greater weight to one over the other, for any one of them can be utterly destructive, but to introduce the mathematical principle of discord."

"But the circles indicate concord. Especially the four medallions."

"Certainly. In this life discord and concord are at conflict, just as are sin and grace. One seeks to subsume the other; yet one loses full significance without the other. This balance is held by the circles."

"And the four medallions?"[16]

"Quite honestly, these were required by my patron. All of my energy went to the dynamic tension. But I suppose he was right. One does, after all, have to consider the end of all this tension."

"I appreciate your willingness to talk about your work," I said. "It seems sometimes that—"

"That the thoughts were already there? In your own mind?"

"Yes. But one more question, if I may. Something I've always wondered about. Just suppose that here . . . here? I guess I mean hell. Or one of your paintings. Suppose Satan, or one of his demons anyway, got the wrong one?"

"The wrong person, you mean? One who does not deserve to go to hell?"

"Yes. Something like that."

15. See Gen 26:12.

16. The four medallions to which the narrator refers are scenes set in circles at the corners of the table. They include: "The Hour of Death," "The Resurrection of the Dead and the Last Judgment," "The Kingdom of Heaven," and "Hell." Of these, "Hell" forecasts most clearly Bosch's later work. It contains the prototype of his anvils, torture racks, cauldrons, the furnace tower, and the demons that appear in similar shapes later. Here, each of the seven sins is labeled with the fitting punishment.

Bosch reflected for quite some time. I had begun to notice the pattern. When speaking of his art, he responded quickly and to the point. But, at other times, almost as if divining something more behind my question, he would look for the best way to frame it.

"First of all," he said, "I think we have to return to the point we made of God being just. Not 'perfectly just,' or 'he acts justly.' God *is* just. It is the inviolable character of God himself or else he is not God."

"Right. I remember."

"Now, if he is just, as we argued, he is faithful to his word, is he not?"

"True."

"That is to say, he doesn't change his mind about his standards—his very nature—willy-nilly. Now. This God has also made certain claims about the nature of his justice and how it relates to us. For example, God has established covenants with his people. They are of that very clear sort where God tell us that if you do this or that, there will be the consequences.

Another pause before Bosch continued. "We have been focusing upon hell . . ."

"Hard not to, being in it."

"True, Pilgrim. But even this quest is coming to an end. I was about to say that sometimes we have to travel the negative road in order to find the right path to truth. For there is the other side of the covenant—the promise of blessings."

"What do you mean?"

"Absolute security from the very fear of hell, for example. You see, if God is by nature all powerful, necessarily so if he is Creator God and if he bears the standard of justice in his own being, then nothing that is created—not angels, demons, height nor depth—can ever snatch us out of God's hand.[17]

"But even that is not the end of the matter. For we live under a new covenant.[18] That of grace. I find grace far harder to understand than sin. Humans will always surpass themselves in inventing new and creative

17. It seems that Bosch collates two biblical passages here. The first echoes Romans 8:38–39: "For I am convinced that neither angels nor demons, neither the present nor the future, nor any powers, in all creation, will be able to separate me from the love of God that is in Christ Jesus our Lord." The second echoes John 10:28: "I give them eternal life, and they shall never perish; no one can snatch them out of my hand."

18. A reference, no doubt, to Luke 22:20 and the institution of the Lord's Supper, but see also Hebrews 8 for the theological discourse on the covenant.

ways to make the same old sins look appealing. We are, after all, gifted with imagination. But how does one grasp grace?"

"Tightly, I suppose."

"Maybe it's the other way around. Grace refuses, as long as possible, to let us go. Can you imagine the grief of God as one more sinner plunges headlong toward the pit? You see, if sin is that insidious worm that destroys our relationship with God, grace is the creative agent that restores. We can be gracious to other humans, we can receive grace from God, but one thing we can't do is supply the grace that cancels sin on our own."[19]

"We can trick ourselves into believing we're pretty good people, though," I observed. "I once heard of a man who engraved on his tombstone: 'He Wasn't as Bad as Some.'"

Bosch laughed. "As a matter of fact," he added, "many of us humans are 'pretty good people.' At least according to social standards. Tell me, you've never murdered anyone, have you?"

"Of course not!"

"Then you're probably a better person than those on death row, aren't you?"

"Ah, I think I see where you're going."

"Answer anyway."

"Yes."

"Now, a second question. Have you ever done wrong?"

"Of course . . ."

"No details necessary, please. Now, both you and the murderer have done wrong, right? But his wrong may be more *bad* than yours."

"Yes."

"But how does one come to that judgment? How do we measure 'badness'?"

"Hmm. Conscience is one way, I suppose. That is, my awareness of my own wrongdoing."

"Very interesting, but perhaps limited. It does seem, doesn't it, that there are moral cretins adrift on this earth, those who for one reason or

19. In *The Riddle of Grace*, Scott Hoezee provides a clear and workable definition of grace: "We could define grace as being first of all that power of God, rooted in his abiding love, by which God forgives the sinful, accepts the unacceptable, revives the spiritually dead, and enables a reunion between the Creator and his wayward creatures" (4). But, Hoezee adds, "Beyond forgiveness, grace also aims to transform our way of life. Encountering God's grace is a formative, creative moment as a result of which a person is not only graced by God's love but also becomes *gracious* because of God's love" (ibid.).

another have conscience seared from their souls. Still, an excellent point. Can we add anything else to the measurement?"

I thought hard about this. Bosch seemed to be getting sleepy and I didn't want to lose him again. When his head nodded slightly, I noticed the hues of gray, almost like brush strokes, running through his hair. "I think I have it," I said. "I'm remembering our talk about grace, how divine grace allows or requires us to be gracious to others. Then maybe what we have here is the reversal principle again. The *badness* of a sin can be measured by the degree of harm inflicted upon others."

"Ah," Bosch grinned. "So it may be wrong to murder and wrong to shoplift, but it is more wrong to murder than shoplift because of the effects on others?"

"Yes!" I exclaimed.

"Yet," he cautioned, "*both* are ethically and morally wrong. Both violate God's justice. And both merit punishment."

How easily he could deflate me. "Okay," I sighed. "That's true."

"Suppose, moreover," Bosch continued, "that the person on death row realizes both his wrong and the degree of badness of his wrong. He repents. Is he forgiven?"

"He still has to be punished."

"Of course. Because of the degree of badness. No one will deny culpability. The issue here is forgiveness. Does he merit that grace?"

"I don't know. A murderer. I mean, I'd like to see him suffer a bit. It should cost him something."

"Oh. And how much should you have to suffer, or pay, for *your* wrong?"

"It's hardly in the same league."

"Not as bad. Yet nonetheless wrong. If you expect full grace for yourself—that is, if you repent—how can you deny it for the murderer?"

"I guess I couldn't."

"No. You couldn't. I'll tell you why. First, grace has to be utterly sufficient. Remember the distinction between being gracious, which is what humans do, and grace in absolute terms, which is always sufficient and meeting all necessary conditions. Understood thus, no human can merit grace, no more than he can create a universe."

"Okay. I take it this has to be grace beyond human ability, perhaps the other side of justice and therefore of God."

"Close, Pilgrim, but it is the true companion of justice. More, they intertwine like one strong cord. But, here's the second part. To meet any sin, to cover any wrong, to effect a reunion with God, this grace has to issue from God himself. Now, the tricky part, for there is a cost indeed. The price of Christ's sacrifice and this new covenant that he instituted."

"I see."

"But don't forget this. If indeed Christ's atonement is as the Bible claims, then eternal God enacted it in time. He entered time, and had to do so to reunite with time-bound creation. But if, as the Bible claims, God entered time, then the act of grace was once for all time but also ongoing for all time. And finally, then, in answer to your question of whether there are undeserving people in hell, we say impossible."

"Weren't we going to talk about that also—the eternal and temporal thing? The problem of time?"

"The riddle of grace is quite enough for now, Pilgrim. I find I need a nap. Keep watch. Yonder is our destination."

He waved his hand vaguely toward the growing red patch and was instantly asleep.

CHAPTER THIRTEEN

The Pit of Hell

AGAIN I HAD THE sense of vast distance—of endless height and depth and no awareness of cardinal directions. We seemed, roughly, to be heading toward the brownish-red patch. If I looked hard enough, it almost seemed to grow, but this may have been an ocular deception as we floated through . . . nothing.

I corrected myself. Not nothing as in a vacuum, but sheer emptiness. A vast and terrible loneliness. For the first time I felt a strange claustrophobia of isolation. Bosch snored comfortably beside me, and I took some small comfort in his presence.

Then I thought—suppose I awaken from this dream, and there is no Bosch beside me but I am in hell. My skin grew clammy.

Unmitigated darkness. No stray bursts of fire. Only the raw blister ahead that slowly, ever so slowly, increased in size. A scabrous red sore in the darkness.

While Bosch snored, his head leaning against the membrane, I found my thoughts wandering. So absorbed had I been in this perilous drama that I had not given thought to what I had left behind. Janie's face exploded into my mind. We were on the elementary school playground, that day when we had left our books on the carrels on the eleventh story and went out to play in the sun. She was looking back over her shoulder at me, her face full of laughter, overfull, spilling over in frolic, as I pushed her on the swing. Her auburn hair snapped out behind her like a banner, casting bits of reflected sunlight. She pumped out her tan legs, her khaki shorts high on her thighs, and my heart was full.

An ache deep in my chest pulled me back. Back to reality, I guess—life on the other side.

I remembered the day Lincoln told me about Rose.

It was one of those days when humidity hung in the air like gray wool. By the time I got to the library, after climbing the long hill, I could have wrung my shirt out.

"Reminds me of the mountains," said Lincoln when I passed his carrel. "Up high, the air would be clear, maybe seventy degrees. You could look out and see clouds settled in the valleys. They wrapped around every rise, following streams. It'd be ninety degrees down there by noon."

"Feels like one of those today," I said. "Although I think it will be in the nineties all over."

"My daddy called it a day when it rains upside down. See, when the sun started breaking through to the valleys, the wind would take these long chimneys of cloud and carry them up the sides of the mountains like smoke. And they'd leave this long, wet trail as they went."

"I felt like I was breathing underwater the whole way in," I said.

"Tell you what. I'll come and get you after awhile. We'll get some coffee. People drink all these soda pops on a hot day. Coffee's the right thing for you."

I had my doubts. Besides, the best cup of coffee around here was at The Oak Room, or, on occasion, in my thermos. Now my thermos was full of ice water and I didn't much feel like walking all the way to The Oak Room in the heat.

But we did. At eleven o'clock Lincoln hovered over my carrel like a giant cloud.

"Put that pen down and put on your walking shoes, brother." He growled the words.

I made to punch him in the stomach. He flicked out one hand and caught mine.

"Okay. I'm trapped," I said.

Fortunately, it was downhill to The Oak Room. I tried not to think about walking back up. The street gradually wound down and alongside the river. A thick haze curtained the water's surface. It was hard to see the other side. Mosquitoes and deerfly began to swarm out of the brush. On a stubby gravel point, two old fishermen with cane poles and bobbers smoked cigarettes and watched their lines. I almost said aloud, "There isn't anything in that river except carp and catfish." But I didn't. Some people liked carp and catfish.

The Oak Room was dusky and quiet. From a square cut in the wall, a monstrous air conditioner with laryngitis painfully gurgled cool air. We got our coffee. I treated myself to a Danish. After all, we had to walk back *up*.

Lincoln was quiet; hadn't spoken a word the whole way here. When he spoke, his voice had a tension in it. "I need your advice about Rose," he said.

His comment surprised me. Rose had joined us to play pinochle a few months after Shelley left me. Admittedly, it was a peculiar entrance. Janie had invited her. She first met Rose as her student in her freshman comp. course. Although friendships between teachers and students were decidedly frowned upon—a full hour session led by an attorney at orientation for teaching fellows made matters clear—that would not deter Janie.

"She's bright as can be," Janie told us before inviting her. "But she's been through some things. In fact, she's about the same age as us. She'll probably be pretty quiet at first. So don't scare her, Lincoln."

"What do you mean! Me? I'm as harmless as a newborn babe."

"Frankly, sir, you don't look like it."

"I'll put on my best manners."

"Please. Try anyway. I believe she'll be worth it." Janie grinned. I wonder if she plotted things already then.

"Sure," Lincoln said, "but tell me why."

"Because she doesn't dare trust. Especially not men."

She may have been quiet, this Rose Lara, but she was beautiful. Her black hair waved around her face, falling forward into her eyes when she studied her cards. Her eyes were large, the deepest brown I've ever seen, and her teeth perfect behind a timid smile that grew wider each week.

And within a few weeks she was a perfect shark with a pinochle deck, able to memorize every card laid and plot her moves. We always played men versus women, and we men started to lose steadily. One night I drew Lincoln aside, after a series of particularly humiliating gaffes on his part, and told him: "This is war, partner. Remember that instead of drooling over the enemy."

I have to hand this to Lincoln: he's the most patient man I know. Slowly, very slowly, I could see him draw Rose into a circle of trust. What started as a sly smile on Rose's part, developed into a grin behind her hand, and finally into outright laughter.

Still, I wasn't prepared for what Lincoln talked about that morning.

"It's sort of obvious, I suppose, that Rose and I have developed a relationship."

"Go, Lincoln," I said.

He smiled. "Yes, well. But I'm not sure how to play this."

"Ah, did you miss the lecture in fifth grade?"

Lincoln toyed with his cup of coffee, head down. Stupid, I said to myself. Putting my mouth in the way of my mind.

"I'm sorry," I said.

Lincoln nodded. "See, Rose has some issues, and, honestly, I don't know if I'm the right person . . . if I'm big enough to handle them."

I was tempted, but I bit my tongue. "Care to tell me about it?" I asked. I took a bite of Danish and leaned forward.

"It goes back a ways. When Rose was six—her parents were migrant workers in Texas—they had driven into town to buy some groceries. Her mother and father and baby brother rode in the cab. Rose was in the back holding the groceries. They weren't driving fast, but a white sports car came sliding out of a side street, her father wrenched the wheel to avoid it. The old truck hit the drainage ditch, rolled over, and burst into flame. Rose was catapulted over the ditch where a fence post impaled her in the abdomen. She was conscious just long enough to see the horrified, screaming, upside-down faces of her family. They perished in the fire.

"She was in the hospital for several weeks, largely because folks didn't know what to do with her.

"Finally the owner of the ranch where the Lara family was working came and got her. When she arrived, she saw the white sports car parked by the barn. The owner's son."

Lincoln took a moment while he sipped his coffee. Then I realized he was choked with emotion. "Take your time," I said.

He nodded. "Well, to make a long story short, the owner's wife had her own little live-in maid, no expense. Rose found her parents' locked box of papers and belongings in the migrant quarters, and was given a tiny room in the ranch house. The thing about Texas, though, is that it had a law that *all* children had to be enrolled in school. Rose was eight before they caught up with her and started her in first grade.

"Then . . ."

I waited. Chewed the last of my Danish. The waitress came and poured fresh coffee. "Yes?" I said when she left.

"She was nine the next spring. It was obvious she didn't belong in first grade, but they kept her there, even though she was doing work several grades ahead. And the owner's son was graduating from high school. Big party at the ranch. And little Rose was there, bringing out food, clearing dishes, dressed in a little white maid's outfit."

Lincoln took a deep breath. "The owner's son and several of his friends got her in the barn and raped her in a horse stall. When they were done, she slipped into the house, put on her work clothes, and started trudging down the dark highway. She fell asleep by the drainage ditch.

"In the morning she saw a migrant truck—old, paint faded, a pickup—and waved it down. She wound up staying and working with the family, even going back to Mexico over the winter.

"They took decent care of her. Uncle Hector and Aunt Maria Garcia, although they weren't relatives. They had three small children. Rose was a godsend to them since she was bilingual. And the Garcias were to her. For one thing, Uncle Hector was strong as an ox and always kept his protective eye on her. And she loved to care for the children.

"Here and there, Rose picked up more education. She located libraries and read when she could. During the winter she went to school in Mexico. Then, when she graduated from high school in Mexico, she came back to the states and took her GED and began working. Saving money for college.

"Now, here's the other thing," Lincoln said. He took a deep breath and drank half his cup of coffee. "In her parents' box, she had found her birth certificate."

I raised my eyebrows.

"Beaumont, Texas! Seems they regularly worked the fruit groves through that area."

"Then she's a citizen."

"Yes. Which also cleared her for financial aid at the university."

"So what's the problem?"

"I love her."

I buried my seeing in my coffee cup a moment. Then I looked at him in his deep, confused eyes. "Forgive me, but what's the problem here?"

"I'm not sure how to tell her."

"Lincoln, for being the most brilliant person I know, you're as dumb as North Carolina dirt."

"We've got good dirt there."

"Just tell her. Have you thought of that radical approach? And believe me, Lincoln, though I'm surely no expert. Women, see, have different wiring than men. They pick up these signals long before we send them. I mean, they're like several evolutionary eons ahead of us in this game. But there's one problem."

"What?"

"All the time they're thinking and reflecting, but you've still got to say it."

"That's not really the problem. I'm pretty sure she feels that way about me too."

"So what *is* the problem? Talk to me big guy."

"Well . . ."

I swear I saw a blush on Lincoln's dark skin—if that were possible.

"It's just that, after what she's been through, whether she can trust me. I mean as a male. I mean . . . if I'm good enough for her."

"Lincoln, let me say this. First, by questioning yourself, you're questioning Rose. By thinking of the possibilities of your limitations, you're limiting Rose's capacity to forgive, to be whole. You have to trust her by trusting yourself."

Lincoln stared at me as if mulling over the Pythagorean theorem.

"Tell me. Have you been intimate with Rose?"

He shook his head. "I mean," he said, "we just started enjoying each other's company. It seemed we started bumping into each other. Then taking walks. Laughing! Oh, my, but that little girl can laugh. Never thought I'd hear it at first. Then the parting became a hug and then a kiss. And that's where it'll stay."

"Seems pretty obvious to me," I said. "Although for the life of me I can't understand why."

"What's that supposed to mean?"

"She's in love with you."

Strange, but I don't think I realized the full impact of my comments until this . . . journey. I too had become friends with Rose, had seen the deepening relationship with Lincoln, but now my admiration for the way she had faced pain and fought for life and joy nearly buckled my knees.

But the fish boat didn't permit that. I nudged Bosch, who came haltingly awake.

"That red thing is growing larger," I said.

"I'm not surprised. That's where we're going. But it will be some time yet."

"Earth time?"

"That old problem. I spoke figuratively. I meant to say that we'll arrive there when we're ready."

"I have a question," I said. "Something I've been thinking about."

Bosch nodded. "Some questions I can't answer, you know. Even if I have the answer."

"What's that supposed to mean?"

"Well, there are many levels of answers. I have been permitted to guide you on this tour. But only the one who has given me permission knows why and to what end."

"Who is this *one*?"

"You have to discover that within yourself. Some answers you have within you; some are too great for you. No . . . don't be, as you put it, 'put off.' It is not a criticism or judgment of your intelligence."

"What then? Sounds that way to me."

"As distance and time on this voyage are judged by readiness, so too is understanding. One needs the cornerstone, the foundation, to ascend."[1]

"What else? What else can't you give answers to?"

"Obviously I am not assigned to anyone else—at the moment. Consequently, I cannot tell you about other people. We speculated about the actions of your ex-wife, Shelley, not to understand her story but to clarify your own.

"I cannot tell you when the gates of hell will be eternally shut, for that I don't know."[2]

I interrupted. "This is just a simple question. Well, not simple at all. I was wondering about my friends Lincoln and Rose . . ." I briefly sketched in Rose's background.

"Yes, I am quite familiar with her," he said.

"I thought you just said—"

1. I suspect the allusion here is to Ephesians 2:19–20: "Consequently, you are no longer foreigners and aliens, but fellow citizens with God's people and members of God's household, built on the foundation of the apostles and prophets with Christ Jesus himself as the chief cornerstone."

2. Cf. Matt 24:36.

"That I couldn't tell you another's story? True. But this is part of your story also. I can guess the question, but, please, I'd prefer it in your words."

"My question is only partly about Rose. I see the suffering—the torment—here, and I guess that by now part of my mind can justify it. After what we talked about. I mean, each of these . . . damned . . . are, or were, bad people."

"We all are," Bosch said.

"Well, I'm not so sure I agree with you on that. But I wonder why a good person, like Rose, for example, had to suffer so. Why she had to carry so much pain."

"Ah, yes. The hardest question of existence, that one. Why do the good suffer pain? Why does the ninety-five-year-old great-grandfather lie on a bed that is a rack of ruin? And why is his great-great grandchild stillborn? Why do we suffer disease, heartache, and worry so intense it blinds the mind? Why do we have the black plague of death? On and on it goes. Yes, I understand the question. It is the timeless howl flung to the heavens."

"So what's the answer?"

"The answer is that there are no glib answers. Oh, don't protest. I know that theologians, and indeed Scripture itself, tell us that in the fall of Adam and Eve we are all fallen.[3] In Eden the primordial sin played out: Satan tempted Adam and Eve to turn from God. His tool was an appeal to pride—'Surely you will be like God.' Then a perfect creation twisted, and it will not straighten out until the end of time as you know it. Yes, they are quite right. But I don't think the answer does full justice to the question."

"Why is that?"

"Consider that some pain is the direct consequence of sin. For example, the damage inflicted on the brain by drug or alcohol addiction is self-inflicted. Perhaps the pain itself may be the event that calls the person to repentance."[4]

"But that doesn't explain why *good* people suffer."

3. In addition to the Genesis account itself, the central doctrinal belief derives from 1 Corinthians 15.

4. The familiar argument Bosch advances here received its hallmark with C. S. Lewis's famous lines from *The Problem of Pain*: "Pain insists upon being attended to. God whispers to us in our pleasures, speaks in our conscience, but shouts in our pain: it is His megaphone to rouse a deaf world" (93).

"True. Although some would want to debate what we mean by 'good,' I don't find that very helpful."

"There's so much confusion about suffering," I added. I also pointed ahead. The red growth, like a warped tumor, appeared to be expanding. "I've heard people say that we should praise God for suffering. That makes me sick. Why praise? Did God cause the evil?"

"God does not *send* evil. For a time and within a space, he permits it. Evil is already confined, both on earth and in hell. No, I think the point, once again, rests on the fact that humans live in a time that God created. If God created time, then he himself is timeless. Eternal. Which is not no time at all, but if anything it is fuller and richer than time as we can conceive it. The further point is that God did not forsake us to time. Humans are not on their own, for God himself entered time and that changed everything. By his doing so, you see, his power continues to work in this world. Indeed, sometimes he acts directly through miracles to alleviate suffering. Sometimes he enfolds us until we ourselves enter eternity. Remember, Pilgrim, your life is but the blink of an eye to God, but in that blink nothing escapes his attention."

"What about Rose?"

"What do you admire about her?"

"Her sense of survival, for starters. Her tenacity, her faith, her hope."

"I can't give you Rose's story had she *not* suffered. But those qualities you mention surely grew out of it."

"Still . . ."

"Yes. I know. How we hate suffering. But this curse of evil will be lifted. The gate of hell will be slammed shut forever. There will be no more suffering, no more need for voyages such as this. For you will have all the answers and no more need for questions."

If I found his words reassuring, and I'm not sure that I did, they were quickly pushed away. The red disc had expanded more rapidly, the brownish-red crust now filling the space before us like a constellation. Long tendrils fell from its edge like drapery, or the poisonous barbs of some incongruously large jellyfish.

"We're going through that?" I exclaimed.

"No. That is not our journey. In this case we will not be going 'through,' but truly above."

Small comfort. As we floated over the serrated edge, the brownish-red flow seemed to move counterclockwise, an enormous dense mass like glowing lava. As the fish boat dipped lower, then appeared to settle into a long glide, I noticed figures upon the outer disc. By some process unknown to me they appeared to drift past the very edge of the membrane. They were stunning. Beautiful. I stiffened in my seat, feeling an unsettled fear at their stark beauty.

Each stared outward beyond the disc toward the gloom. One surpassed the other in the beauty of physical features. Sheer garments, like translucent satin, draped from perfect figures. Hair flowed like long multihued banners. Their mouths seemed to open in a blissful expression I could not fathom.

And as we passed each one, they were transformed. A gaping skull atop a wracked skeleton body. Snakes crawled within a diseased nest of bones. Hair changed to ropes of worms piercing the skull.

"Keep looking forward," Bosch ordered.

I had been mesmerized by the vision. The disc before us was now a roiling mass of red, glowing like a blacksmith's forge. Bubbles roared by, spouts of fire exploded, and I realized that this central mass was moving *clockwise*. I had the sense of inexpressible energy, and willed the fish boat to greater speed.

Ahead two spaced hillocks arose, flaming red. It was like peering into the heart of some immense conflagration that could never diminish. This appeared to be our destination for, as we approached, the distance between the raised mounds widened.

Now I could make out figures on what appeared to be paths, or at least worn spots on the carpet of flame. These paths were not solid; on the contrary, it seemed that a viscous fluid oozed across them.

Wheelbarrows! The figures were pushing wheelbarrows. Slowly. Shoulders stooped. There, behind each one. A creature more horribly misshapen and malevolent than anything any human artist dared to or could represent. It raised a massive arm as it crept along and brought a whip crashing over and over on the backside of the figure trundling the wheelbarrow. Strips of flesh fell burning to the ground.

I know why no artist could paint this. This wasn't representation. It was evil itself.

If anything, the fish boat went slower. Horribly slow as we passed over the wheelbarrows and saw the human damned stacked like cordwood. It reminded me of pictures I had seen of concentration camps.

And all the wheelbarrows, a steady line from countless directions, began converging at a point between the two rises. No color can describe the *sense* of that heat, the sheer intensity and pulsating energy.

A blistered declivity fell inward from the two rises, a raw and ulcerated circle of fire. As the load-bearers tipped their barrows into the declivity, the damned writhed uncontrollably. The circular sides poised between the two ridges throbbed angrily, sucking the forms in. One would sink down, then bob in anguish to the surface, then disappear altogether from sight.

I turned to Bosch, who stared without emotion upon the horror.

"I want to go home," I whispered.

He appeared unmoved.

"I want to go home," I repeated more loudly. My voice seemed to ring off the sides of the membrane.

He nodded. Suddenly I felt a powerful surge in the fish boat.

"What *was* that?" I asked. I felt drained, utterly spent,

Bosch paused a few minutes, as if pondering the best way to answer. He turned and looked at me. He seemed older somehow.

"Do you remember when we discussed the hellmouth image?

I nodded.

"That is how we figure Satan on earth. The great jaws snap and snare sinners. Demons poke and shove those sinners down Satan's gullet on the passage to hell. There is a fair amount of truth in the image, as there is in nearly all of our imaginative representations.

"But remember also our principle of reversal in hell. That was not Satan's jaws."

"You mean that was . . ."

"Yes. And the jaws open far below, held by the curtain of flame, encased by the gates of hell, surrounded by the outer darkness, where he vomits forth the damned to their eternal home."

I felt sweaty. A nervous tremor twitched in my hands. "Are we heading home now?" I asked.

Bosch pointed ahead. A vague shaft of silver light hung tremulously in the darkness. I realized, for the first time really, that everything I had seen had played out on a horizontal plane. The silver beam appeared to be the first vertical intrusion on that.

"That," Bosch said, "is the shadow of heaven."

"You can't have heaven in hell," I declared. "Not after what I have seen."

"No one here can see it," Bosch replied. "They have all turned their faces from it long ago. But once, just once, the Light of Heaven penetrated to this pit of farthest remove."

"Ah, you mean the crucifixion."

Bosch nodded. "It was necessary."

"For what? To give the damned another chance?"

"There are no second chances in hell," Bosch said grimly. "They have chosen, and can never return from their choice. No, it was necessary for other reasons."

"Such as?"

"When the Light of Heaven descended into hell, he took upon himself the darkness of the world so that those who come to him for mercy can rise with him to heaven. It is for the living that Christ died, not for the damned."

"I see."

"And also this. Remember this. The Light of Heaven did not remain in hell. Instead, he established his rule over it."

"But . . . I thought Satan reigned here."

"One might say that. But Christ rules over him. This is where God's complete and perfect judgment *against* is enacted. Remember that for all his horror, Satan is a created being, over whom God rules absolutely. Satan suffers the full wrath of God here as much as anyone."

The silver shaft far ahead grew in brightness, even as we still seemed draped in the cloak of darkness.

"I can't believe that these others can't see it," I said.

"As I said, it is but a shadow of the glory of heaven. As they chose not to see it on earth, they are forever blinded to it in hell. They are forever, eternally, separated from the Light of Heaven.

CHAPTER FOURTEEN

Satan, Being, and Time

"Our time here is running short, Pilgrim."

"No time for eternity?"

"Something like that."

"We never really got to the heart of that issue, did we?"

"Actually, it's not really an issue, but an understanding that should be rather simple to arrive at, given the foundations we have already laid. God is eternal. Being eternal does not meaning being timeless, for that would be merely 'being there,' a state of profound stupor in which nothing happens."[1]

"Like the rocks we saw in the tube."

"Yes, indeed. In eternity, events happen. There are causes and effects. There is activity."

"Yes. I understand that."

"Ah, but maybe not the implications. You see, our human time is not circular, as many believe."

"Who believes that?"

1. Perhaps it is fair to say that time and eternity are far more important issues to us humans than to Bosch, who seems to have awareness of human time, appears in it, yet somehow transcends it. Two fundamental views conflict in how Christians see time after death. The traditionalist view sees time as eternal. The conditionalist view applies specifically to the damned and holds that after a period of torture those in hell will be annihilated. One prominent proponent of this view is Edward William Fudge in *The Fire that Consumes.* The issue raises all sorts of difficulties, it would seem, including the eternality of heaven. In *Two Views of Hell,* Fudge and Robert A. Peterson, a traditionalist, provide a lively debate on the topic.

"Every sort of reincarnationist, for example."

"I'm not entirely sure what you mean by that word, *reincarnation*. It's another term that I hear from every direction," I observed.

"Yes," Bosch said. "And usually used with so much emotional fluff that it means nothing at all. Actually, I was thinking of Plato. Even when he's wrong, he gives a good case."

"For example?"

"I trust you've read the *Phaedo*? It seems few people do anymore. The colleges all seem to teach careers instead of the person who performs in a career. That's why we need Plato. But I may be mistaken."

"Probably not. We have to make a living, though."

"No! Not first of all. First, you have to live."

"So what does that have to do with Plato?"

"Well, the dialogue of *Phaedo* takes place in the prison of Socrates, where thoughts of life after death come readily to mind. Socrates, you see, was well aware that he would soon die. Now, what do you remember about Plato's teachings on the body and the soul?"

"Not a whole lot, I'll admit. It seems to me, though, that for Plato the body and soul are in conflict. The body weighs the soul down into unjust acts; consequently, pure knowledge arrived at through soul is attained after death. Does that sound about right?"[2]

"Close enough for the moment, Pilgrim. But remember that the soul is always hindered in that goal by the body. Plato's soul aims—unlike Christianity's, which claims a body/soul resurrection—to purify itself from that body through successive reincarnations and thus arrive at immortality.[3]

"We should point out, in fairness to the esteemed Plato, that his cycle did have an end point. For example, those who are merely bad might be plunged into Tartarus for, say, a year. And those who are incorrigibly

2. See Plato, *Phaedo*, where Socrates says, "When I have come to the end of my journey, I shall attain that which has been the pursuit of my life" (*Plato: Selections*, 160).

3. See ibid., where Socrates argues for successive reincarnations: "Then here is a new way by which we arrive at the conclusion that the living come from the dead, just as the dead come from the living; and this, if true, affords a most certain proof that the souls of the dead exist in some place out of which they come again" (168). And also, Socrates argues reincarnation to higher states: "But I am confident that there truly is such a thing as living again, and that the living spring from the dead, and that the souls of the dead are in existence, and that the good souls have a better portion than the evil" (169).

evil and unjust may be locked in Tartarus forever lest they wreak further evil on the earth."[4]

"How about the good guys?" I asked.

"Well, they too can escape the cycle, and be united with the Ideal. They are the ones who obtain justice and virtue in this life. But that might be another argument."

I must confess that it was growing harder for me to follow Bosch's arguments, as if my mind had already taken in too much. Instead of overflowing, it felt like it was collapsing.

"I don't want you miss the very simple point," Bosch added. "From Hindu to New Age. It's almost a primal scream by billions of voices insisting that life goes on."

"Well? Doesn't it?"

"Yes. But not to relive another life on earth in an endlessly circular and inescapable pattern. Your time is not circular; it is linear. Consider. When did time begin?"

"As far as I know, it has always been there. I don't know. That's confusing."

"One kind of time surely has always 'been there.' The Eternal, which, to a large degree, is beyond human conception. Let me phrase it differently. What time do you know and experience?"

"The time of the clock. The day and night, seasons, years."

"Yes. And each of those is a measurement of your life in which you have only the present moment, which, even as you think of it, is past. And with it, a bit of the future disappears. That, my friend, is linear time. And it is the only time you know on earth."

"But clocks go around measuring those moments. The earth rotates. And it revolves around the sun. The moon revolves around the earth. All those circles affect us."

"Oh, my, Pilgrim. Just when I think we're making progress, you come up with something like that. All of that is a matter of the laws of physics. Yes, we measure time by them, but physical laws are altogether different than time."

4. Plato makes the point on the immortal destiny of the wicked clearly, and on this point he also differs from modern reincarnationists. In *Phaedo* (in *Plato: Selections)*, he says: "But those who appear to be incurable by reason of the greatness of their crimes—who have committed many and terrible deeds of sacrilege, murders foul and violent, or the like—such are hurled into Tartarus which is their suitable destiny, and they never come out" (228).

"Okay."

"Okay? That's all you have to say for yourself?"

"I suppose I'm getting tired is all. Unlike you, I still live in time."

"Not much fun discussing something when the other party is too time-worn to discuss time."

"By the way, Bosch. What kind of time are we in right now? Eternal?"

"No, no, no. You haven't guessed? There is a third kind of time which is called the Vision. It is the time of the Old Testament prophets when they spoke the word of the Lord. It is also the time of artists who see beyond the physical structures they work with to the idea by which they put those structures—pigment, metals, words—together. It is the time that holds time past, present, and future at once even as time passes. That's the time that you inhabit here. It is no time and all time."

"My head is spinning."

"Then, perhaps we should finish our discourse on time. Our conclusion thus far. We—all humanity—live in linear time. It is time with a beginning and an end."

"What!"

"Let's approach this in an altogether different way. Maybe logic will help us."

"Why is that?"

"Don't you see, Pilgrim? We have been discussing the human point of view again. It's bizarre, really, how you humans insist upon that."

"I don't *have* too many other points of view."

"Oh, I'm not saying it's altogether bad. But notice: we talked about Hinduism, about New Age, about reincarnation. Do you see my point? These are human constructs and all are held without necessary and sufficient proof. Let's use logic to talk about time."

"All right by me. I don't follow the other ones much anyway."

"Now, we commonly say that God is timeless, don't we?"

"Yes."

"And what do we mean when we say such a thing?"

"If I remember right, it's that God created time. At least, I think we established that. Therefore God has to be above or outside time itself."

"Very good. But a baby step. Yes. We say God created a rose, but he is not the rose itself. God created the order of the stars and other heavenly bodies, but he is not those stars and bodies that mark time itself. Furthermore, other galaxies, with their physical laws, most certainly have their own measurements of time."

"Even if there is no one there to measure it," I said.

"Even so." Bosch seemed to be gazing into some untold distance, the rim of which I could never see. I sensed it like that thin prickle of fear that dances along the spine when you walk somewhere you shouldn't be on a dark night. You whistle in the graveyard and pretend you're braver than you ever thought you would be. But then, I reminded myself, that might be exactly where I was.

"The big assumption here," I said, "is that there is a God who created anything at all."

"Oh, really, now. Must we go over that ground all over again? So much of which is a prattling subterfuge for dragging the heavens down into your tiny laboratories. Now don't look chagrined! You are not a puppy dog."

"But it is a valid assumption, is it not? That there is no God?"

"Well, certainly. Regardless of the fact that it is wrong, the assumption may be valid. You may assume that you can jump off a cliff and fly by flapping your arms. You even have evidence for the assumption."

I laughed aloud. "What evidence? That I'm deranged?"

"No, you've seen birds do it. We make assumptions every moment. You assume even now that you are riding in a fish boat. If your assumption collapses, you collapse."

Not a pleasant thought. I stared into the darkness. It was not a "netherworld" as the Greeks taught. It was all encompassing. I was "within," and the only barrier was the cellophane skin of the fish boat. A new thought dawned on me. Maybe I was within my present environment the same way temporality is "within" eternity. If so, then we always are, have been, and will be with God in eternity. God is eternal and has created. But so too he is eternally loving us, is crucified for us, and is resurrected for us. Only in temporality is there future, when we will be resurrected with Christ. Whatever happens to us, God neither began nor will cease to exist. I felt like I was dancing on a spider's web.

"Yes," Bosch broke in, "two seemingly valid assumptions—after all, a thing either exists or does not exist—but we are exploring only one assumption at the moment. Doesn't that seem the wisest course?"

"Why?"

"By knowing one to be true, we know the other to be false. Right? Or, by seeing the merits of one, we see the defects in the other. Of course, we could take the long course of the *via negativa*, as we have done before. As we saw, it is rather cumbersome and takes a bit too long. So, back to the subject. I asked how we know that God is timeless, and you answered that the Creator is not the thing created. What else?"

"Well, if God is timeless, or without time—"

"Bravo! A far better way of saying it."

"I don't get it. What's the difference?"

"Timelessness is a concept from within time, something of which we cannot conceive since we are in time. How, after all, does one measure that which by definition cannot be measured by any laws we have? 'Without time' signifies that God is the creator of time and not, therefore, bound by its strictures. Nothing in God's existence is either earlier or later than anything, whereas our existence always is."

"All right, then. We could describe God's existence as eternal."

"My dear Pilgrim, you're doing better all the time."

"A pun?"

"Only in part, for we reason from step to step, necessarily a time measurement, while God, being without time, must necessarily be all wise. But, *eternal*—what do you mean by that?"

"I'm not sure. I always thought that God existed outside of our time and therefore was eternal."

"Two problems, then."

"What? I come to the plate with two strikes against me?"

"What on earth are you talking about?"

"Never mind. I forget that you didn't have baseball in your day."

"Oh, baseball! No, we walked. Often."

"They still do in baseball. So what are my two strikes?"

"Problems, friend. First, *eternal* implies some different sort of time, other than your time. A supranatural time, if you will. Second, *eternal* implies existing through unlimited time. That is, eternal time is time that cannot be measured. It is time without limit.

"Let's try another approach—logic abetted by revelation. The Bible uses the word *eternal* many times. In nearly all such cases, it describes God in the sense we have used—without measurable time. Then, it also refers to *our* life after we die. That's the tricky point and we may want to return to it. Obviously, in eternity we will not be God. So what does that word mean for us? Maybe we should first define what it means in relation to God.

"It might help if we look at one description that appears twice: 'From everlasting to everlasting you are God.'[5] In the first reference the psalmist speaks to the existence of God; in the second to his love. But that is easily solved, isn't it?"

"I would think so," I said agreeably. "We've seen before that one of the intrinsic qualities of God is love."

"So?"

"So his love is from everlasting to everlasting as is his existence. But remember that I'm not entirely sold on this love business. Nonetheless, the obvious conclusion is that God exists in love without beginning or end."[6]

"Without time?"

"Right."

"Now, how do we define the beginning of time as we know it?"

"The first day?"

"Close, but not quite. The first day had a definite length. Before that, there was no definite length, so no measurable day."

"You're losing me."

"It's quite simple. 'From everlasting to everlasting' has no measurable, definite length."

"But then what of eternity?"

"Ah, yes. Now I think we're ready. Consider. You now live in measurable time."

"At the moment, I'm not sure."

"That's to be expected," Bosch said. "What is our evidence for even thinking of eternity?"

"I suppose it can't be anything that emerges from measurable time."

"Truly, for this is time as you know it. You have no experience or concept of eternity starting from that framework."

"Why not? Eternity is just no time."

"Not quite true. Eternity is no death. But consider this. From the everlasting unto everlasting of God, to the measurement of time that we know, God is the 'why' time began. You might say that every moment of your time, from the first cry of life to the last, is a process within eternity.

5. Pss 90:2 and 103:17.

6. The most helpful resource in this complex discussion of time and eternity is a book by Brian Leftow, *Time and Eternity*. But that book also is not always easy to understand.

"There is more, however. You see, the first event was when God without, or outside, or transcendent over time created time. That was the beginning. The second time God entered time, time itself changed. That was when God entered human form, and by so doing redeemed not just all creation, but time itself. By his death and resurrection, Christ radically changed time. First, because he entered time, there are still those moments, by prayer or by revelation, for example, when the divine intersects with our time. And, second, the death and resurrection pointed time toward the end of time as you know it and toward eternity. This will be the third, and final, time that God enters your time. Time as you now know it will be no more."

"Why do you say *your* time?"

"Surely you have already guessed."

"Well," I said, not at all certain that I understood anything, much less everything, he had said. Bosch's words seemed strangely speeded up. Not that he spoke more quickly, but that my ears were slower to catch them. It felt like that fuzz you have sometimes after you dive into a lake and water clogs your ears.

I glanced out the side of the membrane. I had no sensation of going faster or slower. Certainly not the way I had when the shark attacked the fiery bolts of the gates of hell. The only sensation of movement was the gentle but powerful propulsion of the fish boat's body.

That, and the light seemed to be growing oddly more distinct, more bodily, if that makes sense.

"Well," I said again. "If I do have 'time,' I do have a final question. You yourself said that 'our time is running short.'"

"True. But, then, I'm aware of your time and Vision time, since I'm bound by neither. I'm merely here to serve."

"My question wasn't about time."

"What then?"

"Satan. The devil. Lucifer. Whatever you people call him."

"'You people?'"

"You know what I mean."

"I can guess. But what is your question?"

"I was just wondering what some people at the university would think if they saw what I've just seen."

"'Some people' couldn't see it at all."

"How so?"

"They have so perfectly wrapped their minds in lies that the truth can no longer penetrate."

"Lies?"

"Satan is an old wive's tale. Or, Satan is a projection of our inner guilt."

"'Repression,' as Freud said?"

"Exactly. Or, Satan is just an invention of religion to make us feel guilty and keep us 'on track.'"

"What about him, then?"

Bosch sighed. "Yes, what about him? And where do we start? Let's see."

He reflected a moment. I was wondering how he would come at the question.

I thought Bosch was simply going to ignore it, when he said, "You are working on a dissertation. Nearly completed."

"Yes. Nearly."

"And when you complete it, will it be your creation, your making?"

"Sometimes I'm not so sure. All the research I have to do, you know? Sometimes I feel like I'm just scrambling eggs. What I really like, though, is when I study a painting of yours and just think my way through it. See how it fits into the work I'm doing."

"So the dissertation is undeniably yours? When finished, it will have your name on it."

"True."

"Or is it the other way around?"

"What on earth do you mean?"

"Does the dissertation own you? Are the title and author reversed?"

I couldn't help laughing. "Sometimes," I admitted, "I feel like it owns me, but where on earth are you going with this?"

"Patience. Think a minute, then try to answer the question."

"It is sort of a double-edged question, I think. Yes, I have to say the dissertation is mine. Definitely. I have done all the work on it. And I suppose too that it is mine because my ideas are in it. The argument represents my thoughts."

"Very well, Pilgrim. You see, I find this happening to my work all the time. 'Ah, this is a Bosch.' 'Look at that Bosch. Isn't it awful!'"

"Well, true, Master Artist. We are judged by what we produce."

Bosch narrowed his eyes at me.

"Sorry," I murmured.

"Don't lose the point here. Follow the steps, for we are on a path. First, the creator or maker leaves something of him or herself in the work. It lies within and also apart from the work."

"Pardon?"

"Say it's a long poem. The author arranges plot, character, themes. But to what end? The idea in the mind of the maker discovering itself in the making itself. It is distinctive to that maker. Thus, we say a certain long poem or a drama is a Virgil or a Homer."

I nodded. After all, I had written several hundred pages on those ideas about Bosch and his works. A systematic theology, after all, has to be systematized by someone. It has to be observed, calculated, and expressed. Or, I wondered, does it exist unto itself even if no one observes it? The old tree falling in a forest syndrome.

"But now," Bosch continued, "let's ask what it means to 'own' a work. Can I really say I owned my art? A patron paid me and I turned it over to him when completed. Let's imagine that you publish your dissertation, despite its self-challenged subject matter. Do you still 'own' it after you sign the contract? Can you walk into a bookstore, pick up several copies, and walk out saying you own them? Could I go back to my patron after he has dutifully paid me and say, 'Sorry, this is mine. I want it back'?"

"No need to answer, Pilgrim. I'm sure you see the point."

"Please point it out anyway," I said. After what we had been through, I was not sure I saw anything clearly.

"The point is this. The creator or maker 'owns' the work in terms of complete authority over it. Until such time as he freely gives it its own freedom."

"Hah! I'm not sure about 'authority.' My committee has revision suggestions on each chapter."

"Yes, of course. But suppose you were the one perfect Creator. Suppose that what you created was flawless, good, unique, and given freedom?"

"Ah. I think I see it."

"Such a case is Satan. He was one of God's perfect creations. God had, and still retains, complete authority over him. He was created, like all other angels, to be a servant in the glorious realms."

"What happened?"

"Instead of a servant of God, he chose to be a slave to himself. The case with Satan is not dissimilar to that of humanity. God created us, and put his imprint of ownership upon us. We love. We know good. We sense justice. But we too choose against God."

"You said that God, unlike us, retains complete authority over what he has made. Do you mean this applies to Satan also? Why is that so?"

"Because God's standards are perfect. We may do exceptionally well on occasion, but never perfectly. Moreover, God alone has the authority to call being out of nothing. All of our making is with things already made. We may create like God, but never as God."[7]

"So why is Satan condemned to hell, to . . . what we saw?"

"'What exactly was the turning point?' might be the question we should ask. When did he cease to be an angel of light and become the Prince of Darkness? At that very moment when he thought himself equal to or higher than God. Now, simple logic will tell us that this is impossible, or else God is less than that by which we name him."

"Explain, please. Logic sometimes confuses me rather than clarifies. I feel that tricks are being played on my brain."

"Oh, this is no trick, Pilgrim. Consider all those attributes of God that are revealed, either by himself or by the gift of reason he has given to humanity. And please understand that the gift of reason is not limited to Christians alone. It is given to all humanity. Even if they have not apprehended the one true God, they have a logic that there is a God, someone who transcends this life, someone more powerful yet than the greatest power in this life."

"I'm not sure of that at all. Many—no, most—of my colleagues deny God altogether."

"We can get back to that in a moment, if you wish. Our present question is the logical inadequacy of Satan's effort to be like God. And, we were going to discover certain qualities of God that define him as God and without which he would not be God. Consequently, we will discover also why no created being can take the place of God—neither an angel, nor a dictator, nor a sea turtle."

I smiled at the idea, but then I saw Bosch's point. "Okay," I said. "I suppose that the first response is that God is Creator, and that no created being or object can take the place of its creator."

7. I assume that Bosch's reasoning here derives in part from Jeremiah 18, one of the central biblical expositions on the relationship between the Creator and the created. See also Isaiah 45 and Romans 1:25.

"Especially when the creation is called into being from nothing and shaped and ordered by certain laws."

"Right. A second point," I observed. "The presence of natural laws to order creation."

"Very good," Bosch said. "And you see that even the aberrations in those laws, the moments of disorder, in and of themselves testify to a larger order. Natural laws are not a chaos, even though chaos may occur within them. Think now. We call a tsunami devastating for what reason? Because we think it violates some assumed order in natural law. Yet a thoroughly reasonable, scientific, and orderly account may be given for its occurrence. The devastation is a tragedy, not a transgression."

"There's almost an analogy there," I said. "Just as a tsunami might occur by a shift in tectonic plates far below the ocean surface, sin occurs from a fracture in the heart of a human."

"Hmm," Bosch murmured. "This is interesting. Notice the shading of light outside."

"Yes. It looks like one of those winter mornings when you get a half-light just before dawn. After being in that blackness . . ." I shuddered. I know it's impossible, but it almost felt like a thick, sticky residue adhered to my skin.

"I think we should make conclusions," Bosch said. "Our argument to this point is this. First, Satan's sin was trying to be like God. He sought power. Therefore, it was an act of pride.

"Second, we said that neither Satan nor anyone else can be like God, because of the very definition of what God is. We started calculating those definitive qualities. God is creator, and no created being can take his place. Furthermore, he is a God of order, which not only encompasses natural laws as one evidence but also his divine plan for his creation. In this case, we say that that divine plan unfolds in the linear course of time. And, notably, only God has the power to enforce his own, perfect laws. We call this omnipotence. He has all power over all that he has made. What might we add?"

"Well. . . " I hesitated. "You can also add those other 'omnis'. God is omniscient. He knows all things. This is like catechism classes in junior high. It comes back to me now."

Bosch nodded.

"I can't believe how much I hated catechism. Sitting there on a sunny afternoon with my ball glove tucked under the chair. I stared out the window like I was in a jail cell. And I couldn't memorize anything then. I tried for awhile, then figured I was just too dumb."

Bosch looked entirely undismayed. "Yet you have recalled two of the 'omnis,' as you call them. Omnipotence. Omniscience. See what else you can do."

"Ah, omnipresent. You know, these really freaked me out. Here I'm in junior high and my hormones are chugging away like a runaway locomotive and I'm thinking, 'Whoa, God! Give me a little privacy here.'"

Bosch laughed outright. "Oh, yes," he said, "those are the bad teachings on those good qualities. They are meant to be comforting.[8] Unfortunately the good thing of human guilt developed by God's gift of conscience makes them seem threatening. And many use them as threats."

"God can see what you do and he's going to get you."

"Precisely. But let's get on a new set of tracks here to speed us to our destination. All of these qualities help define, insofar as our minds find possible, the nature of God. There are, of course, other ways.[9] But now we ask the question, how does Satan stand in relation to God in the present? That is to say, we have examined how he fell away from God. Now let's explore the consequences."

As the light shifted to a silvery gray, I felt myself growing tired. The nervous shock of our passage now enveloped me as we seemed to slide into safety. It wasn't so much that we were heading toward the light, but that bit by bit it was drawing us in. It was like we were granted admission, but still had to undergo some process, some procedure in order to enter. And, as I did while standing in slow moving lines anywhere, I began to feel unbelievably weary. The world itself was running away, leaving me in dazed stupor. My very mind seemed to be slipping into a void. Often this was a delicious moment—when I took a much-needed nap, for example. Sometimes it was merely escape into a fog of weariness. I

8. Cf. the many references in the Bible to forms of "I will never leave you nor forsake you"(Deut 31:6, 8), which is the logical consequence of God's omnipotence in the lives of those who love him. See also Joshua 1:5; Psalm 37:28; and Hebrews 13:5. The parallel pattern that those who reject God will be forsaken by him also appears. See 1 Chronicles 28:9; Ezekiel 8:22; and Isaiah 1:28.

9. Consider, for example, Alvin Plantinga's use of symbolic logic to construct proofs for God. In *Warranted Christian Belief*, Plantinga discusses whether it is rational, reasonable, justifiable, and warranted to accept Christian belief. His earlier work, *Faith and Rationality*, introduced readers to his method of constructing logical proofs for the existence of and necessary belief in God.

answered Bosch's questions in an effort to stay awake, not even altogether certain what he was asking at points.

"Pilgrim!" he said sharply.

I turned toward him.

"It's very important that you do *not* sleep now," he said. His voice was sharper than I had heard it before.

"Why? I'm tired. Besides, we're on the way out. And besides again, you've snored through half the trip." I didn't disguise the petulance, and immediately regretted it.

"Don't you see, foolish human?" His words were like lashes of a whip. "That is the great temptation! That is the final hook in you. Resist it. If you think this is *only* a dream, you will never escape it. Focus now, so we can end it."

His eyes held me with some strange, primal power, as if he entered me and scoured the walls of my mind. I noticed that the light silvered his gray hair. I fought off the shades of weariness. It was like writing the comprehensive exams for my degree. Eight hours in a small room with a half-hour lunch break. The biggest battle is not how much you know, but how well you can organize and focus.

"Recap," Bosch ordered. "The one thing to avoid, Pilgrim, is the notion that because Satan has been cast out of heaven, he is therefore insignificant.[10] It is not for nothing that he is called the enemy. Remember that he was cast out of heaven for very good reasons. First, he believed he could be like God.[11] Second, because God cannot abide sin—especially

10. In *The Real Satan,* James Kallas is one of those who advances the argument that Satan is insignificant (15–16). If one meant by this that God retains final authority over Satan, the belief may be construed as true. If one understands that Satan has no power on this earth, including upon the life of believers, the belief is patently false.

11. Although many passages in Scripture allude to this pride of Satan, one of the central proof texts may be found in Isaiah. As is typical of his prophetic vision, he holds time past, present, and future in one moment:

> How you have fallen from heaven, O morning star, son of the dawn!
> You have been cast down to the earth, you who once laid low the nations.
> You said in your heart, "I will ascend to heaven;
> I will raise my throne above the stars of God;
> I will sit enthroned on the mount of assembly,
> on the utmost heights of the sacred mountain.
> I will ascend above the tops of the clouds;
> I will make myself like the Most High."
> But you are brought down to the grave, to the depths of the pit.
>
> (Isa 14:12–15)

the grievous sin of pride—in his presence, God cast Satan out like a fiery bolt.[12] His one-time presence in heaven was purified by fire, and by fire he will be chained.

"What Satan has is what he always wanted: power. What Satan will never have is what no created being will ever have: the authority of the Creator. Do you see how it ties together?"

"I think so. Although my brain is a little woozy. I feel a bit drunk. Or that I'm getting a cold."

"That's understandable. Soon you will be safe again. We must finish. We need to examine the work of Satan today. What you saw was his final destiny . . ."

"His final end, I'd say."

"Well," said Bosch, "maybe you're not as 'woozy' as you said. Yet, I must move quickly here. I will posit some conclusions we can make from our examination of the relationship between Satan and God. You may qualify as you wish or feel necessary.

"First, I have observed that this modern world, and much of modern Christendom for that matter, has tried to ignore Satan by depersonalizing him.[13] There is only a random 'force of evil,' bad circumstances, unfortunate events, or bad luck. What they fail to realize is that in the process they also depersonalize God as revealed in the Bible and received by tradition.[14] In the naturalistic world view that dominates in your time,

---

For further discussion on this topic, see Lewis Sperry Chafer, *Satan*.

12. Cf. Luke 10:18.

13. It is expedient, perhaps, to mention several prominent thinkers who have argued the existence of Satan out of Christian theology. They have spoken in volume and volumes. One might say that the belief grew generally out of the Enlightenment (during the eighteenth century) with its emphasis upon deism and focus on natural law. But specific religious figures certainly heaped their scorn on the idea of a devil. The specific argument acquired momentum early in the nineteenth century through Friedrich Schleiermacher, who argued that Jesus' references to the devil were simply to meet the superstitious mind of his audience; but Jesus certainly knew better. There is no reasonable argument to include Satan in a reasonable theology, or we degenerate once again into myth and superstition (see *The Christian Faith*, 1.1.1.2). Rudolf Bultmann remains, perhaps, one of the most prominent demythologizers of the spiritual world. In *Kerygma and Myth*, Bultmann develops this thesis: "Now that the forces and the laws of nature have been discovered, we can no longer believe in *spirits, whether good or evil*" (4). One of the more aggressive voices advocating the demise of Satan in modern, popular theology belongs to Peter Berger, who notoriously claimed that it is "naughty to believe in the Devil." See "The Devil and the Pornography of Modern Consciousness."

14. By this term, I gather that Bosch refers both to the doctrines, creeds, and

no room is left for spiritual realities. Doing so, as one of your modern writers put it, twists the entire foundation of the Christian faith.[15] Nor can we say that one half of the spiritual world is real—that is, God and the angels—and not those who have turned against God. Again, this would skew the logic of all we have discussed. For example, we would have to have a good God acting badly by creating an imperfect world. Jesus would be a cosmic joke, having died for nothing.[16] The conclusion for the first step, then, is that we have to accept the evidence and the logic and agree upon the reality of Satan. If we agree to that, we also, necessarily, agree to the reality of his work in the world.

"Second, what is the nature of that work? We can define Satan just as much by what he does as by what the Christian tradition has asserted about him. That is, from Scripture we know that he was cast out of heaven. But consider this, Pilgrim. Our concern is how his work affects us, right? So, let's divide the issue into two parts, and then I believe we can find a conclusion. Don't get woozy on me now."

I could not. The silver light grew steadily brighter. It flashed off the scales of the shark like brilliant flakes. Strange. I had always thought sharks were colored dull gray and white. But now I saw flashes of color, no doubt raised by the eerie light, everywhere on it. It seemed to catch the entire spectrum of light and color as it moved like silk. "Go ahead," I said.

"Consider Satan's work on earth. We know well that his work is to tempt, thereby subverting the design of the Maker. Very often he tempts with the very thing he wanted most—power.[17] Even while masquerading as a messenger of light, Satan works to turn our hearts to darkness.[18]

---

catechisms of the Christian church, and to those seminal thinkers whose work has elucidated Scripture and illuminated our knowledge of God.

15. This vital concept is also developed by Carl E. Braaten in eds. Carl E. Braaten and Robert W. Jenson, "Powers in Conflict: Christ and the Devil," *Sin, Death, and the Devil*. There Braaten argues that: "Any theology that does not take the Devil seriously should not itself be taken seriously" (96). He goes on to say that "We simply cannot subtract the Devil . . . without doing violence to the shape of the Christian faith. . . . No room is allowed for these spiritual realities in a strictly materialist or naturalistic worldview, nor for any other secrets of the Christian mystery, for that matter" (97).

16. This argument is thoroughly developed by Nigel Wright in *The Fair Face of Evil*, and also by Kirsten Nielsen in *Satan—The Prodigal Son?*.

17. See Jesus' own temptation by Satan as a prototype. Satan tempted through individual need, appealing to Jesus' hunger as he fasted before starting his ministry (Matt 4:3). Then he tempted Jesus to flaunt his own power (Matt 4:6). Finally, he tempted Jesus with power over kingdoms (Matt 4:9). See also Paul's advice in 1 Cor 7:5.

18. Cf. 2 Cor 11:14.

"We know, furthermore, that he tries desperately to frustrate the spread and the work of the gospel.[19] My friend Paul testifies to that. Remember when he wanted to visit the Thessalonian church? He tried, as he said, 'again and again—but Satan stopped us.'[20] Oh, yes, Paul has some stories. He didn't just have a thorn in his side, he had a whole briar patch.

"But even that is not the end of it, Pilgrim. Satan wages warfare—yes, Pilgrim, that is the correct term—on earth. Listen. Do you think for a moment that all the guns and bombs deployed on your earth are more powerful than Satan? Hah! If anything, one might call them his tools.

"Remember this. Even though cast out of heaven, Satan is ever mindful of what he lost and he continues to rebel against God. He is the spirit of rebellion. He continues in his warfare with heaven. But he will be crushed utterly.[21] Why? Because he has been crushed already on the cross. Jesus has, and always will have, final authority over him."[22]

"The light," I said. It now seemed tangible. The membrane vibrated with its silver glow. Beneath us the shark shivered with a collage of color no artist dared dream of. The colors were not just *applied*, nor an image apprehended by the eye. They were solid, a reality unto themselves, those things to which our application of color points. As if to say, "This is how things truly are." Tongues of flaming color hovered over the shark's body.

19. Cf. the parable of the Sower, especially Mark 4:15. See also Paul's comment about the cunning of Satan. He urges people to be forgiving "in order that Satan might not outwit us. For we are not unaware of his schemes" (2 Cor 2:11).

20. 1 Thess 2:18.

21. Cf. Rom 16:20: "The God of peace will soon crush Satan under your feet." The verse seems to imply that human agents will be involved, perhaps the Christian church as one body.

22. The wrath of Jesus is decidedly understated in modern Christianity. Yet, repeatedly, the New Testament speaks of Jesus as the agent of God's wrath (most powerfully, perhaps, in Revelation). The very one who provided grace to escape God's wrath also serves as the supreme judge. Nowhere is this more pronounced than in Hebrews 10:26–29:

> If we deliberately keep on sinning after we have received the knowledge of the truth, no sacrifice for sins is left, but only a fearful expectation of judgment and of raging fire that will consume the enemies of God. Anyone who rejected the law of Moses died without mercy on the testimony of two or three witnesses. How much more severely do you think a man deserves to be punished who has trampled the Son of God under foot, who has treated as an unholy thing the blood of the covenant that sanctified him, and who has insulted the Spirit of grace?

To the mind of the writer of Hebrews, on the other side of grace stands the efficient, authoritative, and inescapable wrath of the Lamb.

"Pilgrim," said Bosch in a weary voice. "You have made a good journey. You may rest now."

Editor's Note: Bosch never did say, the narrator told me in a phone call years later, what the silver light was, nor was the narrator himself willing to speculate. His comment, "It was the way we took out," seemed to me simply pragmatic. I couldn't let go of it. I finally thought of two possibilities. First, maybe it was the path Christ took in the so-called "harrowing of hell," the liberation of noble souls from the Old Testament era who did not know the Lord. Such a light would shatter that darkness, perhaps even leaving this afterglow. And, it seems to me, that would be a perfectly legitimate view, even though more mythic than evidentiary. After all, if Christ came to earth without the taint of sin touching his life, so too he could enter hell. His purpose, if this happened, would be to rescue his own from the "underworld."

Second, according to some theories, the light represents a general, ongoing escape route, a second chance for those in hell.

But there seem to be all sorts of problems with either view, which appear chiefly as a statement in the Apostle's Creed, although it overtly appears in Catholic and Lutheran catechisms also—though only in one very vague Scripture passage. The Creed and the doctrines merely state it as fact, without elaboration of any sort. In order to support it scripturally, some theologians point to one of the seven last "words" of Jesus—"*Eloi, Eloi, lama sabbacthani*," or, "My God, my God, why have you forsaken me?"—repeated in Matthew 27:46 and in Mark 15:34. However, the words are cried out to his Father and almost certainly lament his abandonment to the cross and bearing of believers' sins. It was his task alone; no other could take up or endure the punishment. Even in his abandonment, however, the perfect man was perfect God (who else could say, "Father forgive them, for they know not what they do"?). Scripturally, however, nothing in the crucifixion begins to suggest that Jesus *entered* hell. The very idea of perfect God in the pit of hell is a bit repugnant.

I turned to certain troubling passages in Scripture that might support the harrowing of hell—the doctrines about which, by the way, were largely developed during the Middle Ages with the full effects of the Black Plague, and in regard to limbo, not hell itself. The first of these passages occurs in 1 Peter 3, where the apostle teaches on the efficacy of Jesus' salvific work. Then he adds: "He was put to death in the body but made alive by the Spirit, through whom also he preached to the spirits in prison who disobeyed long ago when god waited patiently." Peter relates it to those people destroyed in the great flood of Noah's time. A few verses further, in 1 Peter 4:6, we find, "For this is the reason the gospel was preached even to those who are now dead." Such verses seem to suggest some second chance for those who died and were then exposed to a saving grace.

Yet, the harrowing of hell presents difficulties. Some we know; some we only speculate about. If, for example, Jesus suffered abandonment by his Father on the cross, this would parallel the suffering of hell, which is eternal separation from God. But it does not necessarily follow that he entered into hell itself. Furthermore, the miracle of the incarnation is that God became man. At the hour of the crucifixion he was still God and man. If not God, his claim that he forgave sins would be preposterous; if not man, the means for that forgiveness would be logically impossible.

God works in mysterious ways, to be sure. But not in ways contrary to his own nature. If we are to believe that Christ descended into hell, his stated purpose changed. Virtually anyone, Christian or not, has heard the words of John 3:17: "For God did not send his Son into the world to condemn the world, but to save the world through him." Fewer people read several verses further to meet this: "Everyone who does evil hates the light, and will not come into the light for fear that his deeds will be exposed." The stated redemptive purpose is clear, but so too is its exclusion. Surely, God has a means prepared for dealing with the "noble dead" and for those Old Testament saints asleep in the Lord. It is called the judgment day. But it doesn't do to make of Christ something other than he is, something other than he said he was, and to assign to him a task different than he declared by plunging him into hell. He himself created its unbearable, apophatic darkness as separation from the unbearable (presently) brightness of heaven. Then heaven were not heaven; hell were not hell; and Jesus a self-deceived God playing a game he ultimately loses.

I certainly don't claim to solve the problem; I only claim to detail its challenges. While I have some difficulty, then, with the strictest interpretation of the harrowing of hell, favoring the doctrines that on the cross Jesus conquered sin, death, and hell, I was still faced problematically with the shaft of light riving hell's darkness. A second option occurred to me.

This view derives from sources already quoted in the text—Isaiah 14:12–15 and Luke 10:18, two stories that relate the fall of Satan from heaven to hell. Jesus describes it thus: "I saw Satan fall like lightning from heaven." It's hard for me to wrap my mind around this. Lightning shatters. Lightning dazzles. We don't have to understand the physics or the chemistry behind it to be stunned speechless. Knees tremble. We run for cover. Maybe, just maybe, I thought, that white shaft the narrator witnessed on his journey was something like the ozone-laden residue of the bolt, still burning since the time the angel of light was pitched into eternal darkness.

Foolish humans. How we beat our brains about the merry-go-round as we run in circles. We dislike mystery. It is the nature of our world, the tumor in our soul. Of one thing I am certain: hell will never be anything other than the everlasting darkness of abandonment. Heaven will never be anything other than the bright light of love.

And what of our present home? At times the fires nip at our heels. We feel we walk on nails through hell itself. At times the waves of love wash us like a benediction. It is the lurid intermixture that at once torments and promises, holds hope and helplessness. Grief and joy stand in opposite corners of one room, each beckoning us to eternity. Earth is the beginning of a pathway that goes on forever.

Only minutes after I finished drafting these paragraphs, the narrator returned my call.

"Come up with anything?" he asked.

I read though parts of what I had written, summarized the rest. Pretty dull, I thought. And I thought about just cutting it out.

"No. Don't do that," the narrator said. "But I had a thought." Silence.

"Go ahead," I prompted.

"Remember when I told Bosch I just wanted to go home?"

"Twice."

"Yes. When I think about it now, it wasn't so much to Bosch. It was a prayer. I really, truly wanted to go home. The light in the darkness was the way."

"Hmm. Sounds reasonable."

"That's only part of it."

"What's the rest?"

"I saw the light even before I started praying."

I had nothing to say to that. Nonetheless, we both still held on the phone, listening to each other's breathing.

"My friend," he said, "there just might be unicorns."

We laughed and hung up.

NARRATION RESUMES: The membrane was suffused by a purifying glow. I longed to bathe in it. I felt every tense knot in my body release, warmth seep into me like a massage of sunlight.

I glanced at a smiling Bosch. His hand was moving, as if he were the artist dipping from an infinite palette and conducting this dance of color. I felt I could live in this world of wonder forever.

I felt solid ground beneath me. Blades of grass tickled my cheek.

CHAPTER FIFTEEN

The Pasture

PERHAPS YOU KNOW HOW it is on those warm summer days when you think you're just going to lie down and rest a moment and wind up falling asleep. You wake up in sort of a mental fog. Where am I? Shouldn't I be in my bed? What did I miss?

That was precisely how I felt, as if coming awake between two adjacent but dissimilar worlds.

I sat up slowly on the bank and looked out at the pond's surface; not a ripple broached it. From the cattails at the southern edge, bullfrogs took up their sonorous roar. In the center of the pond sunlight reflected off the water so powerfully that it seemed to penetrate to its depths.

It was not a good day for fishing. The fish would all be hiding deep, unmoving. On a day like this, with the heat rising and the crickets and bullfrogs singing, I would have to get to the pond well before dawn. Run a purple worm slowly along the edge of the cattails or maybe drop a hula-popper right across by that old stump that just poked through in low water. It sounded like a wobbly frog when it hit and the bass went nuts over it.

I was smiling to myself. My skin was itchy from sunburn.

Fish.

Suddenly I had this preposterous idea of a fish carrying me.

A fish boat.

Carrying me on a journey.

It may have been the sun. I felt dizzy and short of breath as other thoughts, strange thoughts, flickered through my mind. Then I realized that they weren't thoughts in the rational sense, but more like pictures, a film perhaps, that I saw inside my mind.

I stood up, unsteadily. I would make it up the hill and get something to drink at the Nolans. I had been out in the sun way too long. My skin felt scorched by it.

As I climbed the slope my feet seemed to drag through the grass. "Hay," Ed had corrected me once. "It's grass with only natural fertilizer." But I was surprised how high it was. Here and there clumps of Queen Anne's lace bobbed in the slight breeze. It was a sign either to cut the pasture or turn the horses loose on it.

I reached the road and turned toward the Nolans. Ed was wearing overalls and a T-shirt. He was muttering to himself while going through layers of used wool stacked against the south side of the barn. When he saw me, he called out, "Leaving already?"

"Already?" I asked.

"Well sure. You've only been here fifteen minutes max."

"Got any water handy?"

"Sure. I put a fountain right in the barn."

He followed me in, carrying a weathered piece of wood. It looked like it had once been a trapdoor or some such. "What do you think?" He said as he studied the surface. "Did you know that artists once painted on stuff like this. Once I get done, I might make it into a tabletop."

"I look forward to seeing it, Ed." I turned and walked to the Toyota. It was a miracle that I made it home without falling asleep.

I'm sure that that Saturday night, as I tossed in my bed in the Hollis's back room, then simply got up and sat in the garden feeling the night alive all around me, I felt at times I was going insane. What sustained me?

If I didn't *understand*, I nonetheless *knew*. As night lingered toward a frayed dawn, I felt, to the marrow of my bones, a release from questions. Somehow they had been answered without being fully asked. The heartache and fear that had blistered inside me since Shelley left felt like a miraculous salve had been placed on them. And the unguent went deep, to the very root.

The sun crept over the ridge on slow-moving legs, dragging pieces of copper and brass through the treetops. The rose bushes tossed handfuls of perfume in greeting.

I couldn't wait until Janie got home. I mean, back with me. Home.

I wondered if she would think I was crazy if I tried to tell her.

I decided that she wouldn't.

Epilogue

It is the nature of time and distance to separate us from memories. Not entirely, of course, for our memories shape who we are. Sometimes memories are all we have left.

My mother, for example. When she died, after the funeral, I found myself paging through her Bible. There unfolded the story of her faith but also much of her own personal self. Her wry observations on Scripture flowed in one margin. Somewhere in the second book of Kings she penned, "What a bloody, ungodly mess!" In the left margin were penned notes traced to the many events she experienced that day, each time she forced her way through the "bloody mess." Most of these seemed innocuous, like "3/18/98: picked first bouquet—hyacinth and daffs." Just an ambivalent note, unless one understood my mother's intense love for nature in general and her gardens in particular.

In spring the house on Black Gap Mountain seemed to have sprung up in some misplaced Eden. The yard rioted with color.

So too, certain memories shape the mind. When my mother died that year, Janie and the narrator drove straight through for over a thousand miles to attend the funeral.

They stayed on for several days afterward, taking long horseback rides with Rose and me on the mountain trails, hiking to waterfalls and groves of untouched rhododendron. It was early June. The tourists hadn't come yet. The forest trails seemed untouched by all of time. One morning we hiked into a rhododendron grove that I used to visit as a boy. The pink blossoms canopied over us. Periwinkle mountain flowers poked their bright heads through any ray of sun that hit the earth. The sound of water was everywhere. At points we stepped from rock to rock as small streams converged by the trail and overflowed the banks.

No one spoke. Then we heard the larger sound of rushing water. Rose had been on many trails with me, and had developed the mountain-dweller's instincts for direction. Sometimes she would awaken before me and I wouldn't see her again until late afternoon. But for some reason I had never taken her down this trail. Maybe, subconsciously, I had saved it for when we four could meet again.

And now we could see the glint of silver ahead. The roar of water over the great river stones was listened to from some remote, primitive place deep within us.

We immediately took off our shoes and stood ankle deep in the water by the gravelly shore. I was always surprised at how frigid it was. Then it seemed to simply numb the lower legs and brought a pleasurable sense of abstraction from earth.

Janeen, I recall, immediately starting forging deeper into the river until I called her back. She stood in water nearly to her knees and said—a bit petulantly, I confess—"Why?"

"Come back and I'll tell you," I said.

I swear, even though she was Professor McClatchy now, she was still a little kid. And a little brat, for all that.

When she didn't move right away, I said, "Because I'd like you to live to enjoy your baby."

Janie's face flamed red, but she turned and made her way back.

"How did you know?" my friend asked. "We were going to tell you as a surprise."

"Me medicine man, paleface," I said with a glare. Then, "How long have I known you? I can tell. I inherited if from my grandmother."

"Well, you got good genes."

When Janeen got back to shore, we congratulated her heartily on the new addition. "But I hardly show," she said. "I'm only three months."

"See those rocks," I said, "just beyond where you were standing?"

"They look like silver."

I nodded. "That's mica. And it's as slippery as ice. And this part of the river has a surprisingly powerful current.

"When I was a boy my friends and I would ride our horses down here and set up camp. I was about eight or so when I got the idea that I could wade the river by stepping from rock to rock. I got about halfway before I slipped, landing square on my butt. By the time I realized what happened, the river was pushing me from rock to rock, bouncing me along like a tennis ball. Let me show you where I wound up."

I led them through the maze of tumbled rock by the river's edge. Rose was an old hand at this. She could thread her way up and down rock piles without a second thought. But today she held Janeen's hand protectively, leading her on the most gentle route.

"I'm not going to break just because I'm pregnant," Janeen protested.

"Right," said Rose. "Especially when you're the toughest Irish mama around. But I know these rocks and you don't. Besides, it's not much fun hobbling out with a broken ankle."

In this way we made it over the rocks, down an easy cliff, and back to the river. The roar of water cascading down over the rocks was deafening. The falls dropped a full thirty feet into a pool. Where the water crashed against the pool, foamy white spray splashed in the air. But past the ring of spray, the pool was eerily still, as if planed out of dark green glass.

"And this is where I wound up," I said.

"I can't believe it," my friend said. "How did you survive?"

"I'm not sure, honestly. I remember that I was still sitting upright when I went over the falls. So I could still get a deep breath as I went over. Just sort of shot out as if from a cannon. And then, by that little point over there, there was a man fishing. No one I knew. He dove in and dragged me out of the water. I'll never forget what he said to me."

"What?"

"'If that's all I'm going to catch today, then I'm done.' He left me on the bank, gathered his gear, and left."

"Why is the water so still?" Janeen asked. "Look, just outside the falls there's hardly a ripple."

"I wondered that too," I said. "Usually falls in these mountains sort of tumble over more rocks. There are rapids all the way. In fact, this pool doesn't outlet until where those trees narrow over there. Then it's fairly flat for a mile or so. I found out later that where this falls lands in the pool, the water is close to fifty feet deep. The depth takes all the impact.

"And if you got caught down there, it would be pretty grim getting out," Janeen added.

"I don't think you could," I said.

We spent that evening, our last together, at the cabin. Perhaps *cabin* is a misnomer. People tend to think of those as rundown shacks. I admit, some are.

Daddy knew better than to bring his new wife into a shack. Before he even proposed he started building the place. Everything by hand, from setting the concrete blocks for the foundation and crawl space to felling and shaping the lumber. It had two large bedrooms and these were hung with drywall. Everywhere else, save for the huge fireplace built from native stone, was dressed timber, chinked and as tight as if he had used some industrial glue. A porch stretched across the entire front of the cabin, hung with flowerpots overflowing with New Guinea Impatiens and wave petunias. Mother's domain. I had hoped Dad would remember to water them, and was pleased, after she died, that he devoted scrupulous care to them.

We had a super-efficient wood-burning stove and three cords of wood stacked behind the shed to burn in it. For summer we had windows and overhead fans. Even on the hottest days, the temperature never got above eighty degrees on the mountain.

Just across from the gravel road to the cabin, a waterfall cut a narrow rocky path down through the forest. Our second summer there I designed and built a gazebo that extended out over the falls. Dangle your legs over the edge, listen to the birdsong up and down the ridge, the water foaming down over the rocks, and you will believe that this is the most peaceful spot on all the earth. Rose tells me that every day she finds fingerprints of God and records them in her journal. I have never seen her so happy, so free from worry. She is wildly in love with living.

So it was, however, that when Rose and I decided to move here for a few years, my father helped me build our cabin on an acre of his land just beyond the ridge from theirs. We built it in the same slow, methodical fashion, although I admit I was anxious to drive over to Asheville and buy some power tools on more than one occasion.

"Does a power tool understand the wood?" Daddy asked.

His touch was still flawless, and even though his work with the Cherokee Tourist Bureau kept him away most days, I found that I also loved the labor. It was like writing. Each day you had to finish something polished. Else you have no business trying it.

Rose mostly stayed with my mother, then, though some days she would hike over the ridge with me to work, often bringing starter plants for flowers. Mama's diagnosis that spring had made firm a decision we had been troubling over for some time.

I had taught at the university for two additional years while Rose finished her bachelors degree in social work. The blessing was that my appointment relieved her of the part-time jobs, and she graduated with highest honors. We wed a week after her graduation, with our two best friends standing by our side. We had stood up for them a year earlier. But unlike their wedding, which was a gala affair in Janeen's hometown, few others attended ours in the university chapel. Some colleagues, some friends. Rose had no family that she knew of.

So we wed, and in the fall took an appointment at an Ivy League university that had given me an open offer two years prior. She wouldn't complain, not once, but I sensed Rose was unhappy. She got a job with a social agency checking on welfare mothers. She became quiet. She refused to complain.

I thought perhaps it was related to the fact that we had found out that Rose was unable to have children. Significant damage had been done to her tubes and ovaries during the incident when she was a child, and the subsequent surgery had left irreversible scarring.

Very well. We submitted adoption papers. Yes, of course, we would take any ethnic background. Look at us.

Then one day Rose came home with some papers she had printed out at work from the Internet. I remember she was trembling with excitement.

I was doing the cooking that afternoon. Rib eye steaks. A big one for me and a tiny speck for Rose. She'd want it rare. I thought about holding a match under it.

Rose splashed the printout down on the table, and put her hands on her hips. "What do you think?" she demanded. Her smile dazzled.

I read it carefully. "Is this something you want to do?" I asked. Granted, I can be fairly dense at times.

The printout advertised two positions at a newly founded elementary school in Cherokee County, North Carolina: One for a counselor and teacher; one for a principal and teacher. It had organized as a charter academy designed to give greater individualized care to the Native American children in the county who too often got lost in the system. The school would teach traditional ways of the Cherokee as well as a regular curriculum.

"Think it over," Rose said. "I know you have the most to lose."

Actually, as long as I had Rose I had nothing to lose. I made inquiries in my department. They would—gladly—hold my position for two years, the chair said.

By this point money was not an issue. The linguistics textbook I had worked on while Rose was completing her degree was now a standard text, used at hundreds of universities. I was well into a textbook on theory for which I received an advance more than my annual salary. Between us we had saved a substantial amount toward a down payment on a house.

I was really, genuinely intrigued by the work. Excited in more ways than I was by my daily Professor Jefferson role.

With all the obstacles met and overcome, we wired the bank account to my father and asked him to sell us the acre and buy supplies.

He called me on the phone.

"The land's yours," he said without preamble. "You'll inherit it all one day, anyway. And you don't gotta buy much supplies. We're gonna do it o'selves, you and me, in the good ol' way."

My daddy's smart as a whip. I'm sure he pulled out North Carolina talk now and then to keep me from getting—as he put it—"more uppity than a mule with a burr on its butt."

And so it was that the two years passed and I responded to the university's inquiry that we intended to stay here for a while.

Our one regret is that the greater distance had made it impossible to visit with our dear friends.

The narrator and Janeen had taken a joint appointment in a New England state far north of where we lived. They liked it there. As the narrator wrote me once, "It's a beautiful place—for five months of the year." As a native Southerner, he had a hard time with cold weather.

Sometimes we or they made weekend visits. We would stay up most of the night playing pinochle. They had been fortunate, having bought an old rundown house just a block from the campus when they moved, and spent a year renovating it to its early-twenty-first-century splendor.

As Janeen said, "Throw together an English teacher and an art historian, give them a house to renovate, and it's a wonder the marriage survives."

"Well," I said, looking around the gorgeous rooms, the wood detailing stripped and gleaming, "how did you two, of all people?"

"Easy," she said with that sparkle in her eyes. "We worked in different rooms and locked the doors."

Those were wonderful visits, and we felt we had never parted. Until, that is, Rose and I moved south. We realized this parting would be part of our decision; we never realized how hard it would be.

For a time we exchanged letters. Then the letters became cards—birthdays, Christmas. So it was that when my mother died—and we had all met each other's parents at our weddings, of course—I sent them an email more or less as news. I never expected them to make the 1,000-mile trip.

They pulled into Maggie Valley a little after 3 a.m. and when I heard his voice on the line I had no idea he was that close.

"And Black Gap Mountain would be where, exactly?" were his opening words. Typical.

"North Carolina," I said sleepily.

"How about from Maggie Valley. I'm standing at a pay phone by the tourist office. Deserted of course. The whole place is. Does anyone live here? Give me directions and put the coffee on."

That was how, after several years, we got back together. And in time they had to leave again. It is hard to make promises of seeing each other again. They're so very easily broken. So we made no such promises. We hugged each other, holding on.

When their car bounced down the gravel road that final morning, brake lights bright against the predawn fog, Rose and I went for a long walk. Hand in hand and, for the most part in silence.

It wasn't until much later that morning that I went into my study and found the bulky bundle tied with gardener's twine on my desk. This typed note was attached to it:

This is a manuscript of my experiences, which I believe truly happened. You may have guessed something of the matter from discussions we had and the questions I asked in the months following. For my own sake, I needed to write it out. It has been a long struggle. Needless to say, hell is not a comfortable condition. But, if this is true, I believe Hieronymus Bosch was entirely correct about one thing at least. This was a quest, not an adventure. What I found was myself. Having done so I am able to give myself away to others as I never could have before. So I give this manuscript away. Thanks, friend. You have always been my guide. Do with it as you will.

I had pondered the manuscript for some months before I decided to edit it and try to publish it. I had a vague notion that, if the memoir didn't provide all the answers, it at least posed many of the right questions.

Linguistics, properly understood, is a scientific undertaking. Few people understand that. I suppose you could call me a man of science, although I never would. I'm the principal of small school and a man wildly in love with this woman who consented to marry me.

Rose and I use the second bedroom as our study—temporarily, I hope. Above the desk, Rose has a needlepoint quotation from Shakespeare:

> There are more things in heaven and earth,
> Horatio,
> Than are dreamt of in your philosophy.[1]

Everything found in these pages defies science, yet they may contain the most elusive scientific pursuit—the truth.

Some days after I first read the manuscript—handwritten in the narrator's almost inscrutable scrawl—I called him and asked his permission for my project. "Even if nothing comes of it," I told him," I'd like to do it for my sake."

He assented, but was not particularly forthcoming when I asked him additional questions. "I don't know what to say beyond what I've said," he protested. In further calls, he carefully limited his responses to technical questions on art or reading materials, not the experience itself. The writing must have been a kind of therapy for him, and having found some restorative state he now wanted to live there without fear.

Janeen, on the other hand, was most helpful. She readily volunteered opinions, both on her husband's comments and also his state of mind at the time. But then, Janeen was seldom without opinions.

To both of these dear friends go my undying thanks for their trust. Friendship is one of the most precious gifts we have. I mean true friendship—when your trust and your love go out to another person in such a way that you feel your spirits interlock as one.

1. *Hamlet*, I.V.166–67.

I want to thank Rose, my best friend, who is by far the stronger one of us. She broke through my fear and taught me what commitment means.

Finally, I want to thank the publisher of these pages. It was a risky undertaking and, I confess, I am probably not the easiest person to work with. When the publisher asked me to write this epilogue, I groaned, looking for ways out of it. Now I'm glad I did. It provided both the narrator and me the opportunity to talk about the alternate path—more narrow to be sure than the downward plunge that appears so pleasurable and frolicsome at the time. That narrow road is love, sometimes a hard path indeed. But I have found this to be true also: it gets broader and smoother with each step.

Respectfully submitted,
Lincoln Jefferson

Bibliography

Works of or about Hieronymus Bosch

Baldass, Ludwig. *Hieronymus Bosch*. New York: H. N. Abrams, 1960.
Belting, Hans. *Hieronymus Bosch: Garden of Earthly Delights*. New York: Prestel, 2001.
Bosch, Hieronymus. *Bosch*. Text by John Rowlands. London: Phaidon, 1975.
________. *The Complete Paintings and Drawings*. Translated by Ted Alkins. New York: Harry N. Abrams, 2001.
________. *The Garden of Earthly Delights*. Introduction by John Rowlands. Oxford: Phaidon, 1979.
Dixon, Laurinda S. *Alchemical Imagery in Bosch's Garden of Delights*. Ann Arbor: UMI Research Press, 1981.
Fraenger, Wilhelm. *Hieronymus Bosch*. Translated by Helen Sebba. New York: Putnam, 1983.
________. *The Millennium of Hieronymus Bosch: Outlines of a New Interpretation*. Translated by Eithne Wilkins and Ernst Kaiser. New York: Hacker Art Books, 1976.
Francis, Anne E. *Hieronymus Bosch: The Temptation of Saint Anthony*. Smithtown, NY: Exposition, 1980.
Gibson, Walter S. *Hieronymus Bosch: An Annotated Bibliography*. Boston: G. K. Hall, 1983.
Silver, Larry. *Hieronymus Bosch*. New York: Abbeville, 2006.
Snyder, James. *Bosch in Perspective*. Englewood Cliffs, NJ: Prentice Hall, 1973.

Works Cited

Adams, James Luther, and Wilson Yates. *The Grotesque in Art and Literature: Theological Reflections*. Grand Rapids: Eerdmans, 1998.
Alcorn, Randy. *Heaven*. Wheaton, IL: Tyndale House, 2004.
Aquinas, Thomas. *An Aquinas Reader*. Edited by Mary T. Clark. Garden City: Doubleday Image, 1972.
Aristotle. *The Basic Works of Aristotle*. Edited by Richard McKeon. New York: Random House, 1941.
Augustine. *City of God*. Edited by Vernon Bourke. Translated by Gerald G. Walsh, S. J., et. al. Garden City: Doubleday Image, 1958.
Barth, Karl. *Church Dogmatics*. Edinburgh: T & T Clark, 1957.

BIBLIOGRAPHY

Benton, John. *How Can a God of Love Send People to Hell?* Hartfordshire, England: Evangelical, 1985.

Berger, Peter. "The Devil and the Pornography of Modern Consciousness." *Worldview* 17 (1974) 35.

Block, Daniel I. "The Old Testament on Hell." In *Hell Under Fire*, edited by Christopher Morgan and Robert Peterson, 43–65. Grand Rapids: Zondervan, 2004.

The Book of Hours of Catherine of Cleves. Ms. 945. New York: Pierpont Morgan Library.

Braaten, Carl E., and Robert W. Jenson, eds. *Sin, Death, and the Devil.* Grand Rapids: Eerdmans, 2000.

Bultmann, Rudolf. *Kerygma and Myth: A Theological Debate.* Edited by Hans Werner Bartsch. New York: Harper Torchbooks, 1961.

Chafer, Lewis Sperry. *Satan: His Motive and Methods.* Grand Rapids: Zondervan, 1977.

Dante. *The Divine Comedy.* Translated by Dorothy Sayers and Barbara Reynolds. New York: Penguin, 1962.

Eliade, Mircea. *Myth and Reality.* New York: Harper Colophon, 1975.

Eliot, T. S. "Journey of the Magi." In *T. S. Eliot Collected Poems 1909–1962,* 9.9. New York: Harcourt, Brace, and World, 1963.

Fudge, Edward William. *The Fire that Consumes.* Houston: Providential, 1982.

Fudge, Edward William, and Robert A. Peterson. *Two Views of Hell: A Biblical and Theological Dialogue.* Downers Grove, IL: InterVarsity, 2000.

Hoekema, Anthony A. *The Bible and the Future.* Grand Rapids: Eerdmans, 1979.

Hoezee, Scott. *The Riddle of Grace.* Grand Rapids: Eerdmans, 1996.

Kallas, James. *The Real Satan: From Biblical Times to the Present.* Minneapolis: Augsburg, 1975.

Kierkegaard, Søren. *Fear and Trembling* and *The Sickness Unto Death.* Translated by Walter Lowrie. Princeton, NJ: Princeton University Press, 1969.

Leftow, Brian. *Time and Eternity.* Ithaca, NY: Cornell University Press, 1991.

Lewis, C. S. *God in the Dock.* San Francisco: HarperOne, 2014.

________. *Mere Christianity.* New York: HarperCollins, 2009.

________. *The Problem of Pain.* New York: Macmillan, 1962.

Lunsford, Andrea, and Robert Connors. *The New St. Martin's Handbook.* Boston: Bedford/St. Martin's, 1999.

Nielsen, Kirsten. *Satan—The Prodigal Son?: A Family Problem in the Bible.* Sheffield, England: Sheffield Academic Press, 1998.

Nietzsche, Friedrich. *Thus Spoke Zarathustra.* Translated by Walter Kaufmann. New York: Viking, 1966.

________. *The Will to Power.* Translated by Walter Kaufmann and R. J. Hollingdale. New York: Vintage, 1968.

Packer, J. I. "Hell's Final Enigma." *Christianity Today,* 46. 5 (April 22, 2002) 84.

________. *Knowing God.* Downers Grove, IL: InterVarsity, 1973.

The Pearl. Translated by Sister Mary Vincent Hillmann. Notre Dame, IN: University of Notre Dame Press, 1967.

Plantinga, Alvin. *Faith and Rationality: Reason and Belief in God.* Notre Dame, IN: University of Notre Dame Press, 1984.

________. *Warranted Christian Belief.* Oxford: Oxford University Press, 2000.

Plato. "Phaedo." In *Plato: Selections*, edited by Raphael Demos, 147–233. New York: Charles Scribner's Sons, 1927, 1955.

The Psalter of Blanche of Castille. Fol. 171. Paris: Bibliothèque l´Arsenal.

Schleiermacher, Friedrich. *The Christian Faith*. Edited by H. R. Mackintosh and J. S. Stewart. New York: Harper, 1963.

Schmidt, Gary D. *The Iconography of the Mouth of Hell: Eighth-Century Britain to the Fifteenth Century*. Cranburg, NJ: Associated University Press, 1995.

Shakespeare, William. *Hamlet*. The Pelican Shakespeare. Edited by William Farmham. Baltimore: Penguin, 1957.

Spenser, Edmund. *The Faerie Queen*. Edited by Hugh MacLean and Anne Lake Prescott. New York: W. W. Norton, 1993.

Sproul, R.C. *The Holiness of God*. Wheaton, IL: Tyndale House, 1993.

Stob, Henry. *Ethical Reflections: Essays on Moral Themes*. Grand Rapids: Eerdmans, 1978.

Thielicke, Helmut. *Death and Life*. Philadelphia: Fortress, 1970.

Timmerman, John H. "The Ugly in Art." *Christian Scholars Review* 7 (1977) 138–45.

Trevethan, Thomas L. *The Beauty of God's Holiness*. Downers Grove, IL: InterVarsity, 1995.

Tutu, Desmond. *No Future Without Forgiveness: A Personal Overview of South Africa's Truth and Reconciliation Commission*. London: Rider, 2000.

Volf, Miroslav. *Exclusion and Embrace: A Theological Exploration of Identity, Otherness and Reconciliation*. Nashville: Abingdon, 1994.

Walls, Jerry. *The Logic of Damnation*. Notre Dame, IN: University of Notre Dame Press, 1992.

Wangerin, Walter, Jr. *The Book of the Dun Cow*. New York: Harper & Row, 1978.

Wells, David. "Foreword." In Robert A. Peterson, *Hell on Trial: The Case for Eternal Punishment*, ix–xi. Philipsburg, NJ: P & R, 1995.

Wright, N.T. *Evil and the Justice of God*. Downers Grove, IL: InterVarsity, 2006.

Wright, Nigel. *The Fair Face of Evil: Putting the Power of Darkness in its Place*. London: Marshall Pickering, 1988.

www.ingramcontent.com/pod-product-compliance
Lightning Source LLC
LaVergne TN
LVHW091134080826
845145LV00008B/2153

* 9 7 8 1 6 2 5 6 4 7 3 7 5 *